VOICES IN FLIGHT

VOICES IN FLIGHT

*Conversations with Air Veterans
of the Great War*

by

Anna Malinovska &
Mauriel P. Joslyn

Pen & Sword
AVIATION

For Cynthia

First published in Great Britain in 2006 by
Pen & Sword Aviation
an imprint of
Pen & Sword Books Ltd
47 Church Street
Barnsley
South Yorkshire
S70 2AS

ISBN 1 84415 399 1
978 1 84415 399 2

Typeset in Palatino and Gill Sans by
Phoenix Typesetting, Auldgirth, Dumfriesshire

Printed and bound in England by
Biddles Ltd, King's Lynn, Norfolk

Pen & Sword Books Ltd incorporates the imprints of Pen & Sword
Aviation, Pen & Sword Maritime, Pen & Sword Military, Wharncliffe
Local History, Pen & Sword Select, Pen & Sword Military Classics
and Leo Cooper.

For a complete list of Pen & Sword titles please contact
PEN & SWORD BOOKS LIMITED
47 Church Street, Barnsley, South Yorkshire, S70 2AS, England
E-mail: enquiries@pen-and-sword.co.uk
Website: www.pen-and-sword.co.uk

Contents

Acknowledgements

This volume would be incomplete without the assistance of many who generously provided invaluable information.

Roger King provided inestimable technical support during the original interviews.

Ian Thirsk deserves thanks beyond measure for countless hours spent converting the original videos to VHS format. He showed resolute patience and ingenuity with obsolete media that often resisted conversion. All his colleagues in the library at the RAF Museum in Hendon were unfailingly kind and supportive.

Thanks are due also to the following for their important contributions: Rosamond Clayton; Ruth Cundy; Patricia Dean; Immo Frese; David Goddard; Megan Griffiths; Roberta Hazan; Paul Leaman; Daphne Lee; Phil & Cynthia Morris; Carole Pemberton; Nick Saunders; Mr D. Stratton; Peter Watts; Christine Wells; Philip Wingfield and Elspeth Woolcott.

Without the encouragement, insight and meticulous attention to detail of our husbands, Martin and Rick, this book would not exist.

Introduction

But oon thing there is above all othr:
I gave him winges, wherwith he might vpflie
To honor and fame; and, if he would, farther
Then mortall thinges, above the starry sky;
Considering the pleasur that an iye
Myght geve in erthe by reason of his love,
What shuld that be that lasteth still above?

THOMAS WYATT (1503–1542)

The idea that evolved into a series of portraits of early aviators, eventually presented as hour-long interviews, was stimulated by my first visit to the RAF Museum at Hendon in 1976, where I encountered the collection of First World War aircraft – incredible structures, deprived of function, which had reverted to pure form. Aesthetic appreciation of these exquisite machines aside, I felt an intense curiosity about what it must have been like to fly them. What manner of men were their pilots, the pioneers?

I began research at both the Imperial War Museum and the library of the RAF Museum, and attempted to discover everything possible about early aviation. Having initially been unaware that so many RFC and RAF personnel were still extant, I considered interviewing Second World War rear gunners. There were fewer of these than anticipated, and those remaining were signally unwilling to speak of their experiences. As is sometimes the case when one becomes intensely focused on a particular subject, I began to discover various people who either knew, or were related to, ex-RFC servicemen.

As there was naturally a time constraint on this project, the war having ended some sixty years before, I thought it best to expedite the venture. I borrowed video equipment almost as obsolete as the old planes themselves, and completed the first four interviews. I assumed that the subjects of the interviews would have clearer recall of events occurring sixty years before than of those in the nearer past; this proved correct. As this scheme seemed capable of development, I decided to furnish a comprehensive overview of service in all categories in the first air force, and I submitted a proposal to the RAF Museum that I should create an archive to be used for research by aviation historians, students and other interested parties. This was accepted by Mr J. M. Bruce who was, at that time, Keeper of Aircraft and Research Studies. To his depth of learning in this field, and enthusiasm for the project, I am eternally indebted.

I decided to approach potential interviewees with a written questionnaire to serve as a prompt in the interview. In the main they acceded most generously to my request to record their re-collections, though a few were constrained by the frailty of increasing age or by poor health. The medium of video recording was chosen rather than that of film, with a view to minimizing disturbance of the subjects' home environment. Two clip-on spot-lights were used, with a discreetly placed throat microphone attached to the RFC tie. On meeting, there would be preliminary reminiscence and the display of cherished photographs or docu-ments while the equipment was being set up. The latter would often require some time to register a satisfactory image. The serious business of the interview would then commence, some-times with perceptible nervousness and diffidence on the part of the veterans. Their apprehension usually dissipated as they relaxed into personal experiences of their service, recalling this with increasing confidence. The interview would usually conclude with fresh anecdotes and considerable hospitality and bonhomie.

An MOD moratorium halted funding for the project; consequently, I was able to complete a mere thirty-eight hours of interviews, and these only with British flying personnel. Owing to scandalous curatorial incompetence, this irreplaceable material was allowed to languish and atrophy for more than twenty-five years. Moreover, it proved impossible at the time to interest any publisher in the expansion of this material into print. Fortunately, though, with a new and more sympathetic appointment at Hendon, and with the interest of an accredited historian, this archive has been revitalized, and may now triumphantly assume the role for which it was originally designated – a living record for the RAF Museum, available to researchers of the first war in the air.

Some of the original interviewees have had perforce, and with great reluctance, to be omitted from this book. They are Cyril Britten, Humphrey De Verde Leigh, Leonard Edwards, George Etheridge, Reginald Greenfield, G. F. Hyams, A. R. Johnson, George Moore, 'Bunny' Sharman and Frederick Shildrick. Heartfelt thanks to all of you.

It is hoped that this book will serve as a most salient memorial to all the valiant and beloved men of the first aerial conflict, and to those remarkable chaps whom it was my enormous privilege to meet.

salvete vos omnes!

ANNA MALINOVSKA
London, August 2005

I first met Anna Malinovska in Victoria Station, over coffee and a conversation about Captain Albert Ball VC, in late 2003. Our brief acquaintance revealed an amazing endeavour undertaken by Anna, which resonated with me as a fascinating insight into the world of early aviation. Thus began a long association as we revisited her project of nearly thirty years ago, in order to transform these interviews into print.

I have always been fascinated by Albert Ball. His youth and untimely death prompted my lifelong interest in the First World War and in those first 'Knights of the Sky'. What began as a dedicated interest in Albert Ball for both of us has come to fruition because of him.

This book is the result of our efforts.

MAURIEL JOSLYN
Sparta, Georgia 2005

Sir Herbert Thompson

Sir Joseph Herbert Thompson, born on 9 March 1898 at Wilmslow, Cheshire, was the son of J. Arnold Thompson JP, and Ellen Stewart Fraser. He was educated at Manchester Grammar School and, after the war, graduated from Brasenose College, Oxford. Thompson served in the Royal Naval Air Service as a sub lieutenant in 1916 and was promoted to captain in the RAF in 1918. He became Assistant Master at Oundle School from 1921–22. He joined the Indian Civil Service in 1922 and served in the Madras Presidency. In 1925, he married Kathleen Rodir. They had three daughters. In 1926 Thompson was appointed to the Foreign & Political Department, Government of India. He became Deputy Secretary of the Political Department from 1941–43, Resident for Kolhapur and Deccan states 1944–45, and Resident for the Punjab states 1945–47. He was knighted in 1947.

Thompson retired in 1949, but remained active as General Secretary to the London Council of Social Service 1949–50, Diocesan Secretary, Worcester 1951–1953, and Rowing Correspondent for the *Sunday Times* from 1954–68. He held office at the BBC Appointments Department from 1956–59. Sir Herbert was interviewed at his home at Fair Acre, Haddenham, Buckinghamshire on 19 and 29 May 1977. He died on 28 March 1984.

I wanted to get into the Navy when the war broke out. You couldn't get in early unless you 'fudged' your age, but you *could* get into the Royal Naval Air Service. I met, under my father's aegis,

1

the First Lord of the Admiralty, Winston Churchill. He said to my father, 'Are you going to let him join the Navy?' Father wrote, and I got a recommendation from Winston Churchill. Strangely enough, they accepted me!

The Navy was *gloriously* conservative in those days; they wouldn't have anyone as a pilot unless he was a commissioned officer. I had to wait until I was eighteen. Naturally, I thought I was going to be flying seaplanes, but at Cranwell, which afforded a very good training, they took much better care of you than those poor RFC chaps with all their casualties in France. We started on Maurice Farmans, then Curtisses, then Avros, then BE2cs, and finally the Scout flight, on which you couldn't be instructed. You were sent straight up into the air, and that was your first solo flight. The first Sopwith I ever flew was a 1½-strutter, and I came down and said to the flight commander, 'I want to change and be a fighter pilot instead of flying seaplanes.'

He replied, 'If you want to break your bloody neck, I won't stand in your way.'

So that's how I became a fighter pilot. The reason the RNAS was so good, is that Churchill went into private enterprise, and we had Shorts, Bristols, de Havillands, Handley Pages, and above all, Sopwiths. The RFC and the Army went into the Royal Aircraft Factory at Farnborough, and built up all these other ones, but I don't think they were as good. They were all labelled. An RE was 'Research Experimental', an SE was 'Scouting Experimental' and an FE was 'Fighter Experimental'.

I found flying really exciting, and was a natural airman. Once, though, I was coming down in a Camel and I didn't know that I'd been 'Archied' badly. One of my wheels had been blown off. Of course, you can't see your wheels, so I started to land in the usual way. I didn't know what people were playing at on the ground; apparently they were waving *wheels* at me. Anyway, I made the most perfect landing of my whole career. I came down like a feather on one wheel, but I couldn't understand why the plane suddenly slewed and stood up on her nose. Luckily, nothing was broken, and I flew her again the next morning. The CO came up and I said: 'I'm *awfully* sorry.'

He said: 'Didn't you know you'd lost a wheel?' Thereafter he considered me the most perfect pilot he'd ever known!

We got on marvellously with the RFC. They envied us because we took with us the whole of the prestige of the Navy. When I was at Eastchurch we had a CO who was alleged to have been shot on the beach at Jutland. He was frightfully keen on discipline. He summoned all the instructors to line up and said: 'If you'd been properly educated at Osborne and Dartmouth, you'd know how to behave.' I wondered what on earth was going to happen. He said: 'One of you flew low over a farmhouse and caused a cow to abort!' I was certainly the young man in question, as I was the only fighter pilot there. There were boys there who did all sorts of things that they ought not to have done, and they loved it. I taught them one thing . . . when they'd lost their way, to fly alongside a railway station and read the name off. There was the Maidstone Express, and when I saw it I used to fly alongside it. We were only flying BE2es, which were quite slow, and you could keep up exactly with the train. You had the whole train waving out of the window at you. The boys loved it.

It's quite easy to fly between trees, too, after you've done it the first time. With the first two you go through, you think you're going to hit *both* of them, but afterwards, you realize that your eyesight has exaggerated their proximity. I've never hit a tree. One time when I was instructing, I went up in a Maurice Farman, and immediately afterwards in a triplane, and I could judge exactly where my wheels were when I came down, without seeing them. It's like trying to drive a motor car so that your wheels are aligned exactly with the kerbstone. The idea is that you stall at the identical moment when your wheels hit the ground. That is a perfect landing.

When I went out with Naval 8, I was flying Nieuports. I went out to No. 11 Squadron, which was forming at the time. It never did form, I don't think; we had so many casualties. We had five squadrons flying for the RFC; No. 8 was the first, then No. 1, No. 10, No. 9, and one other. One morning they said to me: 'There's a car coming to take you down to No. 8 Squadron.' I was a replacement for a casualty they'd had the night before. This was in the early stages, so I was considered to be a Founder Member. They'd just got the Sopwith Triplane, which I'd never flown before. Previously, I'd flown Pups; we had a Pup in No. 11, and I flew my first solo in a Pup. She was an adorable little thing. Like all the great Sopwiths, she was really a glider with an engine in it, and she'd float for ever. The first time I ever took one up, the engine completely blotted out and I had to make a forced landing. I've no idea how long she floated. I chose my field and found that I was going to overshoot it; she floated across that field and she wouldn't come down. We ended up beautifully with the propeller just touching the edge of the end of the next field. She was a sweet thing. Call it sentiment, but in No. 8 Squadron we always gave our planes feminine names; always 'she', never 'it'. I've flown other people's aeroplanes when mine was in dock, but as long as I had 'Joan', I wouldn't want to think of anyone else flying her; I would have been frightfully jealous.

The ground crews were absolutely marvellous then, partly owing, I must say, to the leadership of our CO, who was a man called Geoffrey Bromet. He's still alive, and must be about eighty-five now. Curiously he gave up flying. I don't think he liked flight, but he was a very good CO. He was going a long way in his career, but unfortunately his wife had a row with the lady whose husband was Vaughn Lee, the head of the Air Service. I'm told that she was very difficult, and had sacked more Air Vice Marshals than anybody had ever known! This was just before the war. When the war broke out, Bromet came back again, but he could never rise above Air Vice Marshal. They did give him a job which he did extremely well. He ran the Azores and got a Knighthood out of it, but he was still Air Vice Marshal.

We did an awful lot with No. 16 Squadron, escorting them over the lines and so on, and they were dead meat with Richthofen and those people. Richthofen always waited for a sitting duck. He used to attack a lot of two-seaters; he thought them very important, as they were reconnaissance machines. They were dead meat, the poor devils.

Our machines were very slow. At the beginning of the Battle of Arras they had BE2es, which didn't have ring-mounting for the observer. With the BE2e, you could only take a shot if a German got in your way. You chose your combat. With a fighter, his only protection was aggression, so if you were any good, you only got attacked if you wanted to be attacked, unless you got into a fight. If I knew I was going to get into a fight, I found that I always opened fire too soon, but the great thing is that once your guns started, you felt comforted. Once, though, when I had a German in my sights, and he didn't see me, and I had him cold . . . both guns jammed! I put them on both together; one jammed after only one shot, and the other after two.

We occasionally used Buckingham incendiary bullets in Naval 8. It was against the Hague Convention, but we used them, theoretically, against kite-balloons only. They weren't loaded unless someone decided he wanted to have a go at a kite-balloon. We used to load the tracer bullets one-in-two, one-in-three and one-in-four, as far as I can remember. It was a nuisance, though, because you'd follow the trajectory of the tracer instead of looking where you were aiming. You were liable to be shot down from the ground. We had no protection, just a basket chair to sit in. It was quite frightening flying over the Germans and seeing them firing up at you. You'd tingle all over; nobody wants to be shot in the bottom!

With the Camel, we had twin Vickers and we used automatically to fire both at once. The Vickers was designed for shooting on the ground. It was water-cooled. But what they did with ours was to cut louvres into the water-jacket, so it wasn't water-cooled; the air cooled the gun down. Then there was the problem with mass production of cartridges. They used to disintegrate, and then the load might not be exactly dead accurate, and you could shoot your propeller. The interrupter gear was designed to interrupt when the propeller was in front of it, but if the ammunition was just slightly under loaded, you might shoot the next blade. We were allowed five bullet holes per blade!

The jams in the air were a problem, though; we didn't have a machine which was designed for firing in the air. One of the things we learned was to have no oil in the gun, because oil froze at altitude, and this was no good for the gun. It was quite difficult to operate the controls in such extremely cold conditions. You saw

5

the button that you were supposed to be pressing, and you saw your hand doing it, but you couldn't feel it. It was sort of an automatic response. Your feet were like blocks of ice and, when you came down, the temperature changed so quickly, that they would be in agony. But you were young; it didn't matter.

From time to time, I used to fly up to the Sopwith Triplane ceiling just for the exhilaration of doing so. On one occasion, someone had managed to discover that a German photographer was coming over. I was sent out to stay up, petrol permitting, to look out for him. It was absolutely gorgeous. I went up to 23,000 feet and nobody could reach me. I was probably the highest person in the world at that moment. Of course, only triplanes could have done it. I remember looking at this beautiful, blue sky, and singing. I didn't want to come down; I could have stayed up there forever. It was perfectly safe.

The moment you got up in the clouds, with no artificial horizon, you didn't know where you were flying. I always remember the first time I got up in the clouds, the airspeed went up, and so I pulled the stick back to stop it, and it went up faster. I realized that what I'd been told would happen, had happened; I was on one wing or something like that.

When I was instructing, I had some fun with the youngsters and made them pretend to land on the top of a cumulus cloud, knowing that, down below, whatever happened, you'd come out of it. But if you got into a spin and the clouds were below 3,000 feet, you might not get out of the spin in time. I've always thought that doing a loop was a marvellous thing. Your first ever loop just happened; you were stationary and it was the earth that went round you. It's unbelievable. On your second loop, you knew just what to do, but your first came as quite a surprise. The instructors didn't like you looping, though, because you could pull the machine to pieces and pull the wings off. It happened to a member of our squadron. I saw the wreckage when it came back, and I picked a piece of vertebra off the back of the engine. All the wings had disappeared. You had only one set of flying wires, and if one of them went, all three would go straightaway. That's why we were fairly careful, and that's why you'd never spin a triplane.

When people were killed or disappeared, you just had to carry on. In the mess at night, the usual thing was to get drunk. In those days, I was practically a teetotaller, but we had four Canadians in the squadron at one time, and the Canadians were quite different; they would get drunk at any moment. How they managed it, I don't know. There was this fellow I shared a tent with, a man named Thornely, whose father was the Master of Trinity Hall, Cambridge. One day, the clouds were very low and he went up to 5,000 feet after having had a glass of port for lunch. He never usually drank if he was going up, and most people didn't, but he said: 'D'you know, when I got up to 5,000 feet, I was as tight as a Lord.'

Portal was jolly careful about his men, without actually ordering them about. I remember we had a 'blind' one night, and he had a gorgeous brew of mulled claret with all sorts of stuff poured in and he was stirring this, and years later I came to realize that what he had done was to boil away all the worst parts, so that people thought they were being he-men, but they weren't at all! It was quite innocuous.

We didn't go into town for the nightlife; it was too far away. You could only go if you had a tender, and being a small squadron with only fifteen pilots, we didn't have an awful lot of transport. But the CO was quite good. If it was a really bad day, he'd say you could take a tender and go down to Amiens, but you couldn't stay the night, because there was no way of getting home. They used to go down to the village, though. One thing about the RNAS was that they were terribly 'Navy'. They flew the White Ensign, had a ship's bell, *esprit de corps* and so on, and as officer of the Watch, your duty was to line up the 'Liberty Boat' and dismiss it to go down the road to the estaminet! The Army loved us, because we had all these Naval gadgets. It was fun being something different.

I knew Albert Ball by reputation, but I never met him. We'd hear news that Ball had brought down another machine, and Little would want to get straight up in an aeroplane. He'd got an eye like an eagle. You'd usually have two or three chaps in a squadron who could spot another plane in the air more quickly than anyone else. Booker was like that; he'd always beat me at spotting. I flew a lot with Booker, and I loved him. He saved me once when I was set on by the whole of the Flying Circus. I was enjoying myself enormously, shooting a German down, and I didn't realize that the rest of his squadron was up above. They all descended on me at once. Suddenly, I was shot into from behind. We concluded that it was Richthofen's brother, because Richthofen himself happened to be on leave. He had pennons on his wingtips and so on. The triplane had only one gun, which was a 'propelled' gun. It fired off the gun when it thought the propeller wouldn't be in the way, so it went 'pop . . . pop . . . pop . . . ' All he got onto me was one shot slap through the main spar of my top plane. When I came to, I saw that wood was coming out of it. He had shot through the aileron balance wires, and all I could do was to chase the thing down. I managed to get home. I landed, and she just collapsed. All six ailerons fell on the floor, and then she just sat down.

Later, I met Mannock, too, when Booker and I between us shot Waldhausen down. Mannock lied completely and said that he'd got up just as Waldhausen was coming down with a damaged engine. He said he'd shot him down, and filed a covert report claiming that he'd brought him down completely alone. I got back and had been told to write a combat report, which was presumably destroyed when Booker got back and filed his combat report. There was a delay and Mannock got in first. Booker was furious, spitting blood; he knew he'd got in the first shot. If he hadn't hit Waldhausen in the engine, he would have escaped over the lines. We were both in an awful hurry to stop him going back over the lines. We'd come down absolutely flat out from about 12,000 feet, and one had a sense of just how well made the Camel was. I was absolutely vertical!

Fifty years after the war, I met Waldhausen. He came out with the idea that we were the last of the Knights Errant. I felt that we *were*. You never saw anybody you killed. You were awfully protected in that way. You slept in a bed. We were very young and very gay, and we did a lot of lunatic things!

After the war ended, there was a place waiting for me at Oxford University, which was a bit of a soft landing, really. Some people couldn't adjust when they left; they couldn't get down to books again. Some people were impatient, but I was eager to learn, and knew that you had to get a good degree, otherwise you wouldn't get a job. It was such a change coming back from a front-line squadron with all the fighting and the combats, but among the youth of the flying squadron it was rather like being an under-graduate. We were gay and light-hearted, and there wasn't really a hatred of the Hun. It was like having an enemy on a game board; you respected him if he was good. We didn't like Richthofen, but we admired Voss enormously.

We were frightened of the Flying Circus because we knew they were good, but they did make the mistake of putting all their cream into the one squadron. We, on the other hand, had one ace in each squadron, who raised the morale of the whole squadron. When you damaged one of them, you were trying to destroy the plane, not the chap, and I remember the one I shot down, Waldhausen, telling me that he was horrified when he saw the dead bodies that he'd caused himself. But we didn't have to. We were delighted and frightfully excited when their planes crashed, because that was another victory and another machine destroyed.

Quite truthfully, I think we were awfully patriotic in that war. We didn't dwell on the evils of war; it was a game to us. We admired the trenches. The spirit in the trenches was superb. We used sometimes to nip up to the front line and have a look at it, but they soon put a stop to that, as we were far too expensive to get killed in the trenches.

I think the war certainly caused a move toward abolishing class distinctions. True, there were officers and men, but the privileges had gone. These days, you don't really take any notice of a chap with a title. Then there's the political side. There was no Labour Party when we went into the war, but afterwards, the polarization in politics changed enormously.

The older I get, and the more of a museum piece I become, the prouder I am to have flown in those days.

Note: Mannock submitted no claim for bringing down *Oberleutnant* Hans Waldhausen, contrary to Thompson's account. The sequence of events is as follows: On 27 September 1917, Waldhausen attacked a balloon of No. 20 KBS at Aix-Noulette and ignited it. Three Nieuports from No. 40 Squadron, including Mannock and Tudhope, ascended to intercept the Albatros. Mannock suffered engine trouble and was unable to keep up. Waldhausen was then attacked by an RE8, which he shot down into Farbus Wood. He abandoned his attack on the balloon and flew to Ablain-St-Nazaire, where he successfully fired a balloon of No. 37 KBS. Here, he was attacked by Tudhope. As the latter disengaged after firing a long burst into the Albatros, the attack was joined by Booker and Thompson. Booker's engine was crippled by ground fire, forcing him down; he lost the Camel's wheels in a shell crater upon landing. He was met by Mannock, who had landed close by to assist him. The victory was shared between No. 40 RFC and No. 8 RNAS. Mannock arrived on foot at the Albatros, which had come down near Souchez, in time to save the wounded Waldhausen from harm at the hands of angry soldiers from a Canadian ammunition detail. The German pilot was relieved of all potential souvenirs, and taken prisoner. MPJ

Sir Herbert – the title 'came with the job' – was hardly the 'museum piece' he claimed to be. Aged seventy-nine at the time of the interview (the first of the series) he was a man of youthful appearance and boundless energy. This was expended on gardening, his great-grand-children, and an abiding interest in Church architecture. After lunch a most informative tour of Haddenham Parish Church was supplied. He held the post of Churchwarden, and was author of the guide to the building. He was an ardent cyclist, using a machine as light and portable as was his favourite triplane, *Joan*.

On the drive from Stoke Mandeville station to his home, the lingering effect of his years as a scout pilot was evident in his swift and accurate handling of the car, and in the constant rotation of his head, as though he was still scanning for hostile aircraft in the skies of Buckinghamshire.

Lieutenant Leslie Latham

Lieutenant Leslie Sawyer Latham was born in Manchester on 22 May 1898. He attended Manchester Grammar School from September 1910 until Christmas 1916. He was interviewed on 25 November 1978, and died in Solihull on 5 April 1982.

I joined the RFC in early 1917. I had left Manchester Grammar School at Christmas the previous year, and joined the Artists' Rifles at Gidea Park in Romford. It was one of the two Officer Cadet Units in the country at the time. When I went in, I had no intention of flying. Owing to a certain ability in mathematics, I opted for a commission in the artillery, and had several interviews by officers from the War Office. At the beginning of February, we were called in and told that all special commissions, such as Artillery, Engineers and Army Service Corps, had been washed out, and that the only commissions available were in the Infantry and the Royal Flying Corps. All those chaps who'd been waiting for the Flying Corps were delighted! I opted for the Infantry. When I got back to my hut and found that the other chaps I'd been knocking around with had all plumped for the Flying Corps, I thought, 'Well, I might as well stay with them as long as possible.' I went back to the Orderly Room and asked if I could change my option. Fortunately, the Company Commander agreed. We were formed into a squad, and sent on a three-week map-reading course. After a day's march to Rainham, to shoot at the rifle range, we got back home to Gidea

Park in a snowstorm, and were ordered to get our kit all packed, as we were leaving the next morning.

We went to Reading, and became the first batch of cadets in the Royal Flying Corps. Hitherto all the trainee pilots had been officers seconded from other regiments, usually after service in France. Fifty-six of us from the Artists' Rifles arrived on the Saturday; this was followed by a similar batch from the Inns of Court OTC the following week. We were billeted in St Patrick's Hall at the University College of Reading, then proceeded with our course which consisted of lectures on aviation, different types of engine, rigging and general aeronautics. One of the instructors there was C.R. Fleming Williams, one of the early pioneers of flying. He was always known for his talk about the joys of flying, and used to say:

Flying's a wonderful game. You sit up there with your engine purring, and you look down at a ploughed field, and think how industrious the farmer's been. A bit further on, you see a field of waving corn, and you think about the bounties of Mother Nature. Further on still, there's a big wood, with all colours of green. Then a lake, and you think 'How cool that would be'.

Flying's a wonderful game, while your engine's running all right. At the first flutter, you look down and you see that ploughed field, and curse that farmer for having ploughed it, because you know if you don't land very carefully on that you're going to go back over top. You also know that if you land on that field of grain you've got to pancake, otherwise, again, you're going to do a somersault. It's not so nice landing on a tree! And even water can be hard if you don't pancake onto it. So, flying's a wonderful game while your engine's going all right!

Just before Easter, we finished the course and they started to post the cadets. Of course, we'd been kitted out with a special uniform with a white headband. And we were told that on no account were we to take that white band off while we were on leave, as we were still cadets. They started posting: A down to about K, then they went to the bottom of the list and started posting upwards,

12

from Y to N. That left six of us: Ls and Ms. We were posted to Tadcaster. We were the first six pupils in a new squadron, No. 68 RS, and upon our arrival there wasn't even a plane for us! That afternoon, the flight commander, Captain A.T. Lloyd, went to fetch a Maurice Farman Shorthorn.

Our instructor was the CO of the squadron, Major L. Dawes. He was a rather disgruntled person, as he'd taken the first DH1 squadron over to France, and half of them were said to have fallen into the Channel! He always carried a hunting crop with him. We pupils had to wear a crash helmet similar to those used by motor-cyclists today. The pupil sat out on the front with the instructor behind. And very often when a plane was coming in, with its engine shut off, you'd suddenly hear 'Thud! Thud! Thud!' When you looked up you could see Major Dawes thumping the pupil on the head with his hunting crop, very often accompanied by the words, 'Put the bloody *nose* down!'

We only had to do two hours on Shorthorns, but because we were short of machines our progress was quite slow. By the time I was due for my solo, it was 5 June! It was just after 5 o'clock in the morning. The Shorthorn was a very difficult plane to taxi for the simple reason that it had twin rudders, mounted on skids. But the skids were not integral with the rudder; they were quite free to move. So if you were moving along and you put right rudder on, it didn't follow that the plane would immediately turn to the right, unless you put a burst of engine on to give it that extra air on the rudder. After my two hours' solo had been completed, I was transferred to No. 46 Squadron at Tadcaster, where we had DH1s, FE2bs and FE2ds.

I completed my tour on 7 July with just over twenty-three hours' flying, was granted my wings and left two days later. I was posted to No. 77 HD Squadron, with flights at Turnhouse, near the Forth Bridge; Penston, near Huntingdon; and Whiteburn, on the Lammermuirs. We had BE2es, BE2cs, an RE8 and some BE12s. The BE2c was the most beautifully rigged machine I flew in all my service. You could open up your throttle and once you got flying speed, as long as you kept your rudder right, you could take off with just a slight touch on the stick. Once it was off the ground it would take its own flying speed for climbing and when you got to the height you wanted, and eased your throttle back, it would straighten up and drop to the right speed. Of course, there were only one or two select people at that time allowed to fly it; but later, I flew it quite a number of times.

At the beginning of 1918, I was transferred back to Penston. By that time, my old flight commander had gone overseas, and we had a new flight commander, a Dutch South African named Van Eisen. His idea of getting his third pip was to make everybody fly! If he saw a pilot hanging around, he'd say, 'What are you doing on the bloody ground!? Get into the air, you young so-and-so!' We thought he was a bit of a 'nigger-driver' at times, but he contributed substantially to the Home Defence. In February, I was sent down to North Weald, near Epping, with No. 39 Home Defence Squadron. They had just been issued with Bristol Fighters, and were getting rid of all their surplus planes. From there, I was posted to No. 36 Squadron in Newcastle, where they had FE2bs and FE2ds. I travelled down late one evening, went to Squadron HQ, and stayed there overnight. At breakfast next morning, a phone call came through from the aircraft park at Gosforth, where they built Armstrong Whitworth machines. The CO there was asking our CO for pilots, so I was shipped up to the aircraft park. The chief test pilot there took me up in an Armstrong Whitworth, an FK8. Those machines were like canal barges to fly! They were so sluggish, and very heavy on the controls. If you felt a bump coming, you'd put some rudder on to counteract it, and the rudder acted about a couple of minutes later! They were especially difficult to fly in bad weather. Mostly, they were used for artillery observation in France. They had a 160-horsepower Beardmore engine, and one of their characteristic features was an adjustable tail plane. I was detailed to fly an FK8 down to Lakedown on Salisbury Plain. It was looking pretty dark when we took off, and before we got down, snow started to fall. We got a very bad bump on landing. The following day, I flew to London, and from there, up to Newcastle. There, apart from flying ourselves, we were training observers for night bombing. I'd already done some night flying with No. 77 Squadron. Night flying is, of course, very

14

different from flying in daylight; you've got to trust your instruments. But even in wartime, with not many lights, it's remarkable what you can see compared with what you expect to see. The first time I did a night landing had been at Whiteburn, with about a foot of snow on the ground. The moon was shining brightly, and the shadow of the plane on the snow was visible from 1,000 feet.

The idea of putting in as many hours flying as possible had seized No. 36 Squadron as much as it had at No. 77. So we were flying around very often, just putting in hours, doing very little except flying, and a few days after I got up there I said to the observer, 'Get a Very gun, and a few Very cartridges.' He did, and we went up to Berwick where I had a number of friends from my Whiteburn days. We flew around Berwick, and the observer fired off the Very lights. The next morning I had a postcard which said it had been officially announced in the local school that afternoon, that the lights flying from our machine were to congratulate the people of Berwick on their magnificent effort in connection with the Victory Bonds!

A couple of days later, I was flying around with another observer, a Welshman called Evans. Coming home from a flight, I said to him, 'Would you like a stall?'

He replied, 'Oh, yes, sir!'

I pulled her up into a stall, and of course even when you're strapped in, and you suddenly go down from a stall into a dive, it's a bit of a thrill, but when you've only got a piece of 3-ply round you, with a steel tube to keep that in place, it's even more of a thrill. The minute I pulled out of it, he turned round and put his thumb up and was grinning over, so I gave him another one. The next thing was I did an Immelmann turn, in which, almost coming into the stall, you stop, kick over the rudder, and come back in the opposite direction from which you were originally flying. We did two of those, and then I thought, 'Well, I've got to get him somehow.' I said, 'Hold on; we'll try a spin!' It so happened that I'd never tried it myself before because I'd never had the chance to try it in training! Anyway, I put it into a spin, which fortunately was successful! We did a second one, and then came home. I went into the hangar to fill out the flight sheets, but Taffy couldn't wait.

He had to dash into the mess where everybody was at tea, and immediately began to turn on the glamour: 'Marvellous flight! Two stalls! Two Immelmanns! Two spins! Wonderful!' By this time of course, he'd succeeded in making all the chaps thoroughly green with envy. When I got to the mess, though, the flight commander was waiting for me. He backed me into the anteroom, and said, 'What's this Taffy says about the stunting?'

I said, 'Yes, it's quite true.'

He said, 'Oh, right. I'm very glad to know you're so happy with the plane, and that you can do it, but I'm going to ask you *not* to do it again. We're a night-flying operational squadron, and I want as many machines fit for flight as possible. I don't want all these young chaps with no experience trying to emulate your stunts, and I *don't* want any crashes!'

A week later, we were hurrying through the tests for one of the Canadian pilots, on an FE. The FE had a gravity-fed tank in the centre section over the planes. Petrol from that tank was used for taking off and landing, because you'd no engine pressure with your engine shut back, so you'd always got a gravity feed. When you switched over, there was a pump. The control cock was down on the right hand side, and reaching forward to get to it, I leaned on the joystick, and also pressed on the rudder. Quite suddenly, the machine heeled over to the right, and I realized that we were going into a spin! I hadn't much height, so I pulled her in hard, as fast as I could, centralized the controls and she came out all right. In some machines, though, you couldn't get out of a spin easily. In a Camel, for instance, if you did a turn one way, and cut your nose down, the aircraft would go into a spin and you couldn't get out on account of the engine torque.

The following night, there were two German raids on West Hartlepool. On this occasion, our three flight commanders were the first to go up, each doing their own patrol, and followed by three other aircraft. The North Sea has a rather nasty habit of forming low banks of cloud, and one of the flight commanders, a chap called Carpenter, realized after he'd landed that the mist was coming up, and that soon they would not be able to get back down onto the aerodrome. He immediately rang up HQ in Newcastle, for permission to fire Very lights up to bring the other pilots down. The two other flight commanders both managed to get down, but one of the other three machines crashed into the hills at Anfield Plain. The pilot, a flight sergeant, was killed. The other two both had bad landings elsewhere. One of the flight commanders had been right underneath a Zeppelin at 17,700 feet, and his observer had fired all his ammunition at it, but it wasn't effective. The flight commander got extremely drunk in the mess, and danced up and down, complaining that he'd been beaten by a 'bloody sausage in tights'. That was his description of the Zeppelin and became his nickname for a long time afterwards.

There was quite a fuss, because our planes couldn't reach the Zeppelins. It was decided that we should be equipped with Bristol Fighters. For me, this meant going back to tractors, and I was posted back to No. 77 Squadron again. By this time, there began to be signs that the war might be coming to an end, and they were going to put every plane we had into France to strafe the German trenches. They were going to use Camels and SE5s for this purpose. It was decided that the Home Defence squadrons should be trained for Camels. To prepare for this meant flying Avros to get used to the rotary engine.

Meanwhile in May 1918 the last big daylight raid on the Thames had taken place with the Gothas. This was the first time that radio telephony had been used. Before, it had not been possible to get any communication from the ground to the troops, and certainly not in the dark, but now they were able to direct the pilots to where they were needed. By all accounts, very few planes got back to Germany, or to their bases. It was decided that all Home Defence pilots should have training in radio telephony. There was a wireless school at Penshurst in Kent, and each week, a quota of pilots from the Home Defence squadrons was sent down to dabble with the new equipment. It was a box somewhere about fifteen inches cubed, mounted on the plane. The planes that they were using there were DH6s.

We'd go up in the morning, with half a dozen planes circling round the aerodrome, and we had to go up to 500 feet to give clearance for the aerials. Every so often the broadcaster would say

'Aircraft number so-and-so, if you're hearing me, please dip'. Well, transmission and reception were not very good in those early days, and although most of the other pilots could hear 'If you're hearing me, please dip', they didn't always hear their number, so to make sure, *every* plane followed suit and dipped! All round the aerodrome you could see DH6s dipping!

Major Frederick Powell

Major Frederick James Powell was born on 13 August 1895 at Patricroft. He was living in Blackpool when he enlisted in the Manchester Regiment. He took his certificate at Farnborough on 2 March 1915, and served in Nos. 5, 40 and 41 Squadrons. He scored two victories on the Vickers FB5, and four on the FE8. Powell served as chief fighting instructor with Northern Groups in 1917. He assumed command of No. 41 Squadron on 2 August 1917. After shooting down six enemy aircraft, Major Powell was shot down and captured on 2 February 1918 over Auberchicourt by a pilot of Jasta 10. He was repatriated in December 1918.

Powell was mentioned in dispatches, and received the Military Cross. He flew the Maurice Farman Longhorn, the Shorthorn, Vickers Gunbus, the BE2c, the Avro, the single-seater FE8, the FE2b and the SE5a. He was interviewed at home at Ivy Cottage, Stalbridge, Dorset on 29 June 1977. Freddy Powell died on 13 March 1987.

I was just nineteen when I joined the RFC. I had been in the Leicestershire Yeomanry, battling with horses. After two months, I joined the Manchester Regiment, and whilst I was there, my battalion was asked for volunteers to join the Royal Flying Corps. I transferred, and was sent down to Farnborough. I trained there for about three weeks, before doing my first solo on a Maurice Farman biplane. I graduated onto a Maurice Farman Shorthorn, and then onto a Vickers Gunbus. This was an armoured fighting biplane. The armour consisted of a little square of armour plating which went under the seat. It was an interesting little aeroplane

19

with a Monosoupape rotary engine. The engine had no throttle on it, so you couldn't go slow or fast; it only had one speed – flat out! I went off those old Vickers fighters, and onto the BE2c. That was a terrible machine, with a mind of its own! As soon as you put the rudder on it, it banked itself and it slid round on the turns. With the tractors, about three quarters of the visual sight is blanked out by machinery. I always thought pushers were the best fighting machines for the war, though, as the pilot has to be able to see.

My first posting to France was with No. 5 Squadron, flying the Vickers Gunbus. I had done fourteen hours' solo before I went out to fly, which wasn't too bad for those days; nowadays they do about 500 hours. We used to do two-hour patrols. Our petrol lasted two and a half hours. So we allowed fifteen minutes to get to the lines, did the patrol, then allowed fifteen minutes to get back. The time seemed interminable; it seemed as though you'd been up for three years before the petrol went down and you had to get back.

During my first combat patrols, my laundry bills soared astronomically! After the first few times, though, I felt no more anxiety; it was the most amazing thing. This was made easier by the invention of tracer bullets. There was a little light on the butt end of the bullet, and as you fired the machine gun, instead of firing and trying to aim through the sights of the machine gun, you could see this arc of fire going straight off when you fired at the bloke. Once, I was coming down on the back of a Hun in an Aviatik. I fired my gun, I watched these lights, and every one was going right into the heart of the pilot. He still went on. It took me a long time to realize that, of course, your eye is wrong! You may be about three or four feet to the right or left before the tracer light goes out. One rumour was doing the rounds at the time, that if you used tracer bullets and were captured, you'd be shot. They regarded them as incendiary bullets, which were against the Geneva Convention, and not quite 'cricket'. Occasionally, instead of putting one tracer bullet for every two or three, I used a drum of nothing but tracers so I could really have a shot at it.

We had quite a few entertainments, too. Robert Loraine was a famous West End actor. He was the first man who flew from Liverpool across to the Isle of Man. This was in 1912, when he was

20

producing a play by Bernard Shaw called *The Man From the Sea*. Loraine's engine failed and he fell down in the sea, which was wonderful publicity. He eventually became a squadron commander, which was a major in those days. I remember we found a Red Cross Army hostel building, with a stage. We saw this from our aeroplane, and nobody seemed to be using it, and my CO, Loraine, suddenly thought, 'Well, that's a marvellous thing; let's go and take it.' With all our carpenters and mechanics, we took that building, pulled it all down, brought it back to our aerodrome, re-erected it, stage and all. And who should come to visit the squadron but George Bernard Shaw! He came out as a VIP, and stayed with us for a week. Loraine produced two unpublished plays of Bernard Shaw's, which were very good. One was called *The Inker at Berusalem* (sic), which was a skit on the Kaiser. Every 'Major' on the stage always wore an eyeglass. And damn it all, Loraine suddenly appeared in the squadron with an eyeglass! When I was coming back from my first seven days' leave, on the way back, I called in at Harrods, and bought a cardboard box full of eyeglasses with broad black ribbons. I issued them to all the officers in the mess, and when we sat down to dinner, everybody had an eyeglass. Loraine took it in good spirit.

Another play produced by Loraine was *VC*, a skit on Michael O'Leary. O'Leary was a piper in a Scottish regiment, who would walk up and down the parapet, playing the bagpipes. This inspired the whole of his regiment; they went over the top and did damned well. I still think the finest VC ever earned was by a man who was a 2nd lieutenant in an infantry regiment. While he'd been out in France, his wife had produced a son, and he was due for leave in two days' time. The Boche lobbed a bomb into the trench. He ran for cover, looked round and saw his men, one of whom had fallen over. The men were all piled up, and couldn't get out of the way. He came out of his sanctuary and lay down over the bomb. It went off, and he was, of course, scattered all over the place, but the lives of his men were saved. By God, nothing's beaten that.

I loved flying. A thrill! Because you'd so few people who did it, you felt rather like a pioneer. It was interesting, particularly if you were at the right age, about nineteen. But I think for an older man it would bore him. After years of instructing, I could see straight-away if a chap would make a good scout pilot. You could tell that boy when you put him in the front seat and you sat behind. You had the controls, and you'd say, 'Turn to the left,' and he'd turn, merely doing the correct thing – putting the rudder on and then the bank – but himself keeping straight. I used to say, 'Just like an old GOC bus driver'. He'd never, never be a scout pilot. But when you get the right boy, and you say 'turn to the left or the right' and the first thing that moves is his head and he turns round and the machine follows him – there you've got the scout pilot. Quite a different type of mentality – entirely different people.

I knew James McCudden, VC. Quite a different type. He was a little man, who flew Nieuport Scouts with No. 60 Squadron. He was a brilliant pilot, a young captain, and he had the mind of a general. That boy, he used to lead his flight in. They'd do their ordinary work and get into a dogfight with the Boche, McCudden would break away and come back our side and see how his people were doing. If they were not doing so well, McCudden would fight, then break off and come back. But after that, he used to go out by himself. Oh, he was brilliant. Brilliant. He used to get onto the tail of a Boche, and the fellow would turn round and they'd go round in circles and as they went round in circles, he'd gradually elongate the circles, 'til he brought the Boche over our lines, then he broke away and shot him down. I think it was December 1916, probably, and in that year he shot seventeen Germans down, fifteen on our side of the lines. There's no argument as to whether he shot them down or not. He was the most marvellous pilot of all, you can take Immelmann, Boelcke, Richthofen – in all the fighting air forces, McCudden to my mind was the most wonderful genius of the whole of the air corps.

Albert Ball was a different type entirely. He got the VC, but he was a rotten shot, and couldn't hit a haystack at four yards! His idea was to get so close to a Boche before he fired, that it was impos-sible to miss him. Ball came down many times with German blood on his machine! He was a different type of VC. Mind you, they were all wonderful boys. Comrades' deaths in the squadron were tragic of course. You're sitting rather like in a home, and all the brothers are there. And you come in for your meal in the evening, and somebody's missing. The Vacant Chair. There would be the vacant chair in the mess. It was the CO's responsibility to keep the cheer up, so there was quite a lot of cheer, and quite a lot of booze, too. You had to forget, and think, 'Well, probably tomorrow, I'll be the missing chair.' I don't think that really worried us; we were too young and too excited. It was a wonderful thing for boys, a wonderful life. 'Eat, drink and be merry, for tomorrow we die!' There's no finer life than that thought.

I remember the only time I shot a Fokker down. The Fokkers used to fly at about 17,000 feet, and our ceiling was about 10,000 feet. One morning I went up in my old pusher, a little FE8. I climbed and climbed, and I couldn't believe it. I looked at the altimeter and I saw the thing was coming up to 16,500. I'd never been at that height before. And eventually I got damned near to 17,000! I suddenly saw a machine coming straight at me, and he was about 100 feet higher. It was a monoplane, so all I could see was the engine above his plane as he came towards me, and, of course, I couldn't see the markings.

There were two monoplanes, the Fokker and the Morane. So, what *was* he, Fokker or Frenchman? I had to wait until he fired. Well, he fired, and missed, but as I was going to turn into him, I saw his rudder flick, and I thought, 'God! He's coming back again!' So instead of turning round to the left and following onto his tail, I turned to the right and pulled up. When he finished his turn and I finished mine, he was about 100 feet below me, so I came down straight on him, and fired. And he went down. I remember his face; he was so close I could *see* the fellow. He looked up and he hesitated, wondering how the hell I'd got up there. He went down in a complete spin, right through the bomber formation he was supposed to be escorting.

I think the Fokker was a very good machine. I never thought well of the Germans in the war, but as engineers they were brilliant. I remember when I was learning to fly at Farnborough, going into the office of the head of the aircraft factory. He was an Irishman named O'Gorman. I looked up, and over his desk was a great string coming down from the ceiling, and on the end of it was a connecting rod.

I asked him, 'What's that, sir?' and he said,

'Powell, as you know I'm an engineer. That's a connecting rod from a German Mercedes engine. I look at that and it gives me inspiration. One day, we'll make something like that.' And I thought, 'My God. The Germans must be fantastic engineers.'

There was a time when I was sending out more patrols from my squadron, and they kept coming back and saying 'No H.A' (hostile aircraft.) I couldn't understand it, because squadrons on my right and left were knocking the Boche out of the sky. I think the SE5a was my favourite; it was a beautiful machine, and lovely to fly. It makes me rather sad to think that when I was beaten, I was shot down in the finest machine. Ghastly. That was on 7 February 1918. I organized a patrol of eight machines, myself and three others in diamond formation, and another flight of four, 3,000 feet above. I was flying an SE5a. The idea was that *we* were the bait, and when the Germans came onto us, the chaps above could dive down on them and shoot them up. We went right up to the Front without sight or sound of a Hun. When we got to the very top of the Yser Canal, I turned right, looked up and saw that the whole sky was a mass of black crosses. I came down on the tail of one Hun, and had him right in the middle of my Aldis sight. I was about to fire at him, whereupon another Hun was on my tail. 'Pop! Pop! Pop!' He hit everything. He got me through the left arm. My instrument board went up, and then there was a cloud of smoke and water. The bullet had gone right through my arm and into the radiator.

We'd no parachutes in those days and I was at 14,000 feet at the time. Miraculously, with three Huns on my tail, and no engine, I managed to get down. I landed on a German aerodrome! The chap who'd shot me landed too. I put my cap on, and walked over to this German, who was sitting in his plane with the engine still running. He got out of his machine, and I walked up to him to shake hands, as one used to in those days. He said, *'Verwundet?'* At that moment I looked down and saw blood coming from my sleeve. The force of the shot was so intense, that the bullet had gone

24

clean through my arm; all I felt was just a knock, as if someone had hit me on the arm with the blunt end of an axe. The Germans came running out, and carried me to a Casualty Clearing Station, where they dressed my arm. They hadn't got, as we had, real bandages; they used paper bandages. They put my arm in a sling, then took me to see their intelligence officer.

He was a *Hauptmann*, a captain, and wore a delightful sky-blue uniform with a scarlet lining. I gave my name and regiment. Then I was asked my rank. I said, 'Major'. He couldn't believe that a boy of twenty-one was a major, because a German major was usually a fellow with a big, white moustache in those days.

The *Hauptmann* drove me in a German staff car on the other side of the lines, and it was very interesting. As we drove past, there were lots of German troops marching past, and as the staff car came they all turned their heads, you know: 'Eyes right!' The *Hauptmann* said, 'What do you think of that?' I remember saying, 'Well, I think it's marvellous,' remembering that on our side of the lines, as soon as a staff car came past, you saw all the chaps bunch up and go to the side of the road, and you knew they were saying, 'Another bloody staff car!' What a difference to go to the other side and see the Germans all click their heads round! We all know the Germans are a military nation, so that's what we'd expect. The Germans never had the spirit that the Englishman has, though. The thing that will beat them, every time, is their lack of a sense of humour.

I was in the POW camp at Minden until the end of the war. The Camp Commandant there was *Hauptmann* Niemeyer. He had a great reputation, because some of the boys had gone back to England, and the *Daily Mirror* had published his photograph, and described him as 'the basest scoundrel in the German army'. Niemeyer had a copy of that, and he came in one day and said, 'They know me well in England, you know. They have my picture in your papers.' He was *very* proud of that. I think he didn't understand 'the basest scoundrel in the German army'!

I didn't really miss flying while I was in the camp; in fact, it didn't bother me a bit. What impressed me there was the Germans' lack of humour, and the wonderful, intense humour of the British.

I was put in a room by myself with the windows whitewashed on the outside. Some wag had been in there before me, and done a marvellous sketch of a skull and crossbones, above an inscription: Abandon hope all ye who enter here!

When the war was over, we went back to England in a ship. As we got to the coast, all the little tugboats there hooted like destroyers. We stood on deck, seeing all these people welcoming us back home. I cried. Oh, God, it was marvellous! It was amazing to be back in England again.

My experiences in the RFC and the war changed my life, broadened me enormously and formed my character. I went out to France as a poor little sissy and came back as a man of the world. It was a boys' war, in that to enjoy it, you had to be young. I think if you were an old man, about twenty-four or something, it might have shaken you then. It was a terrific excitement for me, an enormous game. I used to say, 'If I had a squadron of fighters, single-seater fighters, I'd like all of them to be nineteen years old.' You don't want an old man of twenty-four or twenty-five because by that time, he's got intelligence. He's going after a Boche and he's got to be able to go straight to that fellow and shoot him down. But he mustn't have the intelligence to think, "well if I'm close to him, then he's equally close to me!" I don't think that someone who's nineteen now would be at all suitable, though. What we need now is to get rid of all those long-haired gits and hooligans. We need another war for those boys; they're made of the same material, but they've been brought up the wrong way. What's lacking in this whole country is discipline; if only we had discipline now in this country we'd be great again. It wouldn't be as exciting as the First World War, though. It would be much more of a push-button war.

It's the atom which really has saved the whole world. The atom bomb has saved us because no country dares use it. We've got to that wonderful show where we've got a weapon which can wipe out the whole globe, so I think we're safe thanks to the atom bomb. I sometimes think, 'How many unfortunate boys did I shoot down? Five? They were all boys, like I was, with families, wives and sweethearts . . . and I killed them.' I don't feel very proud about that, but I had a licence from the Government to kill the enemy. Anyway, we thought of it in terms of bringing the enemy *machines* down.

I met so many marvellous fellows in the war. Wonderful men! No, they weren't men; they were boys! It's the comradeship that I miss. That goes for any of the services, Army, Navy or Air Force. It's a wonderful life, and what you miss when you come out of the service is the wonderful friendship; you feel lonely to come home as a civilian again. My philosophy is that when there's a war, you have the whole nation, all with one goal, and all together. When you get peace, every rotten little man is out for his own. That's the difference between war and peace, and I think the only really satisfactory life that humans have is war.

> Freddie Powell, secretly a great favourite of all the subjects of these video portraits, was in fragile health when interviewed. As the machine declined to register the first attempt, he gallantly agreed to the second ordeal. In every sense he still epitomized the dashing, valiant and flirtatious RFC major. The great gap of years since 1915 evaporated as he sat with G&T and cigarette in hand, recalling those days with vivacity and humour. By request, he sang *Bye Bye, Blackbird*, accompanying himself on his mandolin.
>
> Other members of the household present were his charming wife, Frankie and a swearing parrot known as Birdy-bo who was banished for the occasion, but when released obliged by punctuating the luncheon table with oaths and raucous cries.

Major Gwilym Lewis

Though of Welsh descent, Major Gwilym Hugh Lewis was born on 5 August 1897 in Moseley, Birmingham, and educated at Marlborough College. The family was living at Hampstead at the time of the war, and he was a student at King's College, London when he joined the 2/4 Northamptonshire Regiment. Deciding to join the Royal Flying Corps, Lewis took his ticket at the London and Provincial School on 27 November 1915, on a Grahame-White Box Kite, after only four hours' instruction.

Lewis served in Squadrons 32, 24, and 40, and flew with famous aces such as George McElroy and Mick Mannock, whom he considered personal friends. He received the DFC, and was gazetted on 21 September 1918. His citation reads in part, 'It is largely due to this officer's ability and judgment as a flight leader that many enemy machines have been destroyed with few casualties in his formation. He is bold in attacking, and has personally accounted for eight enemy aircraft.' Lewis scored twelve in total for his career. In 1925 he married Christine Robertson.

In the Second World War he served in the Volunteer Reserve as a wing commander on Churchill's Joint Planning Staff, where his job was to prepare daily briefing reports on actions of the last twenty-four hours. Lewis was interviewed in London on 18 November 1978. He died on 17 December 1996.

I got my ticket, No. 2116, and went to Farnborough on 3 January 1916, from where I was posted to the Central Flying School. The machines I flew there were somewhat primitive, particularly the BE8. It had a rotary engine with immense torque and swing, and would spin as soon as you looked at it. Later, I flew the Vickers Gunbus, again with a rotary engine, which was a splendid two-seater. I'm surprised that it wasn't more effective at the front, because you had a fellow in front with a good field of fire. But from there I got onto the DH2, and had one rather memorable experience.

I was practising my turns trying to get the steep banks and that sort of thing. And it was an aircraft that had more torque with its rotary engine than I had been accustomed to, and used to swing very badly on take-off. I got into a spinning nose dive, and nobody at the Central Flying School knew how to get out of a spinning nose dive. So I spun down from 3,000 feet and just managed to flatten out about twenty feet from the ground. Meanwhile, the Commandant had seen me coming down. He was rather a fattish man and he ran all the way up the tarmac and got himself very exhausted. He was mightily cross and said, 'That young man, what the hell's he doing? Have that young man see me and tick him off properly.' Of course he was probably more frightened than I was, as the ambulance had been instructed to go out.

I got my wings on 23 April 1916 and was posted to No. 32 Squadron, which was commanded by Major Rees. I was by far the youngest in the squadron, a nice pink and white boy, and they nicknamed me 'Cherub', a name which stuck with me throughout my flying days. Major Rees was a terrific character, tremendously enthusiastic and extremely knowledgeable about his aircraft. I can remember him lecturing us on the rigging of our aircraft so we knew how to rig them ourselves.

It was on 8 May that I joined No. 32 Squadron, and we prepared for our trip to France. On 28 May, fourteen of us took off for Folkestone, had lunch at the Metropole Hotel there, then took off for St Omer. We got the feel of things there, then on 4 June we went to Auchel, and from there, on 7 June, we went to our more per-manent airfield called Trézienne, where we were stationed together with No. 25 Squadron, who were flying the rather large FE2bs under Major Cherry. They were bombers, and they could do a bit of fighting too; they had a gunner up in front. We worked with them very closely, and thoroughly enjoyed doing this. Gradually we got into battle order, towing the lines first of all, and going over the lines usually in singles or twos.

At this time in the war, the Germans were causing a lot of trouble with their Fokker. The BE2cs were very badly equipped to defend themselves. The problem consisted in not being able to shoot straight ahead. A Frenchman called Garros worked out a plan whereby he had mounted deflectors behind the propellers of his Morane, and he managed to shoot down several Huns. This disturbed them immensely, and they called in the Dutchman, Anthony Fokker, who produced, in a very short time, a monoplane with a gearing which allowed shooting through the propeller. So our artillery cooperation, and army cooperation aircraft were having a very poor time indeed. The Huns would dive down on them. Their principal operators were Immelmann and Boelcke, and they caused our chaps no end of distress. We came out as fighters to handle this position, and dealt with it very effectively. The Fokker didn't like to come near us at all, and we had quite a difficult time getting a good fight with them. They'd withdraw. They were beautiful in their dive, and could out-dive us but we could probably out-turn them. The Army were very pleased with us, and we were quite an acceptable squadron on the battlefront.

On one of my first offensive patrols, I was up about 10,000 feet, and I saw an aircraft coming from the south on a parallel course. I didn't know whether he was friend or foe; it was impossible to see, so just in case, I manoeuvred myself between him and the line so I could encircle him in that way. As I got close I saw these black crosses, and my heart jumped into my mouth. I could see his German goggles and his gun and all that there was to see. I opened up with a burst of fire, he turned very promptly and I turned after him and got in another burst. But he was too quick for me; he turned under me again and dived for home as fast as he could. In a sense I was rather pleased I'd driven him home, but when I got back to the aerodrome, Major Rees was far from pleased. He said BE2cs don't require too great a distance and asked how far I was from this Hun. I said about forty yards, and Major Rees said, 'Well, you missed your chance; you ought to have shot that fellow down.'

I wasn't really surprised at his reaction. But I was the first one in the squadron to meet a Hun in the air.

We started getting more contact with the Fokkers when we were escorting No. 25 Squadron's FE2bs. We'd do a regular route over one or two of the German airfields, usually Lille airfield, and come back. The FE2bs never lost an aircraft while we were escorting, and they were quite pleased about that. And finally, they were successful in shooting down Immelmann, who was the leading German performer at that time. There were about seven Aviatiks or LVGs, two-seater fighters in very close formation, and one of our very splendid boys called Simpson pitched into them, regardless of the numbers, and put a bullet in Immelmann's head. *That* fixed him!

Meantime, Major Rees was also flying on the front at the same time, and he really raised hell all around, gaily shooting one Hun after another. He said afterwards he thought they were just juniors learning to fly. Unfortunately, though, he got a bullet in his foot and he lost control of his aircraft; he couldn't control the machine adequately to continue to fight so he had to return. And from there he went to hospital and received the VC.

We were then called upon to move down to the Somme. It was an interesting move. Captain Gilmour took command of the squadron but he didn't last very long because in the evening he was in a scrap and got a bullet in his ear, so that was as long as he commanded the squadron. Tommy Cairnes came over from No. 37 Squadron and he took command. The Somme offensive started, as I recall, on 1 July. No. 60 Squadron were having a great deal of difficulty with their Bullets. They were very difficult little planes to handle. They were the fastest thing in the sky, but very difficult to land, and they had to be taken out of the line and reformed. I was up on a patrol in the morning, landed about 12:30, and received instructions to go down to the Somme. By 2:30 we were all in the air flying to the Somme, and the transport was on the move. This showed the efficiency of Tommy Cairnes; the squadron was highly organized. The next morning we were doing patrols on the Somme. The GOC General Trenchard was there to meet us, and he gave us a talk. He was very pleased; he'd heard what good work we'd done on the First Army front.

It was about this time that I met Lanoe Hawker. My brother became a member of his squadron, and I used occasionally to dine with them. I couldn't say I knew him intimately but I knew enough about him to know I had a great respect for him. His was a jolly good fighting squadron; it had some simply splendid chaps and Hawker had this terrific fight with Richthofen. He was about seven miles over the other side of the lines, and they were fighting very close. Richthofen's machine was a much more powerful one. Hawker could turn well, but if he had turned for home he would have been dead meat. He only had one shot in him and that killed him, which is surprising in the long fight they had.

It was extremely active at that time and we dominated the front. We continued to dominate the front until the Germans began to get out better equipment. Perhaps the big day came on 15 September, when our tanks went into action and we thought we were going to win the war. Certainly they weren't going to be lacking fighter cover as far as we were concerned. We preferred to be up all day, and any time of the day, so the tanks weren't interfered with from the air. But that finish of the war didn't occur; the Army did a marvellous job, but it wasn't finally quite successful.

The Germans brought out new equipment. They had Spandau twin guns, which was a great advantage to them. They had the Albatros, DI and DII, the Halberstadt and the Pfalz. All these aircraft were tractor planes, with fixed engines and two guns firing forward. They had about thirty miles an hour better speed and they could out-climb us. We could probably still manoeuvre but we were always flying over their side of the lines. Trenchard was keen on these offensive patrols to keep the Germans back from their own lines. But we were up against it pretty hard, and the man who commanded this new lot was Boelcke, who was absolutely first-class. He met his death fighting with No. 24 Squadron. What actually happened was he collided with one of his own aircraft. That put him out of business. From then, the Flying Circus was commanded by Richthofen, who was not, to my mind, a very attractive person. He was undoubtedly a fine fighter, but not in the same class as Boelcke.

It was tough going. I was pretty young but I was finding it quite strenuous, there's no doubt about it. It was very tough. My brother wrote home and said all you can do when you get in with this lot is get on the wingtip and go round and round and round, and, according to German psychology, after a certain length of time they go away. But with the odds against you, it was quite difficult. At this time, Albert Ball was coming onto the battle front with his Nieuport. He landed at our airfield. I never knew him particularly well, but he was marvellous with his Nieuport. He had a capacity for diving down and getting under the Hun, sitting about fifteen feet beneath them, and shooting up – it was a very brilliant piece of manoeuvring.

To finish up the year, I had an attack of appendicitis. I was dining with my brother, in No. 24 Squadron, and came back vomiting. It was determined that my appendix was the problem, and I was sent off the front, and bundled off to a hospital on the coast somewhere. It was very comfortable, with nice pretty girls and clean sheets and it was an extremely good place to be. They sent me back to England to be operated on. From there, I was sent up to Scotland. I wasn't passed fit for flying. They used to tell me to put my hand out and if it shook a bit, they'd say, 'Oh, my boy, you want some more leave.' I don't know if they were right or not!

But in any case we opened up a school of aerial gunnery up there. The idea was to run some railways up and down the mountain and to shoot some aircraft down these railroads. Other aircraft were to practise shooting these things as they came down. It was not a very brilliant idea; we spent about £2,000,000 and then it was closed down. It was mostly a construction job, and we had a lot of German prisoners putting up buildings and trying to keep roads under repair. I had a DH2 there, which was more or less my private aircraft. Eventually I did get into some trouble. I received a signal from a fellow overseas, a doctor who was a friend of mine with whom I used to link up at Casualty Clearing Stations on the front and he asked me if I would be his best man. I said I would. Well, being a normal Flying Corps type the obvious thing for me to do was to take an aircraft, and I flew over to Kirkcudbright across the mountains and landed there. That was fun because a lot of the people had never seen an aircraft before, and this caused quite a bit of local excitement. And suddenly, in the middle of this, I realized I was there without leave! As luck would have it, we changed Commanding Officers at about that time. Before then it was Louis Strange who was one of the characters of the Flying Corps, one of the pre-war pilots, and an absolutely splendid fellow. An Army man took over, and he wasn't accustomed to our habits. I had been away for two days and for some unknown reason he had been around the hangars, found I was away, and reported 'aircraft missing'. I suppose he lost his head a bit and sent a cable to the Air Ministry. When you got into that area it was a court martial offence and I was right up against it. Everybody was very much on my side, and I knew whatever report I wrote would have to be presented. So I lied quite a bit. I threw some of the blame onto the CO as far as I could. From that day I was considered fit to fly. They posted me to the Central Flying School as an instructor. I rather thought afterwards that they took a somewhat broad-minded view of the whole incident, that it was about time this young man got into a bit more active sphere of operations.

I went to the Central Flying School and after a time there was one SE5 Flight there. There was the opportunity to take it over and I was given this opportunity. This was frightfully interesting and a tremendous responsibility. The SE5 was in its early stages and we had all sorts of trouble. Apart from the pupils, 'Huns' as we called them, damaging the aircraft, the SE5 had radiator trouble and that would require changing the radiator, which could take all night. I had a wonderful flight sergeant who just kept going as hard as he could to keep some aircraft in the air. Because of the demands from overseas the Commandant probably had his eye on this flight more than anything else on his station. And every day, he or the Assistant Commandant would be around asking me how things were going. Even at the age of nineteen, I'm afraid I was very independent, and completely refused to pass anybody as fit to go overseas whom I didn't consider fit. I had my own ideas of what should be sent to the battle front and that didn't make things any easier. It was jolly hard work, with early mornings, late nights, and the mechanics working like blacks trying to do everything they could to support me. The pilots that I received were those who'd been through the school and were specially selected for training as fighter pilots. They were the best that the school had. We had a fair number of accidents, though; at that time there was no dual control in the SE5. Later on, we built a little two-seater SE5, but at this point in the game, you gave them as much advice as you could and off they went and you prayed to God that they wouldn't bust themselves up or smash the machine.

In November 1917, I applied to go back overseas, and was posted to No. 40 Squadron. It was a steady squadron with an excellent record. One Flight was under the command of Mick Mannock and the other was commanded by J. H. Tudhope, whom we used to call 'Tuttles'. They were both splendid chaps, but the hero of the squadron was Mick. He was about thirty, and he'd been around in the world. He wasn't looked on very favourably for some time but, by the time I joined No. 40 Squadron, he was a hero, and was starting to shoot down Huns frequently. He hated the Germans. He picked that up from his time as a prisoner in Turkey, when the Turks sided with the Germans. I didn't entertain any particular hate for the Germans, though; it was just a contest I had to win. The odds were very great. If you didn't win you were for it. You had to be very intelligent as well, and quick-thinking.

I took over 'B' Flight, from Zulu Lloyd. He was quite well known, he came from No. 60 Squadron, got the MC and took over my job at Central Flying School. It was my good fortune that Mick Mannock was friendly to me, and this made a lot of difference to me in this new area. I was very conscious of coming out from England, from Home Station, to an overseas command. Although I probably knew more about flying SE5s than most of those chaps did, I took a very back seat and a quiet attitude. Mick noticed this, and nicknamed me 'Noisy'. When I finally left No. 40 Squadron, Mick was with No. 85 Squadron, and brought over two of his flight commanders to my farewell dinner. We had George McElroy in our squadron, too. He was brilliant. He was rather a bad aerodrome pilot like other pretty good chaps, and took quite a long time to get going. In fact, one time they thought that they'd better send him home. But he was in Mick's squadron, and got the hang of it, and after Mick left he started to shoot down Huns all over the place. I think he must have got as many as twelve when he was posted as a flight commander to No. 24 Squadron. I was extremely sad when he left. They were a very splendid lot of chaps and morale was extremely high throughout. But as a squadron we were disinclined to overdo the drinking except when it was a day off. I always had the idea that bullets travelled awfully fast and that I'd better keep awake when they were around. I was quite capable of a binge with the best of them, but overseas I was rather strict with myself on the station.

The pace of the war had changed quite a bit whilst I was back in England. There were big formations going on, and a lot of dogfights. I was conscious of my responsibility as a flight leader, and very concerned about the wellbeing of my chaps. I liked everyone to have a Hun to his credit, and I rather inclined to watch over them a bit in a dogfight to see that people didn't get on their tails and that sort of thing. I think the only real claim to satisfaction that I had in the game was that I don't think I ever lost a novice. I knew what difficulties they had; they just couldn't see what was going on, their eyes didn't seem to adjust, and they couldn't fly very well. So whenever I had a new boy in the flight that I was working in, I had him fly alongside me with an experienced man on the outside. The usual thing was to stick a chap on the tail and let him do the best he could and keep a strong fighting head. Well there's something to be said for that, too, but they really didn't know where they were for a while and until they could get a feel for it I always had them right alongside me. I didn't want to lose them stupidly. I don't think I ever did lose one. Looking back I was rather pleased about that.

We were up at Bruay, and back on the First Army front, when the German offensive started in March 1918. We all flew down to the Somme front and carried out our operations there. The worst part of this was the low flying, because we had somehow to stop the Germans bringing up their army, or reinforcements, and they were pushing us back very fast and furiously. There's no question about it, though, the RFC made a huge contribution, but the casualties were very high indeed.

As an interesting amplification to the interview with Gwilym Lewis, I had acquired, while engaged in preliminary research at the Imperial War Museum, copies of three letters from the famous Mick Mannock to one Mary Lewis. I asked Mr Lewis about this correspondence, and he replied, with some amusement, that I should enquire further of the said sister. This was not possible, and is no longer practicable. Mick Mannock, apart from his firm friendship with Gwilym Lewis, to whom he gave the soubriquet 'Noisy', was a welcome guest at the London home of the family, and was obviously much admired by Mary. Gwilym Lewis wrote in a letter home in January 1918 that he would reproach Mannock for talking when his other sister Ruth wanted to dance. Next month he commented that he was pleased to hear that Mannock had visited again, while chiding him for fulsome praise of his [Lewis'] exploits. In a later reply from Mannock to Mary, it is clear that she had requested him for a 'joy ride', something that more intrepid young ladies enjoyed being treated to by a dashing hero of the air. The pioneer aviators, aside from their evident bravery – which was also perceived as alluringly reckless – were extremely popular with young women at this time, the Mannock-worshipping Mary being no exception. There is a later letter of condolence to her from his brother, Patrick.

The letters span the period from February to July 1918. The last one dates from shortly before Mannock's death later in that month. They progress from a formal greeting to 'Miss Mary Lewis' to a more informal mode of address. She had also sent him copies of Plato's *Republic* and the poems of Sappho, from which he begs to be spared. He writes: 'Things are going great out here. My star is in the ascendant. What have I done worthily in this world to merit all these good things?'

He ends his final letter: 'Love to little Ruth, and all the sentiment that conventionality permits from me to you and yours. Cheerily, Mick.'

Sixteen days later Mick Mannock met the end he dreaded both by day and in dreams – burning in his aircraft.

Lieutenant Leslie Briggs

Lieutenant Leslie Albert Briggs was born in North London on 7 December 1897. He served as a wireless operator attached to 3rd, 82nd and 13th Siege Batteries from Nos. 2, 6, and 4 Squadrons. He served with Headquarters, 30th Heavy Group, RGA (Royal Garrison Artillery) in 1917, as visiting NCO liaising between detached signallers and the Royal Flying Corps on the Western Front. Briggs became an observer officer in 1918. He was interviewed on 14 May 1979, and died on 10 August 1985.

I joined up on 18 October 1915, mainly because of the Zeppelin raids which upset so many people, including my elderly parents. I used to worry about this and thought, 'What can I do, if anything?' I'd heard about the Royal Flying Corps wireless telegraphy business, and thought I'd like to do that. I had been working for a bank in Shoreditch for about eighteen months.

On the 19 October, a squad of us, all in civvies, was marched across Westminster Bridge to Waterloo Station, where we caught the train to Farnborough. Then the work started. We were stationed at Blenheim Barracks in Farnborough, and came under the wing of drill sergeants. We did all our square bashing in civilian clothes, which felt a bit incongruous. It was three weeks before we got our uniforms. After about a month at Farnborough, we were posted up to various wireless schools in London; Clapham, Marconi House, and the Regent Street Polytechnic, where I was posted.

At the Polytechnic we were taught how to erect a wireless station consisting of an aerial, a tuner and earth mats. Strength was required to erect the thirty foot mast composed of eight sections of heavy steel tubing. Four guy ropes were attached to the middle section, and four to the top. The aerial was made of seven-stranded copper wire. It was attached to an insulator atop the mast, and ran to the station. It was taken in through a lead-in conduit and connected to a short-wave tuner. The earth mat was made of copper mesh, weighted at both ends and attached to the earth end of the tuner. It was buried as near as possible to the station, parallel to the aerial. The operator sat at the tuner with headphones on, a plane would come over and send a signal, and the operator would have to check this for accuracy of reception. Cloth strips were used to lay out the code for the observer. These were placed on the ground near the station and battery so the observer could see them. They'd have to be whipped in quickly if any enemy aircraft were about.

At Regent Street, I had a 'sleeping out' pass, so I was able to go home to North London each evening. In the morning, I had to catch the tram and tube to be in for roll-call at 7:30 a.m. At roll-call, I sometimes answered in an altered voice for a pal of mine who lived further away and was often late; luckily, I was never caught.

Because we had been so well trained in drill and marching, sixty-four of us were detailed for the twice-weekly recruiting march with a drum and pipe band. Any recruits foolish enough to volunteer lined up behind us and were marched off to Chelsea Barracks. We sang the hit tunes of the day whilst marching. The NCOs at Regent Street were very strict indeed. One sergeant major went too far after a particular recruiting march in heavy rain. We were very tired, wet and hungry, and instead of being paraded and dismissed, we were made to do exercises. This was too much, and we stopped obeying orders spontaneously. The CO reprimanded us all, and six chaps were picked for disciplinary action. Of these, only two were sent to the glasshouse at Aldershot as examples. That SM was posted away after two weeks, and we were horrified to find that his replacement had been sent from the same glasshouse. However, although he was strict, we liked the new chap, and even clubbed together to buy him a gold watch.

We had an intensive course in Morse Code and the rudiments of registration, and to pass out, had to attain a speed of twenty words per minute in five-letter code, so 100 letters per minute. This took some doing. Several of us passed out quite quickly. We were very enthusiastic and thought, 'We'll get out of this soon and be posted overseas.' After passing out, we were posted to Brooklands, and twenty of us were put on a two-week intensive course on the electronic valve. This looked like an electric lamp, and consisted of three parts: filament, grid and plate. It could transmit speech as well as signals, and was really the commencement of broadcasting. We transmitted messages by radio set with microphone from one station to the other, by use of both plain and coded speech. We were both sending and receiving. After this, I expected to be posted on active service, but we were sent back to Farnborough, knowing that wireless telegraphers were needed everywhere, both in France and further afield. However, we just wasted time doing more drilling, and were posted back to the Farnborough school to do buzzer practice.

Some months later, I *was* posted overseas. I was so keen, that when we reached Le Havre, I was first off the boat. We were sent up to Rouen, and I was with No. 2 Squadron under A. D. Newall. The sergeant in charge of wireless took me under his wing there, and introduced me to my first battery, No. 3 Siege Battery. They had 30-cwt, 6-inch howitzers pulled by eight beautiful Shire horses. Later, these were replaced by 26-cwt howitzers with a spade trail, which were moved by four-wheel drive lorries, and the horses were dispensed with. The whole battery was made up of Indian Army troops, real old sweats who put me wise. I learned some Hindustani and some very colourful English. I worked mainly in dugouts with an entrance below the surface of the earth.

In the dugout was a short wave tuner on a table, and our sleeping quarters, because it was a billet as well. It was connected to the Battery Command Post by a D3 telephone, manned by an artillery telephonist who was seconded to the wireless operators to relay observations to the battery commander. The dugout was about six feet by six, with just enough headroom, and was usually built in an old trench. It was sandbagged over the top. To go to the latrine, one would have to walk some distance in conditions of extreme danger. If we were stuck in the dugout for a long time on a shoot, we had to use large cartridge cases to pee in. Either we would visit the Battalion cook to draw rations, or they would be sent round to us. The dugouts were usually reasonably clean, except in the French sector. I was in one at Vermelles, recently vacated by the French. It was filthy, and teeming with rats and lice. There, I became chatty [lousy], so ran a candle along the seams of my shirts and breeches to get rid of the little devils. Occasionally, you could get transport to the regimental baths in the nearest town to bathe and get clean linen.

Any corps or brigade or heavy artillery group had targets to be eliminated. These were usually troublesome enemy batteries. These targets had been previously determined by observations carried out by plane-spotting, spies, or the Kite Balloon Section, and were pinpointed very accurately. Certain batteries would be detailed to deal with particular targets, so a plane would be sent along and we wireless operators would work with them. Registration took place when a battery moved, so the CO knew where he was in relation to enemy positions and was able to register on them, having calibrated his guns so that he could put a barrage down accurately on any trench line or position. Registration did not take so long to do, but counter-battery work I always found more interesting. It was gratifying to know you had made a good correction, for example, ten yards from a target, or 'OK' if spot on.

When you arrived at a new battery, you would have to erect the station if it was not already done. Being a wireless operator was a lonesome job. If I moved, I had to pack up my personal gear and the wireless telegraphy gear, and put my next station in operation immediately. We might also be asked to help with manhandling the guns, harnessing horses, pulling howitzers out of gun pits, loading limbers or moving shells. When we moved, we would make contact with our new RFC squadron, and would be briefed on our new superiors and call sign. The wireless operator at that squadron would visit the siege battery to liaise. For example, we might need spare parts or a new tuner. As this was our only direct contact with the squadrons, we felt cut off from the RFC; we were nobody's children. We might visit the squadron on a rare day off, when transport was laid on, but we did feel unusual and different from the Artillery boys because we were in the RFC. However, the RA chaps I worked with adopted me and were very kind to me.

Once, on the Loos front, I left my dugout to visit a wireless operator in an adjacent battery and, as I was coming back, the Germans were sending over 5/9s (shells) which destroyed my dugout. Seeing this, my RA pals thought I was in it, and done for. When they saw that I'd returned safely, they made a huge fuss of me. This is the only legacy worth having of any war: comradeship. They helped me dig out my equipment and tuner. Another time, on the Vermelles front, I was scrounging for coal among shell-holes up to ten feet deep and full of water, to make a little fire in my dugout and keep myself warm. I had filled a sandbag with coal and, trying to get back, became lost in the pitch dark. I wandered about shouting: 'I'm lost!' in a state of panic, the like of which I've never experienced since. My Artillery pals came out with torches, found me and brought me in.

Later on, there were two RFC wireless operators attached to one battery. In the summer you might work up to sixteen hours daily, so one operator could relieve the other. There were also wide variations in the duration of a shoot; it could last from ten minutes to four hours. My longest shoot was three-and-a-half hours. You might get your OKs quickly, or you might have to abandon a shoot. The wireless operator would deal with one aircraft only per shoot, except in the case of zone-calls. If a corps machine spotted unusual transport or troop movement, they would send a zone-call which broke into our normal transmissions. All operators hearing the call would report to the battery commander, who would pass this on to Artillery HQ in the area, who would then direct the batteries reserved to deal with zone-calls to fire on the points given by the observer.

If the sending was good, the job was fairly easy, but you had to contend with a great deal of jamming. There were umpteen planes in the air, both English and German, all ranging artillery or observing for the Infantry. We were all intermingled, and it was possible to miss your signal completely. By and large we managed all right, though. The Germans' Morse was excellent, and I used to take down their signals as well as ours, to try to follow what they were trying to do. More than once, I was able to tie up their signals with targets on our side that they were ranging on. The trouble was that when the Boche planes came over, we would start firing, and this would give away our position. They would spot the flash from our guns, and pinpoint us. The next day, we would usually be favoured with a counter-battery operation against us.

I was shifted up to the Ypres Salient, and was stationed with No. 82 Siege Battery, just south of Ypres at a place called Kruisstraat. No. 82 Siege Battery was a 12-inch howitzer battery. The howitzer was on a rail, and was pushed into position by a socking great locomotive. Each evening it would be pulled back out of the way. I spent three months there, doing about two shoots a day. The shoots were usually done in cooperation with another battery. One observer would range for both batteries, and the shoots would go on simultaneously; whilst we were ranging with the 12-inch howitzer, the observer would give the other battery a command to fire with the 60-pounder. The muzzle velocity of the 60-pounder was much faster, so if it wasn't timed properly, it would reach its target too soon. The idea was that the shell from the 12-inch howitzer would reach the target and then, almost immediately afterwards, the shrapnel from the 60-pounder would burst in the air. The devilish thing was to catch the Boche troops as they were running for cover; it was quite fiendish, really.

When I was with No. 82 Siege Battery, my station was in part of a ruined farmhouse, in a small room eight feet by eight. I preferred being in dugouts, as you were safer from flying splinters, though a direct hit on either a dugout or a building was invariably fatal. I got into trouble there once. When things were quiet I used to go out with one or two chaps from the Artillery, and kick a football about. We were busily doing this one day when suddenly there was a frantic message from the battery commander: 'Get back on your set; there's a plane calling you!' Conditions had apparently cleared up enough for the observer to get on with his target business. He'd been frantically calling us but could get no answer, as I wasn't on the set. I thought, 'Crikey! I'm for it now.' I had visions of courts of enquiry and courts martial, but the battery commander must have sorted it out, as there were no repercussions for me.

I was posted to No. 30 Heavy Artillery Group, comprising several batteries of various calibres, to monitor and keep records of all shoots in the sector, so that one could judge what was going wrong, and so improve the efficiency of the RFC. Although this could be considered as a 'soft' job, I thought it was a pointless exercise. I was promoted, and my next posting, which lasted from July 1917 to July 1918, was as one of six visiting corporals with responsibility for a number of siege batteries, about twenty-four as I remember, spread over a wide area. I was required to visit as many batteries as possible daily, from a list supplied, to check on their welfare, the state of their equipment, any replacements required, the quality of signals and how their shoots were progressing. This was a lonely, unpleasant job, especially around Ypres, entailing much foot slogging in mud and muck whilst being shelled.

I would return at night to my billet in the ramparts at Ypres, with four other wireless operators, where the cooking was done by an RFC chap assigned to us. On one of my daily expeditions, I lost my way, and to the astonishment of the Infantry, ended up in support trenches with them. They were somewhat bemused to see a young RFC corporal in his 'maternity' tunic; I'm glad they didn't think I was a ruddy spy. Anyway, they helped me back onto the right track, though it did occur to me that I might have ended up in the German trenches. I discovered that although the competence of signallers varied, the standard was generally extremely high. In general, they were well educated, sensible and courageous men.

One day, I had been to Vlamertinghe with a friend of mine, and we were walking back up to Ypres. We saw a GS (general service) wagon coming towards us, so I hailed the driver and he pulled over. I jumped into the back of the wagon. My pal, who was a little

44

shorter than I, couldn't make it, though, and the driver pulled off. I put out my hand in the darkness of this wagon, and felt something cold and clammy. The driver shouted, 'Don't worry. I've got a couple of stiff 'uns in the back, and I'm taking them for burial.' I jumped out of the wagon like lightning, and my friend and I continued to Ypres on Shanks's pony. I certainly didn't want to see another GS wagon again in a hurry.

In July 1917, the Battle of Passchendaele started. I went right through Passchendaele visiting these batteries while the battle was on. It went on until November and was a shocking thing, with a colossal loss of life. There were about 440,000 casualties and it was as bad as the Somme. In the whole time, only about five kilometres had been gained, and the mud was getting worse all the time.

In July 1918, I was selected for a commission, because I had a wide knowledge of my subject, and so was suitable for the work of an observer. This was by request and not by order. I was interviewed by Major General Bowen, and was instructed to report to Farnborough again. There, I took an intensive written and oral course on the technical side. In the time that had elapsed since my previous training, technical matters had advanced greatly through experience of the difficulties in cooperation between ground and air. Also, the wireless sets had become more sophisticated. Working as a wireless operator in a plane, I was often taken up from Laffan's Plain and given dummy targets on which to range and send down corrections. There was a Sterling transmitter in my cockpit, and a winch from which to wind out the 150 feet of copper wire, weighted at the end, which comprised the aerial. The signals were recorded by the control station, and checked for accuracy. The trailing aerial was earthed onto the airframe. The Sterling transmitter had a 6V battery, so the range for transmitting signals was limited. There was also a Morse key to send with. The signals had to be sent in intelligible Morse code.

When flying as a wireless operator, you were the instigator of the shoot and made the first moves to start it off. I remember two particular incidents. The first was when my pilot, keen to get off to see his girlfriend, did not allow me enough time to wind in the trailing aerial before he started doing acrobatics, and I was afraid that it could have tangled round the propeller or ailerons. Another time, in a DH6, the reserve petrol tank became detached and fell into the cockpit, soaking me in petrol. However, we got down safely and I lived to tell the tale.

1st Air Mechanic/
Observer-Gunner A.J. Coleman

1st Air Mechanic/Observer-Gunner A.J. Coleman. He joined the RFC
in 1916 as 2nd Air Mechanic with No. 53 Squadron in Catterick and
later in France. He was seriously wounded in March 1918 and thereafter served with No. 16 Squadron prior to his demobilization in
1919. He was interviewed at home in Croydon on 7 July 1980, and
died a week later.

I was working as an apprentice in a firm of manufacturing
jewellers, and as I was always interested in anything mechanical,
I desperately wanted to get into the Royal Flying Corps. As soon
as I saw the advertisement for a certain type of mechanic required
by them, I went to the recruiting station at Regent Street
Polytechnic and applied to join. I was told that I would be
accepted if I passed a trade test at Farnborough. I enlisted and
then, with about a hundred others, was marched down Regent
Street to Waterloo Station in order to get down to Farnborough. I
can remember clearly the girls waving at us from Liberty's and
various shops in Regent Street; it was quite exciting.

We got to Farnborough, still in civilian clothes, and within a day
or two had to undergo a trade test. I passed, and was delighted to
be enrolled as a Second Class Air Mechanic, the lowest rank in the
Flying Corps at that time. We were shipped off quickly to Ireland
and were sent to the Curragh in order to be toughened up, which

involved much marching and physical exercise. In January 1916 I was posted to Catterick in North Yorkshire, to a newly-formed unit which eventually became No. 53 Squadron.

At Catterick, there were different types of aircraft which we had to service, maintain, and sometimes test-fly. We had Avro 504s, BE2cs, and a clumsy Martinsyde. I spent the whole year there, working on both rotary and stationary engines. The rotary was a pleasant engine to fly, but a little unreliable. It had a peculiar induction system with an automatic valve in the head of the piston and occasionally the string used to break, causing the engine to misfire very badly. It would come down from about 1200 rpm to about 800, so you had to land again quickly. The BE2c was really the forerunner of the RE8, except that in the latter the pilot sat in front and the gunner sat behind, so having a clearer view. In that respect the RE8 was quite a superior aircraft to the BE2c. The engine of the BE2c was an 8-cylinder, V8, air-cooled, 90-horsepower RAF engine; the RE8 had a 12-cylinder, V8, 140-horsepower engine of pretty much the same design. Both were designed at the Royal Aircraft Factory at Farnborough.

In December 1916, I embarked from Southampton to Le Havre with No. 53 Squadron. From there we drove up to St Omer which was the area headquarters for all the local squadrons. Another mechanic and I were detailed to repair an engine of one of the aircraft which had flown over from England to be part of our strength. The following day there were two aircraft there, and we mechanics put our gear in the machine and flew up to Bailleul, which was quite a small aerodrome, about four miles from the front line. We saw quite a lot of activity there. The Germans used to shell us with high-velocity shells; they would absolutely scream over. We were in range, but it didn't trouble us unduly. It was very different from having been at Catterick. Looking back, it was more an adventure than anything else. We were young, but we understood the job that we had to do, and were prepared to do everything we were told.

We had Bessoneau hangars, long hangars of French design, which held about six aircraft. Eventually we had six aircraft to each flight, all RE8s. At first, though, we had BE2es, which had a slightly shorter lower plane. These were phased out fairly rapidly, and in early 1917 we were re-equipped with RE8s for the duration. We were due to get Bristol Fighters in 1918, but they never materialized.

There were two mechanics working on each machine. There was a fitter, whose responsibility was to look after the aero engine, and a rigger who had to look after general maintenance. A pilot might say that the aircraft was flying a bit left wing low, and the rigger's job was to rectify that by altering the stress on the various cables running between the struts. My job was looking after the engine. After every flight, I removed the plugs, cleaned them, adjusted the valve clearances on the engine and cleaned the carburettor. Then I would test the machine. First we'd put a couple of chocks in front of the wheels. One mechanic would lie over the rear end of the fuselage, and a sergeant mechanic would sit in the cockpit. You'd swing the prop, the engine would be started and he would test it. If it ran sufficiently well, he would find a pilot, and say to me, 'Well, you go up with the pilot and see what it feels like in the air.' Engines performed differently in the air. I got quite a few flights in that way.

The early morning patrol used to go off at dawn and, if the weather was good, flying would go on until about 8 or 9 o'clock in the evening. Some of the pilots and observers would do two or three trips a day. The work of the squadron was all reconnaissance. I think the correct term was Army Cooperation. I had to pinpoint the batteries, and direct their aim on batteries on the other side of the line. We did some photography, too. In some cases we used to do a long distance trip to take photographs and drop bombs over Douai, in the German sector. The wind was generally westerly, unfavourable when you turned for home.

In many cases the Germans didn't send up their fighters to prevent our aircraft from going over, but they used to appear on the scene when we were fighting our way back. We had quite a lot of casualties as a result of having to fight back against a stiff headwind. For us, the fighter escort wasn't used until late 1917, when aircraft production had accelerated and pilots were being trained more rapidly. In those days it was usual to see as many as fifty or sixty machines going over the lines with their fighter escort at about 10,000 feet.

The work of the reconnaissance squadrons wasn't glamorous, but it was important because the whole of the war was a static war. Trenches fired away at each other, and nobody made any progress. Our job was the same day after day, just taking photographs or doing counter-battery work. When we had some time off, we used to go into Bailleul, and visit one or two little estaminets where we used to enjoy egg and chips with a glass or two of liqueur.

We were lucky because Bailleul had been used as an aerodrome since about the end of 1914. We had wooden huts, and as bombing became more frequent and worried us a lot, a labour battalion of Chinese coolies built sandbags all around our huts. Later on, when bombing became really severe, we had to live in dugouts, which were located very sensibly immediately right behind the hangars. So if the hangars were hit and set on fire, we had to turn out and look after everything. If, unfortunately the hangar was missed, the bomb would probably go in one of our dugouts. But the bombs in those days were nothing compared to what were used in the latter war; they were relatively harmless. You could almost laugh at them. They weren't very accurate. Nevertheless, the bombing was so severe we had to live in the dugout night after night.

One of the tactics that the Germans used was to attack a particular squadron and try to obliterate it in one night. There are several accounts of squadrons being very badly bombed and sustaining many casualties. The Germans were starting to use twin-engined Gothas, which we didn't have. You could always tell when they were coming; there was a lovely, throbbing sound of the two engines. They were the ones that used to create the damage. Our machines could never be used as bombers.

I was in Bailleul until December 1917, then obtained my first leave to England. When I returned to France I rejoined my squadron at Abeele, near Poperinge, in the arc of the Ypres front. Within a week or two we were ordered to fly down to the south of the line, right down on the Somme, in anticipation of the big

German offensive of March 1918. I remember flying down in my machine from Abeele to an old French aerodrome at the extreme right of our line. We went down in a formation of six aircraft and after we'd been flying for about an hour we ran up against a huge bank of cloud. The flight leader fired a Very pistol, indicating that we had to climb above it. We couldn't climb above it, so eventually had to go down through it. All the aircraft dispersed, and when my machine came out of the cloud at 2,000 feet, I looked around for the other aircraft, and there wasn't one in sight. Two of us landed on the aerodrome, and the others made a forced landing elsewhere.

I never got to do any bombing, though. Towards the end of 1917, there were two squadrons, Nos. 100 and 101, whose job was purely bombing. They had all-black FE2bs, and they would land on our aerodrome, remain for a few days and do whatever job they had to do. Of course, we'd then become the target for German retaliation, so we didn't like Nos. 100 and 101 very much.

On one occasion, the Germans were bombing us and they managed to drop a bomb on the YMCA in Bailleul. For some days after, we could go down there and buy cheap cigarettes and other water-damaged items. There were some advantages to bombing! Another time, our machines were going up on a very gusty day. The aerodrome was on a slight incline, and the aircraft had to take off on a path that took them right over the town. One machine took off, and nearly stalled as we watched him, but managed to keep going until he stalled completely. The nose went down, and he finished up right in the spire of the church. A week or so afterwards, one of our chaps received some newspapers from home, which carried a delightful photograph of this plane. Underneath, it read: 'Another German aircraft brought down in France!'

When we were on the Somme, the whole Front was so quiet that we could hardly believe that there was a war on. It was several days before we got into our stride and started to do the normal work of the squadron. Soon after that, in the early hours of 21 March, the big offensive started. At about 4 o'clock we were woken by terrific gunfire. During the day we went about our normal duties but no aircraft could leave the ground because there was thick mist. On 22 March it was a nice clear day, and the aircraft were ordered to start doing their various duties. In the afternoon we were suddenly ordered to evacuate the aerodrome.

The Germans had broken right through the line, and we'd noticed that a lot of the infantry were on the roads near the aerodrome. We realized we were in a sticky situation and that we had to get the machines off the ground and get away quickly. I was ordered to put the tool box in the machine, get the 20-pound Cooper bombs on board, put my gear in and depart. I was given a map on which was indicated the aerodrome which was to be our destination. That was the end of my flying. I don't know exactly what happened. All I know and can recollect from that day to this was recovering consciousness in a hospital train. I realized then that I'd been in an aircraft crash. I don't even remember taking off, because normally when we used to take off, we used to stand up in the rear seat to look at the instruments. If the engine was giving full revs, you knew that you'd be off the ground fairly soon. On this occasion, though, I have no memory of getting into the aircraft for take off; I don't remember anything. I opened my eyes and found myself in a train with wounded soldiers all around me.

The casualties couldn't be returned to England on account of the great demand for shipping for reinforcements to come from England for the infantry. So I finished up in Deauville, where the Army authorities had built special hospitals for the coming offensive. I had a terrific blow on the head, which must have knocked me out, and my legs were damaged. Otherwise I wasn't badly hurt. I didn't see my pilot again, and I heard from a friend of mine in the squadron that he had been killed. Apparently, the plane had caught fire and crashed on take off. The petrol tank was situated behind the engine and very close to the pilot's compartment. For some unknown reason the RE8 used to catch fire very easily.

I spent five months in hospital. When I was discharged, I went to Wing Headquarters and tried to get back to No. 53 Squadron, but I couldn't. I was sent to No. 16 Squadron, in the Vimy Ridge area, which also had RE8s. The Commanding Officer then was Major Portal, who became quite famous in the RAF. When I moved there, my history went with me, and I did no more flying. I was put in charge of the instrument repair workshop and ended my war days there.

There had been rumours for several days before that the war would end very soon. Of course nobody believed it. On 11 November 1918, somebody sounded a bell, and the Armistice had started. All military flying stopped, but a certain amount of joyriding was indulged in by pilots, for the sheer pleasure of being in the air.

Within a fortnight I was given a ten-day sick leave. I was told that I couldn't get across to England on account of the shortage of shipping, so I elected to go to Paris. I stayed in a very large hotel, still known as the Hotel Diana, and I chummed up with a sergeant pilot who had just come out from England. We spent all our time sightseeing in Paris. In the evenings we all came back to the hotel and usually succeeded in getting drunk.

But there's one tragic little story I must relate concerning another sergeant pilot, a former mechanic at Bailleul. He so worried his Commanding Officer that they allowed him to go back to England for pilot training. He got his wings, and came out to join our squadron. As his mechanic, I flew with him on a number of occasions. One day he suddenly said to me, 'I know that I'm going west.' And he did; he was shot down by Richthofen. His name was Sergeant Whatley.

Demobilization was supposed to be on an orderly basis, but it never worked out like that. In January 1919 I got my official second leave to England. I went to the firm where I'd worked before the war as an apprentice and I saw the boss. He took me into the workshop to see some of the older men who still remained at work. There was one funny old chap there who used to deal out all the various metals required. He looked over the glasses on the end of his nose, and said, 'Coleman? We heard you were killed.'

I thought, 'Well that's a nice greeting!'

The boss said to me, 'Well, we'd like to have you back if you can get out as soon as possible.'

I went down to Chelsea barracks and applied for my

demobilization; it was granted and I didn't go back to France. In a week or two I was sitting at my bench and doing my old job. I don't think the war changed me much. If I'd had the misfortune to serve in the trenches, my life would have been changed, but in the Royal Flying Corps, our lives were cushy compared with the infantry.

Sir Victor Goddard

Sir Robert Victor Goddard was born on 6 February 1897 at Harrowdene House, Wembley, Middlesex. He attended Britannia Naval College and joined the Royal Navy as a boy of thirteen. He graduated as an airship pilot at Cranwell on 7 February 1917 and remained in the Royal Naval Air Service as an Airship Officer during the war, commanding the 'Composite' squadron, which comprised one flight from No. 55 Squadron and two flights from No. 30 Squadron, using airships for intelligence purposes.

Goddard was awarded a permanent commission in the rank of flight lieutenant in August 1919. He served with Cambridge University Air Squadron at Duxford from 1921–28. On 22 January 1920 he was removed from the Navy lists and awarded a permanent commission in the Royal Air Force. He married Mildred Catherine Jane Inglis in 1924. They had two sons and a daughter. The day before war was declared in 1939, Goddard assumed responsibility for establishing the facilities for 'Z' at the Building Research Establishment at Garston near Watford. The following day he reported to the RAF component of the BEF as a staff officer.

He retired on 8 April 1951 and was appointed Principal of the College of Aeronautics at Cranfield. He wrote a number of books including *Flight towards Reality* (1975) and *Skies to Dunkirk* (1982) and acted as a broadcaster for many years in the 1930s and throughout his life. Sir Victor was interviewed on 20 January 1979 in Kent. He died on 21 January 1987.

In April 1915, I was a junior midshipman on the battleship *Britannia*, which was in the 3rd Battle Squadron and stationed at

Rosyth. The Captain summoned me to his cabin. The commander, the captain and the captain's clerk were there. To my astonishment, the Captain asked the other two to leave him alone with me. When we were alone, the Captain said, 'My boy, I have a very grave question to ask you.' There was a pause and I wondered what in the world I'd done. He had a letter from Admiral Jellicoe, the Commander-in-Chief of the Grand Fleet, ordering ships' captains to recommend junior officers, midshipmen or subalterns, 'for special, temporary service of a secret and hazardous nature'. The Captain asked me, 'Are you prepared to volunteer for this?' I didn't think I'd got any alternative; one simply didn't say 'no'. I was ordered not to tell anyone what we'd been discussing. Three weeks later, the Captain sent for me again, and said, 'You're going to leave the ship tonight at seven bells. You're going to leave with sealed orders.'

I asked, 'Can I tell the gun room now, Sir?'

'Yes,' he replied, 'You can tell the gun room you're leaving the ship.'

What followed was very interesting. The gun room were really quite friendly towards me by this time, and I couldn't understand why, when I went up on the quarter deck to get into the boat, none of the gun room was present except the captain's clerk. All the ward room came up to see me over the ship's side, and down into the picket boat. What I hadn't realized was that all the gun room had swarmed over the boom into the picket boat which was lying alongside the ship in harbour, and had stowed away, because they wanted to see my sealed orders which were marked: 'Not to be opened until you get ashore.' When we were out of sight of the ship, they all came out of their hiding place, joined up with me and were very friendly. But the moment I stepped ashore, they followed suit. A fight ensued and they robbed me of my sealed orders and opened them. But the captain's clerk had been wily enough to realize something might go awry, and there was a second envelope contained in the first sealed orders envelope. This was heavily sealed, and marked: 'Not to be opened until 100 miles on the journey.' Consequently all they found there was a blue railway warrant to London. They allowed me to go;

they didn't open the other envelope, and we parted on good terms.

I reckoned that Newcastle was about 100 miles on the journey. And so I opened the letter then; I broke the seals and found out what my sealed orders were. I was to report to the 2nd Sea Lord at 10 o'clock the following morning. I met another midshipman, who said, 'Where are you going?'

I said, 'I'm going to London.'

He enquired further, 'Are you going to report to the 2nd Sea Lord at 10 o'clock in the morning?'

I said, 'Yes, that's right. What are we going to do?' He said, 'Oh, don't you know!? There's no secrecy about it on my ship. We're going to sink some cement boats in the Kiel Canal.' There was a good deal of secrecy to this big nonsense. Anyway, when I arrived at the Admiralty, a whole lot of midshipmen and sub lieutenants came in. They were all my seniors. I found that I was one of a dozen and that I was the youngest of them all. I was a bit horrified by this. Anyway the senior fellow was a chap called Almondy, whom I knew, and he appeared to be the spokesman. We went up to the 2nd Sea Lord's office, and Almondy went into the outer office. reported himself and said he had eleven other midshipmen sub lieutenants. He was immediately turned out into the passage again followed by a commander who said, 'The 2nd Sea Lord is not in the habit of seeing any officer below the rank of Post Captain and then only by appointment!' I said I'd got a letter to Admiral Hamilton, in the handwriting of the captain of my ship. He said, 'Well for goodness sake, here's the 2nd Sea Lord, take it in.'

I didn't know the 2nd Sea Lord. I went into the office and presented this letter to the Commander, who took it into the 2nd Sea Lord, in the inner office. Presently he came out again and said the 2nd Sea Lord wanted to see me; I entered. The 2nd Sea Lord looked over the top of his spectacles at me, and said, 'So you're going into this enterprise, are you?'

I said, 'Yes, Sir.'

He said, 'Well, I don't approve of it. Good morning!' And that's all he said! So I asked him, 'Can you tell me what we're going to do, Sir?' Before that question was answered, the Captain, with the

Commander by my side, put his hand on my shoulder, turned me round and marched me out of the room.

At that moment, a door banged down the passage, and I saw a little man emerging with his hands behind his back with his head bowed. He was obviously a senior officer, because he was wearing a monkey jacket. As he passed me I saw that his arm was covered with gold braid, he had four stripes on top of a broad stripe so he must be the 1st Sea Lord, because that's the only man who could be an Admiral of the Fleet. It was Jackie Fisher. He said, 'What are all you young officers cluttering up the gangway for?' Almondy the spokesman said, 'The 2nd Sea Lord wouldn't see us. We were ordered to report to him at 10 o'clock this morning, and he decided not to see us.'

So he said, 'Ah, you must be my midshipmen. Come in.' We were ushered into his office and he said, 'Stand around this table; I want to talk to you.' Then he continued, 'If any of you young officers ever rise to high positions and have to deal with politicians, don't trust 'em.' He was talking about Winston Churchill, with whom he'd just had his final interview – and final row – about the Dardanelles. Later, it was announced that the 1st Sea Lord had left the Admiralty, having written on his clean blotter, on his empty table, 'I'm off!' Anyway, he'd told us that when he wanted a job done well he always got junior officers to do it because they would do what they're told. Then he said, 'I'm going to read to you boys the finest piece of prose in the English language,' and he read us Nelson's last prayer. This was too much for one member of the party, David Donne, who blabbered out, 'Can you tell us what we're going to do, Sir?'

He said, 'Yes, my boys, you're going to fly airships.' That was the first time the air was mentioned.

We were sent to the Air Department at the Admiralty, and we met Captain Masterman, who seemed a very sensible chap. He divided us up, arbitrarily, into two groups. One group was sent to Roehampton to learn to fly balloons. The other bunch was sent off to Kingsnorth to learn about airships. Later, the two groups changed round; we had a month at each place.

First of all, I went with the ballooning party. We were based at

Roehampton, and went daily to Hurlingham, where some sailors were inflating balloons for us, and we went off in these balloons to various remote places, depending on the strength of the wind. We used to take our lunch with us, and would land about tea time. We used to choose a country house and land in its park and we were royally received. They were very amusing flights, those. It was suggested that some of us could have been disappointed that we were thrust into the air having been sailors, and I had volunteered for the submarine service. We weren't really great as airmen, but were very hot sailors. I think that could have been one of the chief disadvantages of having Naval officers as aircrew. Otherwise, nobody complained really; we remained Naval officers and took what was coming.

Subsequently I went to Kingsnorth, near Chatham, and we learned about lighter-than-air airships and about aerostatics and aerodynamics. We also learned about aero engines, and were told that we were going to rig our own ships. There were hangars at Kingsnorth, and we built these airships on the floor. Our coxswains were there, petty officers from the Navy. Our radio operators were also there, and they were going to work the wireless. Otherwise, we sat on the floor and built our ships. They were non-rigid. They had ballonets inside the main sausage-shaped balloon; there was one ballonet forward and one ballonet aft, and they were inflated with air by a blower system behind the propeller.

The rubber manufacturers, who were making tyres and mackintoshes in those days, were turned on to making balloons. The material they used was rubberized Egyptian cotton. So we had this rubberized cotton envelope with an engine in the front. There was a fuselage with two seats behind. The wireless operator sat in the front seat and the pilot sat in the back. It was rigged up like an aeroplane, and the rudder bar, which you put your feet on, was connected to wires. With that, you pulled the wires back to the tail plane, which put the rudder across one side or the other. There was an elevator wheel, and a statiscope which told you whether you were rising or falling. We couldn't go more than forty or forty-five knots an hour.

The submarine menace had just started. Jackie Fisher, the 1st Sea Lord, had apparently seen an airship in the air, and said, 'That's really what I would like to have; I'm going to make a fleet of airships, and get some young officers to fly them.' So that's why we came out of the fleet. Jackie Fisher got the idea that we could see through the surface of the sea, and that we could see submarines. We would have been able to see through the surface of the sea if it hadn't been so reflective of the sky and the sun, and so turbulent. The Channel water, where the submarines were coming out of Germany, was exceptionally turbulent in the tidal flow; the mud was always stirred up and consequently the sea was opaque.

In my particular ship, a fellow called Lindemann, from Farnborough, came up with polarizing binoculars, which enabled one to polarize the light off the sea so that only a part of it was reflected, and enabled one to see how turgid the water was below the sea. Lindemann was German by birth, and later became Lord Cherwell. We couldn't see through the sea, though, and it was largely a waste of time. We came to the conclusion that we were acting to the enemy as scarecrows. The German commanders were as brave as lions, but they had their limits. They could face all the dangers of being in a submarine, but what they couldn't face was the idea of being bombed from the sky. Immediately they saw an airship, which they would see long before we would see them, they would submerge and stay submerged. We got a spurious reputation of being able to protect convoys, because the German submarine commanders daren't face the idea that they would be bombed.

We carried eight bombs in a bomb rack, and they were 20-pound bombs. They were 'pipsqueak' bombs, and wouldn't have hurt submarines unless they exploded on them. But the Admiralty was so scared that we might bomb one of our own submarines, that they said, 'You mustn't carry explosive bombs, you must only carry dummy bombs.' So we used to carry dummy bombs, which were weighted. They looked fine, just like real bombs, and we used to use them as ballast.

We didn't have any mooring towers, those came later on, and

we didn't have any mooring devices. The ships used to be in a hangar, and the hangar that I used for my ship was built for the *Eta*, which was a much smaller ship. Consequently, my ship couldn't get in. Another hangar was built in the meantime. Being a junior, I had to wait until last for an airship. We dug a tunnel about six feet deep through this hangar so that we could get in. On Sunday inspections the commanding officer would walk along the deck and look down at the crew standing at attention. He used to flick my ship with his finger to find out whether it was up to pressure, and it made the sound 'blimp'. I told this story in the mess at lunchtime, and my ship was ever afterwards called 'The Blimp'. That was the beginning of the word 'blimp'.

In those days, we used to have a handling party; it really meant 'clearing lower deck' as the naval expression goes, it meant getting all the men available from workshops, from everywhere. A bugle call was sounded when a ship was going out, and 100 men would come out from Capel, my station. They would come out to man the guys. There were two guys forward, and two aft. The handling party would stretch them out and walk the ship out of the shed. She was sandbagged down in the shed so that she couldn't waft up to the ceiling. The sandbags were taken off and you would ballast up. Ballasting up is finding out whether she's buoyant or not. When she was just about buoyant, we would go out of the hangar. Then if the sun came up, she would get very light and you'd have to take on a bit more ballast. If it started to rain, she'd get rather heavy, and you would have to ballast up before you started the engines. You'd ease up the aft guys once you got her clear of the hangar, and she was pointed in the direction of the wind. Then you'd ballast up, get the ship in trim, both fore and aft, and start up the engine by swinging the propeller. With the engine ticking over, you'd say, 'Ease up the guys!' and the ship would float up into the sky.

We didn't really want to achieve much height. To begin with, we used to go out for fifteen hours at a time, and we used to be full of petrol, so couldn't have much buoyancy. The ballonets would be empty. If you valved gas, you were punishing yourself, by making yourself heavy right away. The ballonets not only kept the airship in shape, but you'd let air go from them when you went up, because the gas would expand as the air became more rarified, and that would push out the air. We used hydrogen gas, which is highly inflammable.

One flight a day would be all that you could do, especially if you stayed out for something like twelve or fifteen hours. We would take our so called 'lunch' up with us. We weren't allowed to take sandwiches; we had to subsist on malted milk capsules and condensed meat. It was a big nonsense, but the idea was that we could have a jolly good meal when we got back. Naturally, we couldn't cook aboard.

I worked for about eleven months or so at this submarine spotting game, and then I was told that I was going to volunteer for special temporary service in France. It was highly secret. We had a black ship which was so secret it was never allowed to come out in daylight. Then we moved off to Polegate, near Eastbourne. We sat in the hangar and flew only by night. A posse of brigadiers and a general had to come down from the War Office to see that we were suitable to go to France. It was a bitter night, and we took the ship out. They wafted us away, and we sailed up into the sky and turned around. I noticed we'd been flying round in circles for some time, and gradually going downwind. I said to the senior subaltern, a fellow called Chambers, 'What's the big idea? You're flying in circles!'

He said, 'I can't help it! The rudder is jammed full over!'

I said, 'Well all the brigadiers are waiting, and they'll be getting very cold.'

He said, 'Well, can you think of anything?'

I said, 'I can think of something straightaway. When you're beginning to aim toward Polegate, put the engine full on, and when you're aiming away, slacken it off again into idling position, and you'll gradually come back in a spiral.'

That's what we did, and we landed head to wind, on one leg of our spiral. The senior officers were very impressed, and passed us as OK for France.

We went to France the very next day. The whole idea was that we should drop agents in France, bilingual Frenchmen who could speak German like a native. Hitherto, they had been dropped by aeroplanes. They used to come back through the Dutch frontier at night, and then get through Holland, get a ship, and come back to the War Office for debriefing. The Germans realized this was happening, and put up an electrified wire all round their frontier. Trenchard was then asked if he could fly his aeroplanes at night and pick up these chaps, and he said, 'Well, I simply can't do that; they're not able to fly by night.' This is how they hit on the idea of getting an airship to go.

We had instructions from Trenchard's staff never to go over the lines at less than 13,000 feet unless there was cloud cover that we could get into quickly, because of the possibility that we could be shot down at night. I was rather relieved to find that none of the agents was willing to volunteer to be picked up by an airship. They didn't so much mind being dropped by airship, but they simply couldn't face the electric fence around the north frontier of Germany. So there were no volunteers. I thought, 'We're going to get away with this.' Not at all! We were ordered by RFC head-quarters as we couldn't get German-speaking Frenchmen to be utilized for this job, that we should do reconnaissances by night over the German lines. We used constantly to fly over the lines at night, but it wasn't very rewarding because we never saw anything worth a damn. It wasn't worth doing. Generally, we'd go out on patrol as soon as it was dark. It was dark in winter time much earlier than in other times and we'd stay out most of the night. We always got potted at when we were coming back. We didn't get shot down, but we got peppered several times. The envelope got holed with rifle bullets, and we often had to repair them. Then we learnt a device of coming down over the lines, coming down to a very low altitude, to about 200 feet. We would throttle back and we would sing, rather bawdy English songs. This would cause us to be recognized by the troops. We got to be known as the 'singing airship', but we weren't much seen by daylight. It was quite an exciting time.

It wasn't difficult to navigate in the ships at night, because although the Germans were thoroughly blacked out and it was almost impossible to see anything on their side, once you got over our side of the lines, we were lighted up as far as we could see. The French and the English couldn't have been more happy-go-lucky. We had no difficulty in picking out the various towns like Arras; we were based near Arras, and could find our way back to an airship hangar there.

I stayed until the end of the Somme battle. We got out on the last day of June, the battle started on 1 July, it petered out in mud and distress in November and I came home. I flew the ship home and left Chambers to clear up the mess. I expected Trenchard was going to send for us once more, as he had told the Air Ministry we'd be sent for again. I marked time at Kingsnorth, and got a new ship ready, but in the meantime, the RFC learned to fly by night, and so we didn't go back. I went onto bigger and bigger ships, and finally onto rigid airships. We built a lot of rigids during the war. They were supposed to act as scouts for the Navy, but it was difficult to get them to sea.

Captain George Machin

Captain George Douglas Machin was born on 9 January 1893. At the time of enlistment he lived in Bushey, Hertfordshire. He served in the infantry as a non-commissioned officer in the 1 Bedfordshire Regiment, King's Shropshire Light Infantry, and the Hampshire Regiment, before transferring to the Royal Flying Corps. As a draughtsman and artist, with fluent French, he was very valuable in the chartroom, and was posted to No. 23 Kite Balloon Section. Machin also served with No. 17 and No. 39, where he was commissioned as captain, and appointed Acting Balloon Commander on 12 June 1918. He received the DFC on 8 October 1918, and continued to serve with the Army of the Rhine until May 1919.

After the war, he became well known as a sketch artist, with work published in the magazine *Bystander*. He served in the Second World War and was badly wounded at Tobruk.

He was interviewed on 16 April 1979 in Dallington, East Sussex and died on 6 November 1985.

I was seconded to the RFC from the Hampshire Regiment, having transferred there from the King's Shropshire Light Infantry to which I was commissioned. I'd had no training at all. I'd been in the Army for a couple of years before that. When I was wounded, it was by a small fragment of shell, but the thing that got me out was trench fever. On the Somme, we had taken over dugouts from the French, who left a legacy of bugs and disease. Many of us got trench fever and my temperature soared to such a dangerous level that I was sent home. Through that, and being posted to the 2nd

Battalion, Bedfordshire Regiment, I was able to pull some strings. I made a lone venture to dig out a vital colonel, who was colonel of a regiment to which a friend of mine belonged, found the battalion, got his signature and my papers for commission. With that, I became a cadet at Wellington Barracks in Lichfield, and was commissioned into the King's Shropshire Light Infantry. I transferred into the Hampshires to catch up with another friend of mine, and from there, always thinking of something new, I heard about balloons and made my application to go to the Royal Flying Corps.

I had to report to the Somme for my posting. As I stood by the dugouts, in all that mud on the side of the canal, I saw a string of five or six balloons, all coming down in flames. My Colonel, a stout fellow who'd been wounded in Gallipoli, said, 'Captain Machin, I'm sorry for you, but that's what you're going to.' Next day I went down to the Somme, quickly thinking I'd be posted soon to some more healthy sector, but unfortunately I was shoved back into that same salient, to the very spot where I had been standing.

I was posted to No. 23 Kite Balloon Section. We had to pack our own parachutes, which had a rather peculiar 'Harry Tate' harness, comprising Wilson canvas straps with a waist belt and some trouser buttons. On my second day up, I had to jump out in a hurry. It was a beautiful day, with clouds scudding by. Suddenly, a plane came out, 'pop, pop, pop', and I was instructed to jump over the side, which I did. I fell upside down for a few hundred feet, my parachute popped open, and I was very relieved. The German pilot was shot down by an RE8. They had a good field of fire, and they were able to get onto this Hun; as a matter of fact they hit him right through the head.

The Captain commanding No. 23 was quite a character. He was the nephew of Jameson, of Jameson's Raid fame in the Boer War. He'd had a crash in a Shorthorn, and stuttered thereafter. He used to tell the story of his early days in balloons when the Belgians, who were working alongside, had Caquot balloons. There was no winch; instead, they had a team of horses, and a great big drum around which the cable was wound. These four horses were there with their riders, and in the distance a little spot could be seen,

66

which could have been a hostile plane. Well, the Belgians had a colossal wind up. They blew trumpets or something, and the chap on the horse, captain in charge of the four, pulled his whip out, and gave a hell of a crack. This sent the horses off at a terrific speed, and with a direct pull, wound the drum up to the balloon. The poor old occupants up top, without any warning (there were no telephones in those days) suddenly felt 'Bonk!'

I was always up bright and early, too early for many people. I always believed in getting up very early in the morning to make sure everybody was on their toes and to see the possible prospects if we went up with regard to visibility. Our main object, of course, was lining up our artillery batteries onto hostile gun emplacements. Our idea was to inch them gradually onto the objectives until, all going well, we saw the whole outfit go up into the air in a cloud of smoke. We felt if we could finish up a 'shoot', as we called it, with a loud explosion, that was a happy moment. That was the way we worked. We were beset all the time, though; our big anathema was a dreadful gun that the Germans had running on a railway line at Houthulst Forest, which was a blur in the distance. The railway gun ran up and down, firing a 9.2 calibre clockwork-fused shell, which weighed nearly a ton, on balloons. They would range one in front, one behind us, and we knew very well that the next one would be pretty well dead on. We were more or less immobile, because we were in mud, and our movement was more or less limited. So the old guns that ran up and down on the rails were difficult, in fact almost impossible, for our counter-battery people to get because of their mobility. Every day we would encounter chunks of metal from this clockwork Charlie gun. Quite often, we were losing so much gas, that we simply fell down at almost the speed of winding up from the winch. Once I was hanging on a bit too long, I suppose, and determined to finish the shoot, when we came down faster than they could wind it in and we collapsed into a grove of trees. We were lucky to get away with that. When a kite balloon is rigid, it's more or less manageable, but the moment it's lost a lot of gas, its nose caves in, it's at the mercy of the wind and it'll do all sorts of tricks. I've been treated to a loop-the-loop quite a few times.

67

We were up there from 2 or 3 in the afternoon until sunset. The best light for observation was with the sun behind us and we were able to work until quite late on those long clear, frosty days. It was not very comfortable, and extremely cold. We would sit up there for hours and hours. We were intent on our jobs, though, and on knocking out the enemy, which gave us a real kick. That's what kept us going.

We used a pair of six-inch glasses, with graticules, showing the degrees right or left, and steered the shell bursts onto the target. We were linked up direct to the battery through our chart room, which was a great big affair on wheels. We'd talk direct to the battery and say we were short a degree or a degree and a half right and we'd steer them onto the target. When we landed, I'd make drawings from notes I'd made when I was up in the air. There was no time to do any up there; it was all done in the chart room. There was a certain amount of collaboration with the RE8, too. It was quite a slow machine, but did a lot of fine work. The observer had a good field of vision. We never took any photographs from the balloons; all that was done by the chaps in the RE8s, who were properly equipped for that sort of thing. They took a sequence of oblique pictures of the front, then pieced them together to make a continuous map. They took excellent photographs from about 1,000 feet up, showing the trenches, farms, landmarks and ammunition dumps. With our collaboration, we got a very good overall picture.

We had about 150 men to handle one balloon. Our personnel in those days were really first class. The men were brave, disciplined and well turned out. The riggers were all highly skilled chaps, and the equipment people who operated the winch were excellent, too. Many of them had had the chance to go to the Balloon School at Roehampton, and were properly trained. We officers were in command of a fine body of men. But as time wore on, and we suffered tremendous casualties, I'm afraid the calibre of individual they sent us deteriorated a lot. The spirit was there but the ability wasn't; they hadn't been properly trained, as there simply wasn't the time. However, we managed. And that was the case throughout the war. One takes one's hat off to the Britisher, who, when he's up against it and hasn't the material, makes the best he can of his resources. There's no use sitting down crying or waiting for special help. A good soldier makes the best use he can of the material at his disposal, whatever it may be. That, combined with a sense of humour, brought us through many a tight corner.

We very rarely got any time off. If the weather was against us, and it often was, there was a lot to do on the ground in regard to keeping equipment in trim. This applied not only to the gas bags, but the guy ropes and all the paraphernalia and machinery. There was always equipment to be seen to. We lived in tents mainly, which were sandbagged fairly well. Of course, the Germans were always very hot on shooting us up on the ground where the balloon was bedded. They had their own balloons in the distance, and were able to pin down our balloon 'bed' as we called it, so they'd shoot us up on the ground as well as in the air.

My most memorable period of leave had nothing to do with flying. It was freezing like the Devil, and I was in the lines. My leave had been a long time coming, but when it eventually came through, I didn't waste any time. I was a sergeant in those days, and I loaded myself up with stuff from the NAAFI, bottles of whisky, chocolate, butter, lard and good things I knew were short in England. I struck out for the main roads, just as I was, caked with mud from the trenches, rifle on my back, and a German rifle as a souvenir as well, and my knapsack full of all these comforts. And I was lucky in that the first car I hailed was driven by an ATS girl. She was an OC, and on her way to the coast from where my boat would be leaving. I got on board with all my stuff and within a short time found myself at Victoria Railway Station. Eventually, I managed to get a taxi to my home in Bushey, some seventeen miles away. It was snowing, and my people were sitting around an open grate with no fire. Father had not a drop of whisky in the place. He hadn't got any tobacco, either and everybody was sitting, very miserable, wondering where the eldest son George was. I knocked on the door, and there I stood, covered in mud, straight from the trenches. That was a Christmas. I managed to stay two more days, then got in touch with a unit who flew me back on an FE2c, a machine with the propeller behind. It wasn't long before I was back with my unit.

69

When I got my DFC, I forget what phrase they used, something along the lines of 'kept my nerve in spite of setbacks and shelling'. Most of us felt that the old Germans were going to shell us, and that if we were forced down, we had to get another balloon up quickly, so they couldn't laugh at us and say they'd pushed us down. I believed in that, and made it a policy in my unit. Another policy I followed was, if possible, to stay up. When the Germans were attacking a single balloon, if one was hauled down, obviously others were hauled down as well, and it was easy for the Hun to make one straight line and kill off about six balloons. If I left mine aloft, he'd miss it. We liked to show the old Hun that we would not be compelled to land, and that we were still a live force. We didn't have a huge casualty rate, not compared to the infantry. The Hun often used to try to shoot us up on the ground, where they knew some personnel were housed. My flying coat was riddled with bullets when it was hanging up in the tent below. One particularly bad afternoon, a very heavy shell went past our basket. The chap standing behind me, my second-string observer, was a Lancaster man and he was hit. The piece of shell went right through my flying coat and got in behind me. That was the closest I had. The other piece of shell was just a random bit that fell on my wrist on another occasion.

Our normal height for observation was about 4,000 feet. The job consisted mainly in ranging artillery batteries, and noting any particular action or movement on the ground. It was from that height that I was able to observe those two terrible battles, Poelkapelle and Passchendaele, with their colossal loss of life. It was pouring with rain on both occasions, and I saw all the action from up in the air. I was very happy to be up there and not down in the trenches with those poor chaps, I can tell you. It was quite a sight to see the whole line, thirty to forty miles each way, blazing with the first volley of the guns going off.

I always found it exhilarating to be up in a balloon, looking at the scene below. The wind comes along, and there's a shrieking of the wind through the wires, the supporting wires that hold the basket to the envelope. I broke away a few times. Once was when the cable was cut by a piece of shell, and I drifted with my observer over the salient. There's a complete cessation of all noise; you're going with the wind, you don't hear a sound, and it feels wonderful. I dropped down, pulled the valve cord and let the gas out. We were lucky to get over the German-held part of the salient, and dropped down just in time for tea with some artillery chaps. Another time, during a snowstorm, my observer was chucked out in one of the gyrations, when the wind caught the envelope. I was on my own, and bumped about six or seven times. Finally, I got my jackknife out and ripped the envelope. That was rather unpleasant, but the sensation of complete tranquillity is rather wonderful. There's no wind, and you're just silently drifting.

The second occasion my balloon was shot at was on the Somme. We were attacked by nine Albatros planes. I put my observer out, and jumped after him. Unfortunately, our parachutes collided. We managed to get down, more or less on one parachute. In that predicament we were attacked by these planes, who failed to fire the balloon, and concentrated their fire on us. We were like a couple of hams on a hook, hanging up to be fired at by nine German planes. It was most unpleasant. Some Camels came along, brought down two of the German planes, and drove the rest off. Things had certainly become a bit less chivalrous by then.

Then came the final big push when the Germans advanced in March 1918. We were having a pretty grim time, moving the balloon position night and day, and the Germans were cock-a-hoop, thinking that we were on the run. But then the tide turned. With 'our backs to the wall', as Haig said, we drew on all our reserves and pushed the Hun right back. Armistice Day had come.

At the time of the Armistice, I was in the Mons area. We took the balloon over into Germany, and were stationed near Cologne, where we used to fly just the same as before, taking the balloon up to keep in training. It was far more frightening, though, going up with nothing to do, rather than with a specific counter-battery job in mind. When you've got a fight in front of you, there's little time to think about your personal safety. I stayed in Germany for about three months, before returning to England, where I was put in charge of winding up the aerodrome at Old Sarum, and responsible for the disposal of surplus *matériel*. Things were so haywire at the time, that my pay was not getting through, but I had carte blanche to take whatever I wanted in order to pay for food and so on. I availed myself of a large quantity of rubber tyres, a Bosch magneto and a twelve-bore shotgun. During this time, I obtained a commission in the Indian Army, eventually taking the boat out to Bombay in 1920.

Flight Sergeant Bernard Oliver

Flight Sergeant Bernard Oliver was born in London on 3 August 1898. He served in Nos. 2 and 23 Kite Balloon Section, and knew George Machin. After the war ended, he set up and managed a radio dealership in Maidstone in Kent. Oliver was interviewed on 2 May 1978. He died on 16 April 1983.

I saw a recruitment advertisement for the Kite Balloon Section of the RFC and I decided to apply. I had tried to enlist before, but my father forbade it, as I was underage. At this point, though, I was away from home, living in lodgings, so there was nothing to stand in my way. The reply came after two days, but my landlady hid it. A few days later, feeling guilty at hampering the war effort, she handed it over to me. I reported to the local barracks for a medical, and from there went to Whitehall where I met two chaps called Mason and Sheffield. The three of us decided to go in together and sign up for the duration. Mason was accepted immediately, but Sheffield and I were turned away and told to grow up. We went outside the building and grew up in five minutes. Then, aged 'nineteen', we were accepted.

The next day, we marched from Whitehall to Waterloo Station. We were escorted by a bagpipe band, and felt that the Kaiser was already beginning to take fright. From Waterloo we went to Farnborough Barracks, which was very crowded. We had to sleep in schools, chapels and any other building with a hard concrete

73

floor. Soon, we were at the Curragh in Ireland, where we underwent two months' square bashing, drilled by the NCOs from the Guards, the greatest bully boys in the Army.

On 22 December 1915, we were sent to Roehampton for balloon crew training. Mason and I were sent to a balloon factory to be trained as riggers. Most of the staff were girls. On our first day we noticed that their stockings were showing their toes and heels, and that their undies were rather drab. At work they were lying down on the balloon fabric, sewing and sticking the seams. The next day, though, the girls seemed to have undergone a miraculous transformation, with lovely stockinged legs, and undies as easy on the eye as those of a modern tennis star.

After two weeks' intensive training in rope-splicing, sewing by hand and machine, and general balloon manufacture, we were passed out as balloon riggers. Mason and I were posted to No. 2 Kite Balloon Section, where we found that Sheffield was one of the balloon crew, so the three of us were together again. During the following days at Roehampton, Mason took me to his home at Stroud Green. His parents told me to regard it as my home, too. I shall always be grateful to them for their kindness. My parents had been strict Wesleyans, who looked upon the demon drink as the most abhorrent of Satan's sins, and preached every day about its evil effects on mind and body. The night before we went overseas, I and some of the other Balloon Boys indulged in a few bottles of Bass. Next morning, with a guilty conscience, I looked in the mirror, expecting to see a face bloated and poisoned beyond all recognition. Behold, there I was, quite normal. I had clearly been conned.

On 6 March 1916, we left Southampton for Le Havre, and from there we went up to Rouen. We stayed there in a camp behind barbed wire, and were not permitted to visit the 'evil' town. I was rather surprised that the officers and NCOs were allowed out; they did not appear to me to have particularly strong moral fibre. From Rouen, we got cattle trucks to Bailleul. This was a horrible journey; there were forty men per truck, and it took twenty-four hours to go about eighty miles. From Bailleul, we rode in a lorry to Locre, where No. 2 Kite Balloon Section had been manned by the RNAS.

74

They returned home and we took over. The crew slept in lofts over a barn full of pigs and rats. Now barns, pigs and rats might have been all right for the RNAS, but not for the RFC. We built comfortable huts near the balloon mooring, and after a few weeks, we had built wash places, lavatories, a cook house and a canteen. We were about to move into our new luxury accommodation, when we were ordered to pack up and move to a wood north of Poperinge.

We understood that there was a war on, and that the Germans were over the other side of the hill, but at Poperinge we felt even more remote from the war. The fact that the Prince of Wales was in a tent 100 yards from the one occupied by Mason, Sheffield and me, suggested that we were in a very safe place. The Prince often used to watch Mason and me when we were repairing the balloon rigging. We overheard him ask for a trip in the balloon, but this was flatly refused by the CO.

A few weeks later, we were sent back to our camp at Locre. Then, No. 25 KBS came along to share our balloon. We looked upon these newcomers with deep suspicion. Their flight sergeant was an ex-policeman from Liverpool with a voice like sandpaper. In the early days of the war, soldiers were not allowed to shave the top lip. I was too young to grow a real moustache, so used to darken my few hairs with soot. The shaving moratorium was suddenly rescinded, and that night, all the crew shaved. The next morning, on parade, the flight sergeant looked with utter horror, and exclaimed, 'What the hell!? I've got a crew of bloody babies; the Kaiser will be pleased!' Swearing was commonplace, but the flight sergeant's harsh Liverpudlian tones made it sound even worse to us Londoners.

We were beginning to notice that there was a war on, and the gunfire appeared to get closer. Now and again we heard the whine of a shell coming in our direction; something was obviously brewing up. No. 25 left to take up a balloon of their own about a mile south of our position. German planes were coming very close to our balloon. We had two parachutes attached to the basket, but no means of using them, as observers didn't wear a harness. We riggers set to work with rope and webbing to make some kind of safety gear. Our blacksmith, a man called Bates, made us an iron swivel-hook to attach the harness to the parachute.

Inevitably, the time came when the German tracer bullets caught our balloon on fire. To our great relief, the harness and parachute worked. The Germans then started shelling the balloon when it was in its bed at night, so the gardens we had planted by our huts were replaced with dugouts. I can't think what possessed us to build our camp so near to the balloon bed. A few days later, the Germans shelled us in the daytime, as we were walking the balloon back from the flying field to its bed. One of our chaps was killed in the middle of fifty men walking together, holding on to the balloon. Many months later, at Ypres, we practised with the men lying down on command, still holding on to the balloon.

Soon we were going to have to leave our camp at Locre. A new balloon bed was being made in an advanced position. We were to leave a place of very pleasant memories, especially the Frontier Café, where *vin blanc* was 1 Franc a bottle (about 10d in those days). There was a girl of seventeen living there who played the piano quite well. I was a member of the concert party, and she used to be my pianist for rehearsal. One of the conditions imposed was that the door be left open so that her mother could watch, and put a stop to any flirtations that might have arisen. Thirty years later, I found her in Bruges, and she was a grandmother.

We were cut off from all civilians, seeing only the ruins around us. I was now a sergeant, having been a rigger for a year. Mason, my fellow rigger, had been sent home to teach rigging skills. My pal Sheffield was transferred to the Infantry. We took up our advanced position, and after a couple of days the Messines mines went up. An advance had started, and the Army took Messines Ridge. We only got as far as Suicide Corner at Kemmel, where we were bogged down for a long time.

Camping at Suicide Corner had always seemed to me a rather stupid idea. The balloon was put near the ruins of a farm, and we managed in some reserve trenches. These conditions were not good enough for the boys of No. 2 KBS, though, and by scrounging timber, huts had soon been erected, along with washing places, a cookhouse and a canteen. Shortly afterwards, the Germans flew over and shelled us. Up went the huts, wash places, cookhouse and canteen. Even the piano was destroyed. We were all safe in the trenches, and our balloon escaped damage. We moved camp immediately, about a mile up the road.

In December 1917 I had my orders to leave No. 2 KBS and report to No. 23 KBS, just north of Ypres. The flight sergeant of this section was suffering from shock, and the camp was right in the middle of a mud patch which extended as far as the eye could see. Soon after my arrival there, the balloon was ordered up. The flight sergeant was in a terrible state; he shouted and bawled, and the crew shouted back. It was chaotic. The officers didn't appear to be much more disciplined, either, and the conditions were the worst I'd experienced in the war. The flight sergeant took me into the cook-house for something to eat, and the Germans started shelling the camp. We went outside, where we saw a pair of legs minus a body. The flight sergeant let out a mad scream, and ran nearly a four-minute mile. We never saw him again.

I was told to take over, and the other NCOs took a dislike to me, as they had expected to be promoted. At night, all the NCOs and crew crawled into rat-infested holes to sleep. No attempt was ever made to improve our conditions. The officers ignored my repeated requests to make some kind of camp and proper dugouts. The CO had bouts of drinking, and would use the winch for joyriding at night. When no ballooning was possible, he would take out a machine gun and fire at rats, often missing the men by inches.

We used to keep gas tubes on the flying position for topping-up. These tubes had to be collected from base, which could be reached only by going through Ypres. No one was too eager to volunteer to take a lorry through this mass of ruins which was always being heavily shelled. I said that I'd go with a driver and collect the tubes. At base, we loaded twenty or so of these tubes onto the lorry, and after a hectic drive through Ypres, they were stored by the flying position. Next day, topping-up was required, and some of these tubes were connected and turned on. They were empty. I was placed under arrest by armed NCO guards, and charged with neglect of duty. I had no idea how this could have happened, but always suspected that someone let the gas out to spite me. The following morning, I was escorted to HQ for the court martial. On my arrival there, I heard the familiar tones of Corporal King from No. 25 KBS. He was now an RSM, and in charge of the court proceedings. The trial was very brief and discharged for lack of evidence. I received an apology, and was later taken to a local café and plied with champagne.

By March 1918, the Germans were beginning to break through our lines. We were able to pack up in good time and retreat. The German advance continued, and we were sent to take over the meteorological balloon at Boulogne. Our job was to take readings of air conditions three times a day and pass the information to General HQ. This was marvellous. The countryside was beautiful, and we were near a village with two cafés which sold a delightful *vin rouge*.

My trips up in the balloon were usually with a young lieutenant. On descent, he used to sit on the side of the basket which, after my two years' experience with balloons, I thought was a stupid thing to do. One day, when we were down to about 500 feet, there was a sudden high wind. He fell into the basket, kicking a valuable instrument into the air. It fell to the ground, and smashed into pieces. We were both on the carpet for that, and sent back to the lines.

When I was ordered to report to No. 23 KBS, near Abeele, my heart sank. However, on arrival I found a complete change of officers and NCOs. Everyone made me very welcome, but the NCOs warned me to give Captain George Machin a wide berth. I soon discovered that he was very strict, but I respected him as the finest instructor; he was a great help to me. The next three months were the hottest time I'd ever had, and I'm not talking about the temperature. Although it was quiet on the ground, the balloon was either shelled by German heavies, or attacked by German machines in the air. When the balloon was up to its flying height, the AA would put up a barrage of shells in readiness for an aircraft attack. My first flight was with Captain Machin, who gave a general outline of the German occupation. To my sorrow, our original No. 2 KBS site was in German hands. Dranouter village was wiped out. The church at Locre, just inside our lines, was burning, and the village itself was slowly being obliterated by shellfire. It was like seeing my own home village in ruins.

Major Cochran from Company HQ phoned us up with the warning of trouble ahead. The winch below reported very high tension on the cable. Reluctantly, Machin told the winch to haul us down, as we were being heavily shelled. Owing to the tension, the winch was not able to bring us down, so they resorted to the spider. This was a pulley which fitted around the cable, allowing the crew to walk us down. The slow operation started. When we were down to about 1,000 feet, there was no wind, and the balloon crumpled up. Down we came. It was impossible to parachute, so Machin told me to climb the rigging to break our fall. The basket fell through a clump of trees, with us safely hanging above.

After climbing from the balloon, we walked a distance away from the escaping gas and had a smoke. It seemed a long wait before the ground crew arrived, and I shall never forget how they cautiously looked in the basket to see the state of the bodies that they assumed they'd find within. However, we had vanished, and it wasn't even Easter Sunday. Such was my first flight with Captain Machin. He was given leave and awarded the DFC. Soon afterwards he returned with an air force blue uniform, and was referred to as 'Little Boy Blue'. He went to No. 39 KBS as commanding officer. Fifty-four years later, I found him living in Heathfield, quite near my home.

On my next flight, after reaching our observation height of about 5,000 feet, we were ordered on the telephone to look out for von Richthofen's Circus, which had just attacked one of our number. We could see balloon No. 4, just north of us, in flames, and we watched No. 3 go down too. It was a cloudy day, so the German planes could hide easily. Suddenly, machine-gun bullets were all around us, and I could see a red triplane very close. Looking to my officer for orders to jump, I found myself alone. Like a shot, I was over the side; I closed my eyes and dropped into space. On my descent, I could still hear the machine-gun bullets around me, but felt no pain. I opened my eyes to behold the pilot of the plane waving at me. I gladly waved back, and in a few moments, had landed in a hop field. I used my knife to cut myself loose. Initially,

I thought that my knife was blunt, but discovered that I was using the wrong side of the blade. As I was heavier than the officer, I passed him on the way down. He landed in a stream of dirty water, and the wind in the chute carried him quite a distance through it. A motorcar from the section soon picked us up. The officer said, 'Did you hear me tell you to jump?'

I replied, 'Yes, sir!'

By now, I had completed my time in the air, and was sent back to HQ for the examination to qualify for my Observer's Wing. After this ordeal, the colonel sent for me. He shook my hand, congratulated me and remarked upon the tough time that I'd had with No. 23 KBS. He reminded me that, until mention was made in the *London Gazette* of my passing out, I ought not to wear my Observer's badge, but told me to ignore that and wear it at once. He sent me on home leave, the first I'd had in two years.

On my return to Belgium, I was posted to No. 13 KBS. During the next few weeks, I helped the flight sergeant with his ground crew. When the colonel came to inspect the flying log, he saw that my flying time was nil. The CO got a reprimand and was ordered to take me up immediately. Soon after we got into the air, the Germans started shelling us. I had no idea who this CO was, or whence he had come, but he certainly showed his fright. On the second shell, he hid in the basket so quickly that his steel helmet was lost overboard. He ordered the winch to haul us down at once, but the colonel overruled him, saying, 'No you don't! Stay up!' The shelling lasted for about an hour, and I didn't offer the CO my helmet. This, I'm sure, caused our relationship to deteriorate. He was subsequently transferred to another section.

By this time, our armies were advancing very quickly, and we tried to keep up with them. We advanced to Ypres and bogged down in the square there. The flight sergeant and myself were sleeping in a cellar beneath the ruins. One night, a very strong wind came up and the guard came into our cellar to warn the flight sergeant that the wind was getting the better of the balloon. In these cases, the crew would be called out to put a large net around the balloon, weighted down with gas tubes. To my dismay, the flight sergeant said, 'Let the bloody thing go!' I had visions of his being shot at dawn, and wondered what I could say as a witness, when I knew he'd been given fair warning of the wind conditions. Nothing was said, though; there was no inquiry, and within a day a new balloon had arrived.

There was no doubt that the war was coming to an end. The Germans were so busy retreating, that they had little time for attacks on us by shell or plane. I remember 10 November, as we and the ground crew had pooled money to buy some beer, and that was the day on which it arrived. We decided to ration it and make it last as long as possible, but discipline broke down and we drank the lot that same night. We were sleeping in a farmhouse scullery, and that night we slept very deeply. Early next morning, a motor-cyclist woke us with the news that the war had ended. With a heavy hangover, we told him to shut up and get out.

About nine o'clock we heard our guns opening up and firing. We shouted, 'Where is that bloody motorcyclist!?' Then we had the official news from the CO, to the effect that hostilities would end at eleven o'clock that very morning. Our thoughts now turned to packing the balloon up for good. Next day, however, orders came to go up, watch the Germans retreating, and report trains leaving. In a few days, though, flying was stopped. The Germans had retreated according to plan. We packed up the balloon and were on the move. Our destination was a farmhouse near Lille. When we arrived there, we didn't know what to do. As an NCO observer, I was redundant, so helped the flight sergeant with the general running of the camp. As I was drawing my extra flying pay, I was quite content. Passes were given out to visit Lille, which we found to be a very gay playground for us. We ran wild.

My leave came through at Christmas, and in January 1919 I was demobbed at Wimbledon. For many years afterwards I met my old comrades at reunions in London. Forty times I have been back to Belgium, and have felt both deep sadness and great happiness, but above all gratitude for still being alive and for having had the privilege of knowing such friendship as I encountered in the Kite Balloon Sections of the Royal Flying Corps.

Bernard Oliver was still in contact with the six other remaining members of the Kite Balloon Association when we met. They convened annually for a celebratory dinner, and had organized the presentation of an original R-type Caquot balloon, discovered at RAF Cardington, to the Wright-Patterson Museum in Dayton, Ohio. A flight twice round the Bay of Biscay in Concorde, hired for a day by RFC veterans in 1980, he reported as 'the dullest ride I have ever had – there was no movement at all . . . though the food and drink were wonderful'.

Technical Sergeant Major (1st Class) Eric Shrewsbury

Technical Sergeant Major (1st Class) Eric Gordon Shrewsbury was born on 6 January 1894 in Hackney, London. He served as a Territorial before joining the RFC on 29 November 1913, and left a civilian occupation as a fitter and turner to offer his talents to the service. He was wounded and away from the front from 13 August 1914 until 22 February 1915.

Beginning as an air mechanic, he worked his way up to sergeant major by the end of the war. He was in charge of squadron transport, and provides a little-documented facet of squadron life. Of the more famous pilots, he knew Leefe Robinson and Louis Strange. Shrewsbury was discharged on 28 November 1921.

He married Gertrude Hammersmith on 5 September 1918. They had one son, Peter. Eric was interviewed on 17 May 1980 at his home in Warlingham, Surrey, and died on 4 April 1991 in Caterham Hospital.

I was apprentice to John Penns, the marine engine section of the Thames Ironworks. They built the first Thunderer, or the first Dreadnought that was ever built on the Thames. Unfortunately, the company went bust, so I was out of work. Vickers had promised to take over all the apprentices, but my mother, foolish woman that she was, wouldn't allow it, as it would have meant my leaving home. Instead, I got a job at Matchless Motors. At that time I was very, very keen on the new motor cars that were coming in but, my father being a mere schoolmaster, we couldn't afford a car. The British School of Motoring was just starting up, and I took a course there and got my driving certificate. I thought I'd go up and join the Army Service Corps which was changing over from horse to motor transport. When I got up to the recruiting office, the chappie there said, 'Are you an engineer?' and I said, 'Well, sort of.'

He said, 'Well, why don't you take a trade test and join the Royal Flying Corps which has just been started?' I did, and passed the test. This was in 1913.

When I joined up, it was still really a Victorian Army. In our barracks at Farnborough was a barrack room with about twenty-five men in it. We had bare wooden stools and tables, and there were no washing facilities or sanitary facilities in the room. The ablutions were 100 yards or more away, and you had to go there in the morning to shave – hail, rain or shine. Then there was the grub. The cookhouse was probably just as far away as the ablutions. The orderly man had a big tray, and used to go and collect the grub and by the time it got to the barrack room it was stone cold. You just had one plate, knife, fork and spoon. When the pudding came up, if there was any, you just had to wipe your plate and have the pudding on that. What we would consider unpleasant in those days on active service is probably very different to our young friends of today, who've had it given to them on a plate all around.

No. 5 Squadron had just been formed, so I was one of its founder members. It was then stationed at Farnborough, but in early 1914, the whole of the Flying Corps was concentrated at Netheravon, which we called a concentration camp. Our squadron had the Henri Farman, a two-seater, pusher type machine with an 80-horsepower rotary Gnome engine. It was an interesting engine, and actually for its weight-to-power ratio, one of the most efficient engines ever. It made for a very stable aircraft, and we had relatively few accidents. I remember only one chap being killed at Farnborough. Also, we didn't fly if the weather was at all adverse.

The RFC was still part of the Army, and we were under Army discipline. My first month in the Flying Corps was spent on the parade ground, learning how to put the cane under my arm and salute. In those days, one had to salute with the hand which was furthest away from the officer. The Army was distinctly hostile to us. It was very much Cavalry-orientated, and didn't have much time for aircraft, as they used to frighten the horses. In fact, in the early days of the war, HQ refused to believe the reports that RFC pilots brought in, because they hadn't been confirmed by the Cavalry.

At that time, there were very few British-made aircraft. The Royal Aircraft Factory, which originally started as a balloon factory, turned over to building planes. They designed and built the BE machines, and later the FEs and the SEs. At this early stage, though, the plane supplied to the Royal Flying Corps was the BE2a, which had a fixed Renault V8 engine.

The beginning of the war didn't come as a great surprise; everyone thought that Germany would start something sooner or later, but not enough preparations had been made in advance, and we even had to use civilian cars to make up the strength. One of our lorries was from the HP Sauce Company. It still had the HP device in gold paint on one side. We had Carter Patterson lorries, and a number of private cars that had been donated.

Then the squadrons broke up. No. 5 went to Gosport, and from there we went overseas with the original British Expeditionary Force. I can't remember exactly when we went out to France. We landed, and got up somewhere between Mons and Mauberge, and were there in time for the start of the Mons retreat. We retreated right back down, past Paris, and then advanced again up to Bailleul. We were on the move the whole time. All we had to eat was oatmeal biscuits, which were called 'hardtack', and raw tea. Our boots all wore out; the toecaps came off, exposing our toes, and we looked like a lot of old tramps. I remember the first time I was able to take my socks off, the skin came off with them.

There were no fixed aerodromes at this time; we had to try to keep the whole show running while scouts were out looking for suitable fields. Fortunately, it was August, and most of the crops had been cut, so it was only a question of moving stacked corn to make a new landing ground. Our planes were all screwed down in the open. At a place called Saponay, our squadron lost five machines, which were blown over in the night and smashed. It was a terrible mess. We had to sleep under the planes, too. Our working hours were very long, and it was there that I learned the knack of dropping off to sleep at any moment, to catch a nap where you can. I've retained that habit to this day. I remember one night we were issued with a large French blanket to be shared between two men. In the morning, the blanket lifted up as solid as a board, encrusted with ice.

We didn't have much contact with the commanding officers; the sergeant majors were the 'powers that be'. There were two of them in every squadron; one was a technical man, and one a disciplinary man. I remember one of them putting us 'on the peg' as we called it, for having dirty boots. Well, of course boots were dirty from staying up all night, wading in dirty water and pushing the machines back to higher ground. That was the sort of mentality that we had to contend with, as if we hadn't enough problems with the enemy. It was a pretty rough sort of time. Really, though, that was nothing compared with what the real heroes of the war had to go through in the trenches.

I didn't get to see much of the enemy. We did see one or two Uhlans, German cavalrymen who were left behind, during our advance. They used to lie in wait for the Army Service Corps convoys, which had only two men on a lorry, but when it came to ambushing an RFC convoy, that was a different proposition, as there were a lot more of us. We did see a number of German aircraft, though. When we were at Bailleul, we were bombed by one, and once, our squadron managed to bring down an Aviatik. We found a Lewis gun in an abandoned Belgian armoured car, and we rigged this up in an Avro. It was hung with a bit of rope from a bar across the two back nacelle struts, and the gunner fired over the pilot's head.

At Bailleul, the machines were screw-picketed down, and a guard was put on them at night. One gusty, wet night, our machine was lifting a bit of slack in the ropes. I tried to screw the picket in a bit further. I slipped, and somehow got my leg under one of the wheels when it came down. My knee was dislocated, and they

86

couldn't deal with this up the line, so I was sent home. When I landed, I was asked where I'd like to go. I said, 'Anywhere near London,' which is where I lived. I landed up down at a place in Devon. It was an ex-farmhouse, and the nurses were all the daughters of the local farmers. This was a really happy time for me, as some of the girls had got little cars, and as I knew something about cars, I was able to tinker with them. I had a whale of a time. On many occasions we used to crawl back in through the windows after going to shows in Bournemouth. I was quite a long while convalescing. Eventually, I was sent home to our local doctor. My knee had not been operated on, as this would have left me with a stiff knee, and meant that I was not fit to return to my unit. I received an undated pass from the squadron, which I thought extended my leave at home, but I soon received a telegram ordering me to report immediately. When I got to Farnborough, I found that I had been posted as a deserter. I said to my sergeant, 'What shall I do, sergeant?' And he said, 'Oh, soldier on, soldier on!' So I soldiered on.

Soon after this, I was promoted to corporal, and posted to No. 7 Reserve Squadron at Netheravon. At Netheravon in those days the flying sheds were about a mile and a quarter away from the hutments. There was no telephone communication, except to some place further down the line. One evening, I was corporal in charge of the guard. The sentry looked in and said, 'The Officers' Mess is on fire!' I looked out, and couldn't see anything, so I sent a cyclist down there to find out. He couldn't see anything, either, and came back. A couple of days later, the sergeant major said to me, 'By the way corporal, you're under open arrest.'

I said, 'Oh?'

But he said, 'It's all right; you can go on leave.' When I returned, I was court-martialled and severely reprimanded in that as corporal in charge of the guard I did not warn the orderly officer, who was a mile and a quarter away, that the mess he was sitting in was on fire. A fortnight later, though, I was suddenly promoted sergeant.

Just about this time, No. 48 Squadron was formed, and I was posted as its sergeant in charge of transport. In that capacity I more or less built the squadron up. I had to go up to London to get stores, collect the transport, and so on. No. 48 Squadron was waiting for the delivery of a mythical BE12 from the Farnborough factory. We were posted to a place called Rendcomb, near Cirencester, and instead of the BE12, were issued with Bristol Fighters. We were the first squadron to take them overseas.

While I was up there, there was nothing to do of course; it was absolutely hopeless at night. But the transport sheds were behind the flying hangars, and I used to wander down there to see the transport chaps. And there was a chassis frame standing up. In those days the cars were built on a chassis and the body put on that. And I said to him, 'What's that chassis doing there?'

He said, 'We had a crash, and bent the chassis so they sent a new one, but nobody knows how to put it together.'

So I said, 'Well, do you mind me having a go, see what I can do in the evenings?' So I did, and rebuilt this Crossley Light Tender.

When we were waiting to go overseas, all the stores were stowed, and the transport was all lined up in the approach road, waiting for instructions to proceed to the port of embarkation. Orders came through that the squadron was not to show its number, but to have a squadron sign. Of course the sergeant in charge of transport was told to see to the matter. Well, I was in the Sergeants' Mess at the time and I thought, 'Oh, good God, what do we do now?' There were some Bass beer bottles standing round, and the thought struck me that the triangle would just do the trick. It's an easy stencil to cut, and the triangle would obliterate the number we'd already painted on the planes. So our squadron became the 'Boozy Squadron' with the red triangle. I'm rather surprised to see, after being up to the Hendon Exhibition, that that red triangle is still the basis of the No. 48 Squadron badge.

We went off to France with No. 48 Squadron and Leefe Robinson. It's easy for me to criticize, with the wisdom of hindsight, but instead of their acclimatizing themselves and getting used to the Bristol Fighter, they crossed the line on their first sortie, and of course the Germans very cleverly just let them go over and waited until they were coming back, when they brought down four out of the six, including Robinson. All were made prisoners of war.

In France, there were never any aerodromes. We had to build them. And I was very, very lucky in No. 48 Squadron, because the troops coming forward in those days were extremely patriotic people, and I had a crowd of very fine fellows. One of them was a mill owner's son from up North, the other was a cigar merchant's son, one of them was a master builder in his own right, and so on. Of course the cigar merchant's son had large parcels of expensive cigars sent out to him, and they were all used to bribe the sentries at the various railhead dumps, so we could get motor generators, motor pumps, or anything we wanted that we thought we would like.

We used to build our own little hangars, you see; we got timber and tarpaulins, all from these railhead dumps, and built ourselves transport hangars. At Bellevue, we were dismantling a hangar. The squadron commander there – chap named Zulu Bennington if I remember rightly – said, 'What are you doing?'

I said, 'Well, we're dismantling this to move, sir.'

He says, 'Well don't you think you ought to leave a place as you'd like to find it?'

So I didn't reply of course; that was that. And about an hour before we were due to start, he came out and he said, 'Take everything! Take everything. I've seen the new ground we're going to and there's not a thing there!' Which, of course, we could have told him had he asked us. So that was the organization of the Flying Corps, even at that time.

In No. 48 we used to get back to Doullens to get petrol supplies. There were no tankers or anything, so the transport had to go out and get the petrol for the aircraft. It was all in big 3-gallon French cans at that time. You had to go for that daily. We'd bring back a couple of thousand gallons, I suppose.

Soon afterwards, I was promoted sergeant major in the field, and posted back. At that time the Women's Legion was just being taken into the Flying Corps to act as drivers, and I was posted to Hurst Park Racecourse, where I was given the job of requisitioning large houses in the district and converting them into hostels for these women who were coming in as drivers. I was posted away from there, as the RAF, as it was at that time, had decided to build a transport repair depot of its own. This was at Wormwood Scrubs, and I was posted there as a technical advisor.

While I was there, I met Prince Albert, who later became George VI. He had a Lancia and we used to provide him with drivers. If there wasn't a driver about, they asked me to drive him. I was asked whether I would take on the job as his permanent chauffeur, but of course in my own opinion I was far too big a noise for a job like that. Eventually, the job went to a bloke named Wood, a leading hand from the depot, who became the Prince's official chauffeur for many years, and stayed with him when he became King. Wormwood Scrubs was a very nice billet for me; the officers and men there didn't know anything, and as the technical adviser, I was left very much to my own devices. I was asked if I would take a commission, but I thought, 'No, this is too good a job for me to do anything silly like that!' So I stayed a technical sergeant major.

When the end of the war came, I was still at Wormwood Scrubs. I went on leave, and when I returned, I thought, 'Well, when we joined up it was for four years' service and four years' reserve.' By that time I'd nearly done all that. I looked round, and all the troops were leaving, and there seemed to be all Chiefs and no Indians. And I thought to myself, 'Not many prospects here.' I was posted first to Manston and then back to Kenley, before being sent to Hounslow to be demobbed. After this, I went back into industry.

Between the wars, I got my pilot's licence. I trained on Gloster machines with the Civil Air Guard. When old Hitler decided to start something, though, it was decided that I was too far into the sere and yellow, so I didn't do anything in the RAF in the Second War. I didn't keep up with flying after that, as it was far too expensive. In the Civil Air Guard we used to pay 5/- an hour, but one of my young friends is with the Biggin Hill Flying Club, and it costs about 35 quid an hour now. Even if I could afford it, I suppose I'm too old to do anything like that now.

As I said, I went back into industry. One or two of my school pals had joined the Western Electric Company, and they said, 'Well, why don't you do that while you're looking round.' I joined the company for a temporary job, and stayed there for thirty-seven years. I rather lost touch with the Flying Corps until I took an old tunic back to the Shuttleworth Collection, where I met a bloke named Wing Commander Guttery who was a mechanic with me in No. 5 Squadron. From that I got to know the Hendon Museum. It begins to look as if I'm in the hot seat though, because most of my old pals have packed up now. Still, I count my blessings . . . .

Eric Shrewsbury, who was tirelessly active at RFC reunions, kept in regular contact until his death. He lived in a fragile 1920's bungalow, to which was appended a well-equipped metalwork shed, as he still preferred to customize his vehicles. Aged nearly ninety, he took delivery of a speedy Suzuki 16-valve car, and his capacious garage housed a Brough Superior motorcycle that he had owned for years and had always intended to restore. The garden surrounding his house was extensive, and was laid down to grass for convenience. His ride-on petrol mower served to keep it trim. The sole decorative feature was a half-overgrown Anderson Shelter dating from the later conflict.

He would wait, wearing an old British warm overcoat, outside the garage for my arrival, much as he had once waited outside the hangars on various forward airfields in France for the machines to return from the lines.

Captain George Riley

Captain George Raby Riley was born in London on 23 February 1899. He took his ticket, No. 5205, aged eighteen on an L&P biplane at Edgware on 7 September 1917, and entered RFC service as a 2nd Lieutenant. While serving with No. 3 Squadron, Riley was shot down with a minor wound on the day Manfred von Richthofen was killed. He is credited with thirteen victories in Sopwith Camels and was gazetted on 16 September 1918. Riley received the MC for 'four direct hits on a long line of enemy transport, and afterward caused havoc among them with his M6. Several times he attacked troops and transport from low altitude.'

In a supplement to the *London Gazette* of 8 February 1919, Riley's DFC award is prefaced by the entry: 'An officer who shows the greatest dash and gallantry in leading low-bombing and defensive patrols. On 27th September, he obtained two direct hits with bombs on an enemy balloon on the ground which set it on fire. Later he attacked another balloon in the air, shooting it down in flames.'

Riley was interviewed in Croydon on 16 November 1978. He died on 1 July 1983.

I'd always been very keen on flying. My father took me to the Hyde Park Hotel, where I shook hands with Blériot, who had just flown the English Channel. After that, I was even keener to fly. In July 1917 I joined an infantry regiment. For my training as an officer in the infantry, I was sent to Hursley Park, near Winchester. We built the camp there, and I passed all the relevant examinations, going through all the ranks from lance corporal to sergeant, before getting a transfer to the Royal Flying Corps. From there, I went to Reading University to do theoretical courses on engineering, navigation, fighter flying and aerial gunnery. I passed the course there, then went to Stag Lane Aerodrome at Hendon, where I flew the old pre-1914 Caudrons. These planes didn't have ailerons, and if you put on bank to make the machine turn, the wings warped. Needless to say, those aircraft weren't safe to fly if there was any wind at all. When the weather was fine, though, you got a marvellous view of London from about 2,000 feet. I got my pilot's certificate flying those.

At Dover, I flew about half a dozen types of machines. My favourite training aircraft was the Avro, which was safe to fly, and extremely manoeuvrable. After Dover, I was transferred to the Royal Naval Air Station at Manston, and finally up to Turnberry in Scotland, for training in aerial observation. I returned home in January 1918 and got my wings. I qualified as a pilot on the DH5. These had a terrific dive, and were used for strafing the German troops on the ground. But they got nicknamed 'flying coffins', as so many men killed themselves doing their solos on them.

The whole squadron turned out to see me take off. I was about the sixth bloke to go up; all the other chaps had been killed. I took off very carefully and gained about 3,000 feet before attempting to turn. She was very easy to manoeuvre. Shortly after that the DH5 was washed out. I went onto the Sopwith Camel then, which was a difficult machine to fly at first; once you got control, though, they were wonderful machines. They were very fast and tight in the turn. The only thing you had to watch out for was the torque when turning right; it could stall the engine.

I always took a very great interest in the mechanics in my flight; our lives depended on these fellows. I took a great amount of interest in watching them work, so they knew I was keen. No. 3 Squadron was the first squadron to land in France in 1914, and a lot of the original mechanics were still with the squadron. They were of a very high standard indeed. I had a rigger and a fitter assigned to me. I showed a great amount of interest in the riggers, who used to make sure my machine guns were properly sighted. This was terribly important. I would test-fire them myself, on the aerodrome. We had two Vickers guns, and a belt of ammunition. The Constantinesco gear prevented the bullets hitting the propeller. Occasionally, you got a bit of dud ammunition which hit the propeller and if it did, it would break up. But we were lucky. To shoot another machine down, you needed to be within fifty yards; any range greater than that, and you might not be sure of hitting the Hun, as your machine guns would be converging. I had mine converging at about 100 yards. Generally, we'd go out with 600 rounds, so we had to preserve our ammunition by firing in short bursts. You'd hate to be stuck up there with all your ammunition gone after half an hour.

At the beginning of February 1918, I went out to France to join No. 3 Squadron. I was posted to Warloy near Albert. Albert was famous for the spire of its church, where the statue of the Virgin was hanging down, having been shot by shellfire. It was quite a landmark. The French always maintained that they'd lose the war if the statue fell down completely. Later on in the war the whole lot was shot down anyway. At this time we were flying mostly offensive patrols on the German side of the lines. The Huns were really pushing, and drove us back almost as far as Amiens. We were then sent over with 38-pound bombs to drop on the German troops. We were taking huge casualties, but this bombing was very worthwhile, as it had a devastating effect on the enemy's morale. Flying operationally in France was a bit different from training in England, but I soon got used to it.

The other job we had to do was balloon strafing, shooting at the German balloons which flew about seven miles on their side of the lines. They were very difficult to get, as they had a covering battery of about twelve machine guns on the ground. Also, when our machines appeared, the Germans would haul down the balloon at terrific speed. I did manage to get one eventually. I came through the clouds, the Germans spotted me and winched the balloon down, so I flew quite near the ground and dropped my bombs on the balloon. It went up in flames. I got the DFC for my balloon strafing, and the MC for my work as a scout pilot.

At this time, we were very much up against Manfred von Richthofen and his Flying Circus. They were very good fliers, but

I think our chaps were a wee bit better, both in skill and morale. Richthofen had an all red machine, and the other Huns had their machines painted in different colours, but ours were camouflaged to match the ground. When we were in a dogfight, all mixed up and dashing around, we didn't often shoot down a German; usually it was a quick attack, a dive, that was decisive. You could dive up to about 160 miles per hour, but you had to be very careful how you came out of a dive, otherwise your wings could come off. That happened to a number of our chaps and, of course, we had no parachutes in those days. Our squadron had Sopwith Camels, which were most effective in getting the enemy planes down, so we did quite well, I think. We shared our aerodrome with No. 56 Squadron, who flew SE5s. I never got to fly one of those, though. Towards the end of the war, the Sopwith Snipe came out, but our squadron didn't get them.

I knew James McCudden from No. 56 Squadron. He went back to England in April 1918, and was sent up to Scotland as an instructor. I was very impressed with McCudden, who seemed to me a quiet and very modest fellow. He had originally been a mechanic with No. 3 Squadron, having joined the Royal Flying Corps in 1913. He rose steadily in rank, becoming a flight sergeant observer, and then a pilot. It was a great tragedy that he killed himself. He had taken off, and was doing a climbing turn; the machine stalled and he crashed. It was ironic that he should have died in an accident rather than in combat. His speciality was shooting down German two-seaters. He'd fly very high indeed. Of course, it was often rather dicey taking on a two-seater, as you had the observer firing at you. McCudden used to come up from underneath, in the same way that Captain Ball used to. That was his favoured method of attack. The Hun didn't know what had happened until they'd been raked from underneath; sometimes they didn't even know you were there.

Most of our patrols were at 18,000 feet. It was dreadfully cold up there in an open cockpit. I even used to have to put anti-freeze on my nose. I used to wear silk gloves, with a pair of woollen gloves over the top. Even so, when I came down and my hands thawed out, it was excruciatingly painful. There was no heat in the cockpit at all. We couldn't really go up much higher than that. Whilst practising, I did once get up to about 18,500 feet. Of course, if we hadn't been loaded with the machine guns, we might have got the planes up a little higher.

We were doing up to three patrols a day, starting at dawn. We had about two hours' worth of petrol per patrol, with about half an hour's reserve tank. Generally, we were on the lookout for German planes. There were still plenty of Huns about in the air, even though the position on the ground had changed. Their morale was waning badly, though. They tended not to attack us; we'd always do the attacking. There had always been a policy in the RFC of offensive, rather than defensive patrols. This, of course, used to mean that if we were hit by machine-gun fire, or anti-aircraft fire, we were forced down on the German side of the lines. A number of our chaps were forced down, and became prisoners of war.

I was slightly wounded once. We were attacking the von Richthofen lot. There were about eight of these chaps, all in one line. There were only five of us by the way. My flight commander attacked them. Well, I got my bead on a bloke right at the end of this formation. They were about 400 yards away, and they were firing, all eight of them. It was a very short range that you fired from to shoot a German war machine down. And the chap on the right, his bullets hit my machine guns, and cut my cheek, as if I'd cut myself very badly shaving, and got a splinter of the bullet in my left shoulder.

The machine was hit, and two of these Germans followed me down, and fortunately there was a cloud about 3,000 feet below. I went through the cloud and they left me. So I managed to stagger back and get back to the aerodrome and was sent to a Casualty Clearing Station. Fortunately, the wounds weren't at all serious, but I was sent back to England for a month's leave.

The first time I had a forced landing was in Dover. I had been touring round the coast and, when I was coming back, the engine cut out. I saw what I thought was a field just ahead, but when I came down to land, I found I was landing downhill. I had to stall the machine from about twenty feet. She crashed and went over upside down. Thankfully, I was unhurt, and landed in the grounds of a very posh mansion. They gave me a wonderful reception and a great lunch. The squadron collected the machine, which was badly damaged, but not a write-off.

When I returned, the squadron was quite different. In those days, the average life expectancy of a pilot was about three weeks, and most of the chaps had been killed, shot down or taken prisoner. I had a couple of forced landings in France. The engine cut out and I managed to stagger over the hangars, across a cornfield, over a railway line and into a field on the other side. On the other occasion, I was shot from the ground in France. I'd been hit in the engine, so had to come down. I landed in a field about twenty feet from a German gun range.

Only once did I get to fly at night. Every morning at dawn a German two-seater used to come over and take photographs of our line. We didn't say anything about it, but four of us decided we'd go up in the dark one night. Gosh, that was a silly thing to do. There were no lights to show us where we were, but eventually my eyes got used to the darkness. We reached the particular part of the line where this Hun used to take the pictures, but he never appeared. Our only theory was that there must have been spies near the aerodrome that told them we were going up. He turned up the following day, though. We never went out at night again; it was far too risky.

When we weren't flying, I think we had it much better than the poor chaps in the infantry. We had a nice mess and good food. Towards the end of the war, we were billeted in villages, and I found it very comfortable. We didn't have much of a social life, though. We used to have a guest night at the aerodrome, when we'd entertain the New Zealanders who'd come out on rest. We had a gramophone, and used occasionally to bring back records from England.

Armistice Day was really extraordinary. All the gunfire had stopped along the line. We weren't flying of course, and it seemed so quiet. I couldn't imagine that the war was actually over; it felt rather an anticlimax. Some squadrons were sent to Germany, but we remained in France for a while. I was disappointed; I would have liked to have gone to Germany in those days. Looking back,

I feel very lucky to have had an experience that few others had. All the young men were interested in aviation, as it was something new at the time, and they were young. You had to be a young chap for flying, though, as you've got to have split-second reactions. In those days, by twenty-five or twenty-six your reactions were beginning to slow up. I didn't think much about getting killed; I suppose because I was so young at the time. The best thing about it was the sense of adventure we all felt, but it's terrible when I think of all those young chaps who lost their lives.

When the war ended, I was posted to Eastbourne as an instructor on Sopwith Camels. They had a two-seater Camel there. It was a real headache taking another bloke up in a Camel, as it was so sensitive on the controls. I flew there until I came out of the service in March 1919, and didn't fly again after that. I missed it very much; I felt like a duck out of water. I went out to Burma for four years, then returned to England, where I worked with electricity.

Captain Lawrence Wingfield

Captain Lawrence Arthur Wingfield, known as 'Lawrie', was born in Richmond, Surrey on 17 April 1898. His father opened Shoreham Aerodrome in Sussex, and inculcated in young Lawrie a passion for aviation. Wingfield was commissioned in 1915, aged seventeen, after attending Aldenham School and serving in the Inns of Court Officer Training Corps and the Royal Fusiliers. Training on Maurice Farman Longhorns, he was posted to No. 12 Squadron in France, where he flew BE2cs on general reconnaissance duties.

On 1 July 1916, he was shot down after blowing up ammunition wagons at St Quentin station, and became a prisoner of war. After incarceration in various camps, he escaped in October 1917 and reached Holland safely after walking over ninety miles in ten days. Later he was awarded the MC and DFC. He noted, 'I was decorated once for being shot down and once for running away.'

After the war he served as solicitor to the Royal Aeronautical Society starting in 1920. He joined the Institute of Aeronautical Engineers and founded the Guild of Air Pilots and Air Navigators. He retired from GAPAN in 1955 but continued as its legal advisor. Wingfield wrote a book, *The Law in Relation to Aircraft*. He was interviewed at Weybridge, Surrey on 13 October 1979, and died on 23 October 1989, aged ninety-one.

My father started an aerodrome at Shoreham in 1911 when I was a schoolboy, and I became interested in flying. As soon as I could, having the intention of getting into the Air Force, I joined the Inns of Court Officer Training Corps. In July 1915, I was commissioned Temporary Acting 2nd Lieutenant in the Royal Fusiliers, and after a short time at the Duke of York's School in Dover, I was transferred to the Royal Flying Corps, and went up to Castle Bromwich to learn to fly. I learned on a Farman Longhorn, which I found a delightful machine. I was allowed to go solo after about four hours; after eight hours, I got my Aero Club Certificate. I then went to Netheravon for more training, and was awarded my wings in December 1915. I met Billy Bishop at Netheravon. At that time, he was no further advanced than I was, but when I met him many years later in Canada, he was an Air Vice Marshal with strips of medals.

I joined No. 12 Squadron in January 1916, flying an assortment of aircraft, but mostly BE2cs, which were used for gun-ranging and short reconnaissance. They weren't fighter aircraft. We had a couple of Bristol Scouts in our squadron, which were reserved for Flying Commanders, but I was allowed to take them up from time to time. Stationed at an aerodrome a few miles to the north, at Savy Aubigny with No. 11 Squadron, was Albert Ball. I took a Bristol Scout over to that aerodrome to find Ball and get some idea of modern fighter tactics, of which Ball and Bishop were really the pioneers. They had realized that a plane was little more than a gun platform, and that what was required was a fixed gun and a movable aircraft. I never got the chance to meet Ball, though, as he wasn't on the aerodrome that day.

My initial posting had been to St Omer. Later we moved to Vert Galant and then down to just behind Arras. That's where I was stationed at the beginning of the Battle of the Somme. Our reconnaissances were made, in formations of five, about ten miles over enemy lines. One exercise which was set for us was to send one machine every hour to the railhead at St Quentin, and bomb it to prevent reserves coming up. I was by far the youngest in the squadron at the time, but this mission struck me as being tantamount to suicide. I went to see the CO, and asked him for permission to go first; permission was granted. I didn't do this from any heroism, though; I had the idea that maybe only the first plane to do this would have a chance of getting there and back safely. That didn't happen, though, as I was shot down on my return. I had a Fokker on my tail, and the only way of getting back against the prevailing south-westerly wind, was to sideslip. I did this, but the Fokker overtook me and got back on my tail again. I began to see masses of bullet holes appearing in my wings. A bullet smashed into my instrument panel, and a bit sheared off and hit the tip of my nose. My engine began to falter, and I looked about for a suitable place to land. I landed on a parade ground full of German troops. I entirely forgot that I ought to have done something about my plane, such as set it on fire. I was surrounded by souvenir-hunting German soldiers, and was eventually rescued by four officers in a small Mercedes-Benz with a mounted machine gun.

I was very courteously treated by my captors, who took me back to a magnificent château, where I was entertained to tea with the squadron. The man who shot me down, Wilhelm Frankl, was introduced to me. He told me that I was his seventh victory. After tea, I was taken round the aerodrome, and allowed to have a good look round a Fokker. It was a damn good machine. It was very fast, and shot through the propeller. It was altogether a superb fighting aircraft.

The Germans took me to the jail at St Quentin, where I spent three days in solitary confinement. Another member of my squadron, Van Nostrand, was there. He had been shot down the same day as I had. We were taken together to be put on a train to Germany. A German officer told me that my plane would be taken to Berlin to be exhibited. I was rather dispirited; after all, I'd lost a serviceable aircraft and a new Lewis gun. I felt that I had failed. Later, though, I learned that the station at St Quentin was in a terrible state. My bombs had hit an ammunition train, and the consequent explosion was so staggering that I could scarcely believe it. It wasn't until nearly two years later that the official citation read as follows:

FOR GALLANTRY AND GOOD SERVICE
IN THE FIELD
On 1st July 1916, this officer set out from No 12 Squadron's aero-
drome for the purpose of bombing St Quentin. He went entirely by
himself, without escort or observer. His machine was hit. He was
brought down and taken prisoner by the enemy, but not before he
had successfully carried out the bombing of his objective. A report
by prisoners taken later in the year, said that on that date, a British
aeroplane dropped bombs on St Quentin. An ammunition train was
hit, and the greatest confusion and consternation ensued. A regi-
ment which was being entrained fled, took to the woods, and were
not all re-collected until the following evening. It is known that no
other aeroplane reached St Quentin on this date. His work with the
Squadron had previously been excellent . . .

J M SALMOND, MAJOR-GENERAL COMMANDING RFC
IN THE FIELD

Although I hardly recognize myself from that, it vindicates my initial idea that only the first aircraft would be able to reach the target.

I was in about five camps, Krefeld, Neuburg, Rosenberg, Mainz and Strohen, where I ended up in May 1917. In those days, there weren't any escape organizations; all escapes were individual attempts, and tended to fall over each other. At Strohen, the prospect of escape became possible. It hadn't been possible before; the other places were remote fortresses. I managed to escape from Strohen on 4 October 1917. There had been three previous escapes from there that year; G. F. Knight of No. 12 Squadron got out on 16 August, G. W. Insall VC, on 29 August, and Geoffrey Harding on 29 September. These three gave us all tremendous encouragement. I got out with Somerville, Robinson and Fitzgerald of the Gloucestershire Regiment. Somerville and Robinson were re-captured, but Somerville got out at his second attempt, on 6 November, by which time I was back in England.

I had no time for tunnelling. Not only did we sacrifice our bed boards to no purpose, but they always fell in. The plan which Robinson and I had was to make use of a shallow depression in the ground. There was a ditch leading to a steel trellis fence, that was about nine feet high. Beyond that was the main ditch, then a bank and a road, then finally a third ditch, full of water. Our plan was to wriggle through the first ditch, cut the wires and get out. We had a map and a compass, but no wire cutters. Somerville had wire cutters, however, so we let him in on our plan and agreed that he would go first.

We all waited for about two weeks, until we got a really wet night. A confederate signalled the movements of the sentries by rapping on a plate from the canteen. At an appropriate moment, Somerville reached the ditch, crawled along, cut the wire, and got away. Robinson and I crept into the ditch. Having to wriggle seventy-five yards on your front in wet conditions was no mean feat, though. Robinson squeezed through the hole in the fence, but I became stuck. By this time, Fitzgerald was right behind me. A powerful fellow, he grabbed my feet and shot me through the hole like a cork from a bottle, with a dreadful clanging of the wire. This alarmed the sentries on either side, and they came running up at the double. I ran straight at a column of German troops coming down the road; this afforded some cover, as the sentries couldn't risk firing at me. Robinson went past me in a flash, and I dived headlong into the nearest ditch, remaining there for the next three-quarters of an hour. Shots were being fired, and a German guard came right along the bank beside me. I remained very still.

When the hubbub had died down, I climbed out of the ditch and crawled clear of the light. I had no money except for a cheque for £7 I'd won at poker. I determined to go on foot. It rained incessantly the whole time, and I travelled by night, sleeping in barns during the day. After eight days, I came to the River Ems, and resolved to cross that night. At nine o'clock that evening, I was peering through the reeds, looking for a suitable place to make my crossing, when I was held up from behind by a man with a gun. When I made to run, he threatened to shoot me, so I stopped. He asked me in German what I was, and I replied: '*Kriegsgefangener*'.

He asked me if I spoke French, and I thanked God that I was able to say 'Yes!' He said, 'If you'd like to follow me, you'll find a spot where the river is considerably narrower.'

This man turned out to be from Alsace. He took me to the place, where I found a plank. I got out of my clothes, tying them to the plank with my puttees. Before I pushed off from the bank, I asked this chap whether there were any guards on the other side of the river. He replied, 'No. They're out on the moor.' I thanked him, and made the crossing. By this time I was way off my map. I was on a moor, it was very windy and the rain was absolutely tipping down. I pressed on until I reached the door of a farmhouse. I must have been a most depressing sight. The farmer took one look at me, said *'Hollande! Hollande!'* and invited me in.

I was handed over to the Dutch police who took me, after forty-eight hours' rest, to the Consul in Rotterdam. I was given some money and ordered to buy some new clothes. I came back on the next convoy. Fitzgerald was there, too. On the 22 October 1917, I received a letter from Clive Wigram:

> *The King is very glad to hear that you have managed to escape from Germany. Will you kindly let me know what your movements are likely to be, so that I can arrange some time for His Majesty to see you.*

Fitzgerald and I went to see the King on 25 October 1917. He was very interested, and seemed to know a lot. He gave Fitzgerald an MC, presumably for some previous exploit. Later on, when escaping was regarded as something meritorious rather than abandoning your fellow captives, I was awarded the MC. One of the effects of being a prisoner of war was the most terrible constipation; I suffered from this throughout my internment and for three years afterwards.

They never sent one back to the same front, for fear of court martial by the enemy. I went back to Shoreham for retraining. I was sent to Biggin Hill, where I worked on wireless experimental work. We had DH9as, Sopwith Camels, Pups and Snipes. I used to take up wireless operators who were doing experiments with ground-to-air, air-to-ground and air-to-air wireless communication. I was much more interested in looping the planes, though. I didn't really like the Sopwith Snipe, finding it too heavy, but the Camel was a wonderful aircraft. Although I never got to fly it in the face of the enemy, I would have said that, from the point of view of manoeuvrability, the Camel was far superior to the Snipe. I once took a Camel up to 22,000 feet without oxygen. At that altitude, all your reactions are slowed down, and every movement becomes exhausting.

By the time I came back to England, Smith-Barry had started the Gosport School of Flying, where one learned to fly the Avro 504K backwards, forwards, sideways, downwind, crosswind or wherever you liked. It was the most marvellous machine for that purpose. Another plane that I flew there was the RE4. It was a rotten plane, but I don't remember all the details. Most of my logbooks were destroyed in a cellar at Willesden, when a sewer burst. Only my original logbook, from Castle Bromwich, remains.

When the Armistice came, I got demobilized as quickly as I could. I was lucky to have a father who was a solicitor. I had a career ahead, and got down to my studies. At the end of the war, the Air Force was reduced to about a tenth of its former size. About 26,000 planes were left, and most of these were destroyed. The civilian pilot was no longer a glamorous figure; he was just a poor chap without a job.

In 1922, Air Vice Marshal Sir William Sefton Brancker was appointed as Director General of Civil Aviation, and sought to give it every encouragement. In 1924, Imperial Airways was set up to combine the four big aviation companies into one. I didn't have a particular interest in the Airship Programme, until the formation of the Guild of Air Pilots. This arose in 1929 out of the Air Ministry's insistence that pilots should at least possess a Secondary Navigator's Certificate. A time was set for passing the exam, and together with Lamplugh and the Chief Navigator, Johnson, I set up classes. With the Guild of Air Pilots, we had the idea of forming an elite body of professional pilots, divorced from trade unionism.

After twenty-seven years, I was helpful in turning it into a City Livery Company, and I was its clerk for the whole of that period.

Anything to do with airships arose purely because Lord Thomson, the Air Minister, was extremely keen to go to the Delhi Durbar in 1930 on the R101. I dined with Thomson and Brancker a couple of nights before, and they were full of enthusiasm. The construction of these two airships, the R100 and the R101 was all part of the overall Empire plan. In those days, we really believed in the Empire, even holding an Empire Air Day on 24 May every year. However, the R101 had not been extended in length, and wasn't ready.

I'm not a technical man, so I've no idea what caused the disaster, but I believe that the subsequent enquiry found that the ballonets had rubbed against the frame, whereby the gas leaked out. All I know is that it descended onto a slight eminence near Beauvais in the early hours of the morning of 5 October 1930. I heard the news on the wireless at 7 o'clock, whilst I was shaving. I was horrified. I rang Jones, Brancker's secretary, and we went down to Croydon to see what we could do. We found an aircraft there, waiting to take off, and we went with it. Jimmy Jeffs, the airport controller, wrote us out a couple of passes, and we arrived at Beauvais with Henry Tizzard and some important scientists and technicians. When we arrived, the thing was still alight. Of the fifty-four passengers who were on board, the only ones who escaped were the seven who were in the power gondolas at the side. They were able to jump out. The rest were just a row of charred bodies, stretched out.

I've been mixed up in aviation all my professional career; I've learnt a lot from it, but I've never earned my livelihood at it. For those of us who believed in aviation, we had to see what could be done, hence all the different pioneering flights, of which the first was Alcock and Brown crossing the Atlantic. I remember welcoming them at the Aero Club at 3 Clifford Street. I remember many of the subsequent ones, too, such as Kingsford-Smith, Bert Hinkler and Alan Cobham. Later on, women such as Amy Johnson and Amelia Earhart played a big part, too. We held a dinner for Amelia Earhart at the Aero Club. I remember her saying to me, 'The funny thing is, three hours out of St John's, Newfoundland, my compass and altimeter both packed up.'

I asked her, 'Didn't you think of turning back?'

She replied, 'With *that* amount of petrol on board? Not likely!'

All those pioneering flights were flown with heavily over laden aircraft. If you managed to get off the ground, you daren't land; you had to fly for three or four hours to burn off the petrol.

I joined the reserve when it was formed in 1922, flying DH9as. There were three or four training schools set up, of which one was De Havilland's at Stag Lane Aerodrome. The man who used to swing my propeller at Stag Lane was Bob Hardingham, an ex-apprentice of the factory at Farnborough. He eventually became Sir Robert Hardingham, Head of Air Registration, and is now retired. I only visited the factory once, to deliver a plane there. With the machines they produced there, the emphasis was on stability, inspired by one man, Edward Teshmaker Busk. He designed, flew, and was killed on a BE2 type. I think that the disadvantage of the BE2, compared with the Avro 504K, which was not so stable, was that it was far less manoeuvrable. This was fine for civilian flying, but no good at all for a fighting machine.

When I was out in France, the Avro 504K was widely regarded as a death-trap. I've seen chaps spin the thing into the ground and be chased up the tail by the engine. I always loved flying. Flying at 300 feet above the trees in the autumn, when the colours were just right, was an incomparable pleasure.

Though earning his livelihood principally in the law to which he was dedicated by his initials, L.A. Wingfield had pursued other careers as publican, chairman of a greyhound racing track, and fruit farmer. His early introduction to pioneer flying came in 1911, when he saw Cody's 'Cathedral' at Shoreham, the aerodrome set up by his father.

An admirer of female pulchritude, and a bon viveur, he retained a debonair, youthful aspect, together with an incisive legal brain and an undiminished enthusiasm for aviation. He obtained one of the first commercial pilot's licences in England after the war, and as a founder member of GAPAN, upheld the highest standard of rules and practice.

Sergeant Observer Frederick Archer

Sergeant Observer Frederick Archer was born in Burton-on-Trent on 15 October 1896. His family had moved there because his father worked on the railways. Fred was one of thirteen children. He had only one given name because supposedly the family had run out of ideas.

After the war he worked as a joiner for a local company, making fittings for breweries. He married Alice Mary Dean in 1921 and they had one daughter, Patricia. He joined the Special Police during the Second World War, and served for twenty years, becoming a commandant. Archer was interviewed at his home in Burton-on-Trent on 12 August 1979. He died on 15 March 1986.

I enlisted in early May 1915. There was no conscription at that time; we were all volunteers. I met someone who told me that they'd joined the Royal Flying Corps, and I thought, 'That sounds just up my street.' I was an apprentice joiner at the time, and only seventeen. When I went to enlist, I told them I was nineteen. They used to believe you in those days. Everybody had to have some sort of trade. Joiners went in as riggers, steam-engine fitters came in as internal combustion engine fitters, and tailors came in as sail makers. They would cover the wings with fabric, and dope it to tighten and waterproof it. We had painters who used to paint the aircraft. We had some mechanics who had come into the squadron having been steam-engine mechanics on boats. They became internal combustion engine mechanics, and very well they did, too.

It didn't take them long to adapt from steam to petrol. We even had tinsmiths. We all had courses of instruction and lectures on the care and maintenance of aircraft. These were, in the main, given by experts from the factories. Gradually we became acclimatized to handling aircraft.

I was given £1 and a railway warrant, and sent off to Farnborough. Once there, we had to undertake a course in drilling, went shooting at Kingsbury Rifle Range, and then we had trade tests and inoculations. This lasted about a month. I was allotted a regimental number, 5251, which was the total strength of the RFC at that time. The initial training at Farnborough was mostly an attempt to make a soldier out of you. In the evenings, we had lectures on military history. There were some sloppy individuals about, who looked as if they'd never be soldiers, but they developed in later years to be really class mechanics. The ranks were Army ranks; we all wore Army uniform. The RFC was a part of the Army, there's no doubt about that. When you joined up you were all classified as 2nd Class Air Mechanic. This was the lowest rank, but it meant 14 bob a week, which was 2/- a day, and this was a shilling a day more than the infantrymen got.

Then they sent us to a place that was going to become an aerodrome, and I was lucky enough to be sent to Birmingham, to Castle Bromwich where we started No. 5 Reserve Aeroplane Squadron. We had no aeroplanes for the first three weeks, then we were sent some Maurice Farman Longhorns. They were a contraption of bamboo, wire and string, and the rear axles were tied to the frame with elastic rope. I know that, because I've tied a good many. I became a mechanic on Maurice Farmans. One strange thing at Castle Bromwich was that there was a sewerage works at one end of the runway. Sometimes the pilots used to overshoot, and land in the sewage. I can tell you that it was a very unpleasant job to go in and pull them out, because it was liquid sewage.

They sent me away to Avro in Manchester for a course in rigging, and I became a rigger. When you'd been on the job for about six months, and had got used to various aircraft, you were promoted to 1st Class Air Mechanic, which I picked up in October 1915. The advantage of this was not only that your salary doubled to 28/- per week, but that you got a permanent pass out at night. You could go into Birmingham in the evening without having to apply for a pass. And 28/- was more than a lot of people were getting for a week's wages in Civvy Street.

The first officer who came to us at the squadron was Major R. N. Rodwell. He was a very nice fellow, and the only chap in our squadron with wings. He taught two men how to fly in Maurice Farmans, and in turn, they were made instructors. Then we began to get a dribble of officers from infantry regiments, attached to the RFC for flying duties. They found out it wasn't good enough to fly a Maurice Farman; the twin-seater Avro had come along, and they had to qualify on those. They were deadly killers, the Avros. I don't think we had anyone killed on a Maurice Farman, but quite a number died flying the Avro and the Caudron. After some time, we were fitted out with BEs, which were a big improvement.

We developed into a working squadron, and started night flying lessons. Night flying was very primitive in those days. There were no such things as landing lights; we cut the tops off petrol cans, half filled them with paraffin, and lined them up in rows. We had one pilot in particular, William Leefe Robinson, who became very proficient at night flying, and was transferred to No. 39 Squadron to attack Zeppelins. He shot down that Zeppelin over Cuffley, and later on was awarded the VC.

From Castle Bromwich, we went to Netheravon, where they had RE7s. These were big, cumbersome machines. They were no use at all; we had no end of trouble with them, and a lot of forced landings over Salisbury Plain. They were two-seaters. I flew in an RE7 on test flights on a number of occasions. It was meant to carry a large bomb; not a cast iron bomb, but one made of a metal like aluminium, and big enough for a small chap to get inside. The theory was that when this bomb dropped, it would spread liquid fire for about a quarter of a mile. But it was never used; the idea was scrapped altogether.

After Netheravon we went to Filton in Bristol, where they built and tested the Bristol aircraft. We didn't stay there long, but I remember being part of a little crew that used to tow a raft out into the river for our chaps to practise dive-bombing. Thank God our rope was 200 yards long, else we might have caught some of the little bombs they used to try to drop on the raft.

From there, the transport went from Avonmouth, the machines flew across, landing at St Omer, and we ground staff sailed from Southampton over to Le Havre, then went up to Rouen. St Omer was our depot for about a fortnight, after which, in July 1916, we went up the line to the Battle of the Somme. At that time we had terrific casualties among our fellows. The trouble, in my opinion, was that the pilots never had long enough to learn to fly a machine; they'd never had much practice at aerial warfare. Most of the Germans weren't much better, but their crack men seemed to take great delight in shooting our novices down. I used to wonder why these men were sent out to France as combat pilots when they didn't know very much at all about the job, and about their planes. The thing I always found strange was the number of hours' flying that a budding officer would do before getting his wings. Ten or eleven hours was all he would have had in the air.

We were stationed at three different places, Ste Marie Cappel, Bailleul and Poperinge. We moved several times, probably to try to make the Germans think we had more Spads than we really did. We used to make decoy aerodromes to deceive the Germans. We put landing flares out at night so Jerry would drop his little bombs on it. We dug ourselves into slit-trenches, and hoped he wouldn't drop anything on us. It was quite a thrill, but sometimes the bombs would land very near us indeed.

We had a number of very famous people visit the squadron; Lloyd-George, General Pershing, the head of the American forces, Bonham-Carter and Lord Trenchard. Trenchard was OK with the ground staff, but he was very strict with the COs, and they didn't care much for him. But he'd pat us ground staff on the back and say: 'That's the stuff to give 'em, my lads.' Trenchard was a big, tall bloke, and rather a jovial type. At Poperinge, I met the Duke of Windsor on a number of occasions, too. He was Prince of Wales at the time. He was attached to the Brigade of Guards near Poperinge. He used to come to the aerodrome simply to scrounge a flight, but nobody was ever allowed to take him up. He was a lovely looking chap, with the most beautiful complexion, and was dressed

111

immaculately. He was always accompanied by a special guard of four men; he didn't look very big in the midst of these 6 feet 3 inch Grenadier Guards.

One aerodrome I remember was at Le Vert Galant. This is where Captain Ball VC, Albert Ball, was stationed with No. 56 Squadron. I used to talk with Ball every day. He was from Nottingham, and I had come from Burton, which was not too far away. He was always dressed scruffily, and his tunic was always covered in grease. He was an old RFC man, not a transfer. He used to dig a bit of garden on the aerodrome, and plant flowers. They tell me that he played the violin marvellously, too. I got on all right with him, but he was a bit aloof. He was so dedicated to his machines and his work, that he developed a streak of aloofness that not everybody liked, but I found him very likeable. He was only a little fellow: big in bravery, but short in height. He was scruffy, though. He used to work on his own machines without putting any overalls on, and he'd get grease all down the front of his tunic. His CO was Major Blomfield, who used to be a flight commander in our squadron. I've never in my life seen anyone as put out as he was on the night that Ball went missing. They found Ball's body in a field. They didn't bring him to England and make anything of it; he was just buried in France somewhere.

As a mechanic, you didn't have a particular pilot, but you were assigned to a particular machine. The pilots would be swapped over. They would fly any machine that was available, but the mechanic would be permanently on a machine. We were always having to go and reclaim planes that had been landed elsewhere. Along the Western Front, there was an aerodrome about every five miles. Generally speaking, there were two or three squadrons, of eighteen planes each, on an aerodrome. Not only did we have to deal with crashes, but some planes went missing, shot down over the German lines. We had a lot of work to do. The Vickers Gun, on the front of the machine, fired through the propeller; they called it the Constantinesco Gear, and it worked the gun trigger off the overhead camshaft. Sometimes, if a bullet was a bit of a 'hang-fire', it would end up going right through the prop. This meant, of course, that the machine would have to be fitted with a new propeller when it came back, otherwise, the propeller might have disintegrated at any time. As regards the damage done, it was surprising to see how often a pilot would come back with twenty bullet-holes in his machine, not one of them having hit him or a vital part of the aircraft. Sometimes, just the fabric would be torn, and we'd have to patch it up. On other occasions a pilot would get back all right, but with a dead engine, having managed to land at another aerodrome.

Ordinary damage we used to repair by getting the spares from St Omer, and we used to give the engines a minor overhaul, but if it came to a big overhaul, the engine would be sent to the depot, repaired, and returned to us. It was done very quickly indeed. I was always surprised at the speed with which the machines were replaced. The pilots were replaced pretty quickly, too. At St Omer they had a pool of officers and men, especially sergeant pilots. If someone was lost overnight, we'd be sent a replacement the next morning without fail, and also be sent machines to replace the ones which had been lost.

There were plenty of men keen to be pilots and work in the Flying Corps. I don't know what the number got to, but I know that a chap joining in April or early May would have a number in the 5,000s. By October, the number would be in the 11,000s. From a man's number, you could always tell when he had got in. In the case of the officers and sergeant pilots, most were coming from infantry regiments, and were attached to the RFC for flying duty and taught to fly. An officer still wore his regimental uniform, though. The only thing which marked him out as a flyer was the wings on his chest. He wasn't allowed to wear the RFC uniform, and didn't do so. Some of them used not to like this. They would have preferred to wear the more glamorous RFC uniform. In the towns I was in, you were a bit of a novelty in that uniform, and the whole thing used to appeal to the girls.

On our aerodrome we had two machines painted completely black. They used to fly at night and drop a Belgian chap with a parachute. He used to get out of the plane, sit on the wing, and push himself off. He'd come back six or so weeks later, and be dropped again. How these chaps got back over the lines, I don't know. We didn't have much to do with them, except to exchange a few words. One of them couldn't speak English at all; his language was Walloon. The pilots didn't mind being detailed for spy-dropping. They just went over and waited for the signal from the ground. The pilot wasn't nearly so bothered as the chap with the parachute.

Later on, we got Spads. The Spad was fast, but we had no end of trouble with its radiators. When we got them, some of the fitters were lucky, as they got to go to Paris for a course on Hispano-Suiza engines. Four or five of the fitters got to go, and they had the time of their lives. The skid at the back of the machine used to dig into the ground on landing, and this would mess up the water system. The Spads were beating the Germans at that time because of their speed, but some of the pilots weren't good enough to fly a Spad. They hadn't had enough tuition on them. The Spad had very little room, so if the pilot was very tall, it was difficult to get his legs in and out. Personally, I never thought the Spad was much of a success; the engine gave trouble, the radiator gave trouble, the general rigging gave trouble, and we mechanics didn't like it.

In the summer of 1917 I left the squadron and went away. I had volunteered as an observer, and they were so short of observers at that point, that my application was accepted within three days. I was sent to a place to do some aerial musketry with camera guns. To qualify, you'd have to pass map reading, and be able to do six words per minute wireless transmission. You had a machine like a camera, and two of you would stage a mock battle. You'd pull the trigger, and instead of firing a bullet, a picture would be taken of your 'opponent'. When the film was exposed, some of the pictures would have nothing on them at all, because you weren't aiming right. But after a while, you got used to it. After qualifying, you had to do six operations before you got your wing up. I was quite anxious to get these six operations in, because then you'd get flying pay, which was about 4/- a day at the time. I completed my six operations in a Bristol Fighter.

You were a different class of person when you started to fly. As a ground mechanic you were dirty, scruffy and ill-fed, but once you were flying, they started making a fuss of you. You got smarter clothes, and when you weren't flying you did nothing but lounge about with your hands in your pockets. We used to drink a fair bit, too. You led a gentleman's life, really. We had a certain amount of lectures on how to escape if you got shot down. We had maps sewn into our tunics, and one of the buttons on the tunic hid a little compass. Another thing we did was to memorize three or four addresses in Belgium and France. If you could get to these places, you'd reach an organization that would get you over to Holland, which was a neutral country. The intelligence officer, who was attached to the squadron, would come up to you at any time and ask, 'what was that address in Brussels?' Of course all these things were in their infancy, and a new experience for everybody.

When we'd returned from an operation, whether it was bombing, reconnaissance or an offensive patrol, we'd have to go to the squadron office and make a report. Then you'd go into the intelligence office, and the intelligence officer would take details of any train movements you'd seen from the air. For instance, you might have seen four trains going from Roullers to Menin, and you'd report that. The intelligence officer was interested in any movements of troops or guns you'd observed on the ground. He had quite an important job, but I don't think the one attached to us was very clever. He should have been trained as a flying man; then he would have understood what we were telling him.

Doing an observer's job wasn't difficult. The photography section would tell you where they'd want pinpointing, and we had maps, divided into squares. You never saw much of the photograph yourself. You didn't look through binoculars or anything like that; we did it all with our eyes. We'd be up at about 4,000 feet, and the cameras were about two feet long, and pointed down through the bottom of the plane. You'd pull a lever, which would expose the negative, then pull another lever which would load another plate. When these photographs got back to the squadron, they would be enlarged to four times their original size. The photography section could pick out all the details of new emplacements. They used to write on the back of the photographs what they'd asked you to get, and what you'd actually got, which sometimes differed quite a bit. Sometimes we'd take wide-angled pictures at 18,000 feet. You could see for seventy miles in any direction on a clear day at that altitude. You could even see the cliffs of Dover from over the Western Front. It was a very queer feeling.

We also did low-level bombing. We'd have one 100-pound bomb on, and we'd come down to about 2,000 feet to drop it, to make sure we hit the target. We didn't always hit it, of course. We never had a bomb-sight. You'd squint, judge your speed, and tap the pilot for direction, using a railway line or road as a guide. To release the bomb, you'd pull up a little handle, a bit like a cheese-cutting wire. Each bomb used to have a small propeller on the top of it, which would fly off once the bomb had descended a certain distance. This little propeller used to let the detonator drop into the bomb. So when the bomb dropped on anything, the two detonators would hit each other and cause the explosion. On many occasions I nearly fell out of the plane whilst looking for this propeller to fly off. I don't think our bombing was very accurate. For instance, at Roullers there was quite a big marshalling yard. You could hit that easily, but if you wanted to hit the engine sheds, it was much harder to achieve. It was more luck than judgment, I think.

Generally, we had three or four different jobs. There were offensive patrols, where we went looking for trouble, then there were defensive patrols, where we didn't go over the lines, but tried to stop the Germans from coming over our side. Then there were bombing patrols.

Sometimes we used to have a go at the German observation balloons. I used to fly with a chap called Captain Colville-Jones. He was such a good pilot, that he had a freelance job, a roving commission, and could pick up a plane and do what he wanted with it. He often used to take me with him. He used to put the fear of God into me, but he was a daring sort of bloke. His favourite activity was balloon-strafing. I used to feel sorry for the poor Jerries; when they saw him coming they'd climb quickly out of their baskets and go down. But he never used to fire on a bloke who was climbing down. It was never done, that sort of thing. They used to accuse the Germans of doing it, but that wasn't true.

Normally, we'd go up once a day, but when things started to

1. *above:* Lieutenant Latham's crashed Avro D7146, 1919.

2. *right:* Sub-Lieutenant J. Herbert Thompson, 1916.

3. *below left: Oberleutnant* Hans Waldhausen; Thompson's shared victory.

4. *below right:* Lieutenant L. S. Latham, July 1917.

5. Sopwith Triplane N6292, *Hilda,* used by Reginald Soar, Naval 8 Squadron.

6. Major Freddie Powell with his Lewis Gun mounting on the FE8.

7. 40 Squadron RFC. Major Robert Loraine *(seated, centre)*.

8. Second Lieutenant Gwilym Lewis, 1916.

9. Regent Street Polytechnic.

10. RFC Wireless
Telegraphers in a dugout
in France, c 1916.

11. C23a airship in service with the RNAS for coastal patrols, 1917-18.

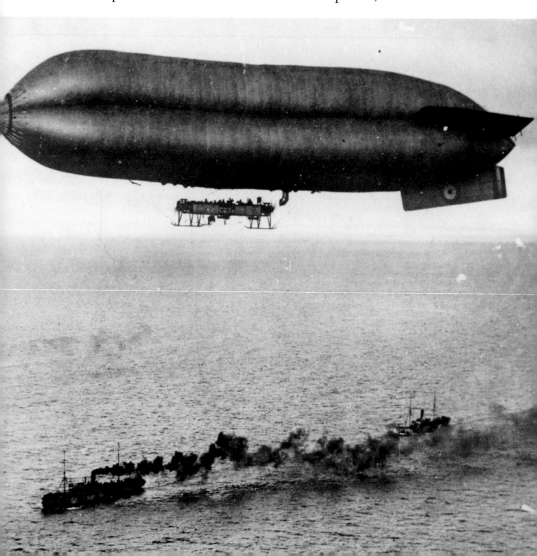

12. Midshipman Victor Goddard aboard HMS *Cornwall* in February 1914.

13. Sopwith Baby with men from the RNAS.

14. Kite Balloon Section observer in parachute harness, France, 1918.

15. Flight Sergeant Bernard Oliver, KBS. 16. Lieutenant Colonel Louis Strange.

17. Two Caquot balloons ascending on the Western Front, 1918.

18. Second Lieutenant
    Lawrence Wingfield,
    1915.

19. *below left:* Second
    Lieutenant George Riley,
    1917.

20. *below right: Leutnant*
    Wilhelm Frankl who shot
    down Lawrence
    Wingfield on 1 July 1916.

21. BE2cs of 12 Squadron RFC, St. Omer.

22. Robert Smith-Barry *(left)* with Avro at Gosport Flying School.

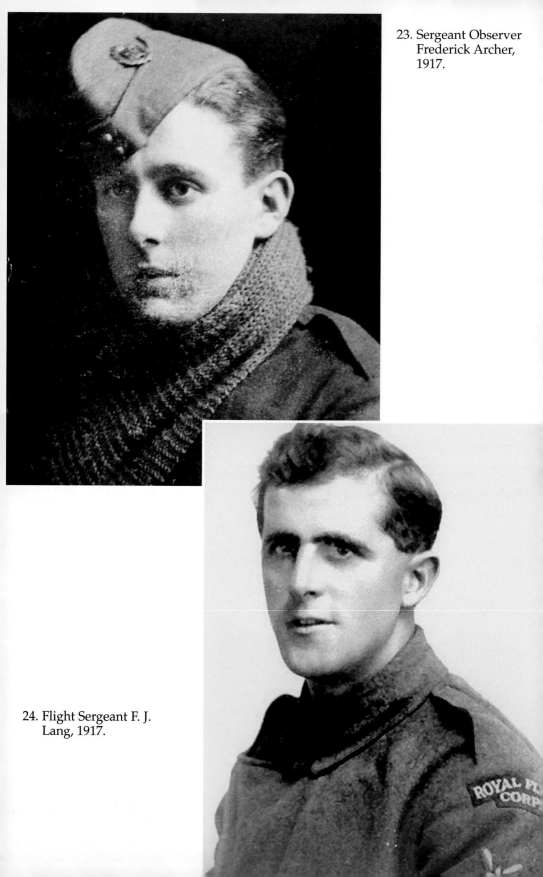

23. Sergeant Observer
    Frederick Archer,
    1917.

24. Flight Sergeant F. J.
    Lang, 1917.

25. Lord H. H. Balfour
    with 50-horsepower
    'Ticket' Caudron,
    July 1915.

26. Captain Robert
    Halley, c.1920.

27. Lieutenant H. E. 'Tim' Hervey, c.1919.

28. Major J. O. Andrews with DH2, Bertangles Aerodrome, 1916.

29. Major Lanoe Hawker with HQ staff and fitters of 24 Squadron RFC.

30. Removal of airecrew from Handley Page 0/100 bomber wrecked by AA fire near
     Bruges on 16 May 1918.

31. The Artists' Rifles.

32. The RE5; a rarely aired precursor of the RE8.

33. Nieuport 17 with over wing Lewis gun mounting.

34. SS Z59 on the aft deck of HMS *Furious* in 1918.

35. FE2b crew about to embark on a night bombing raid.

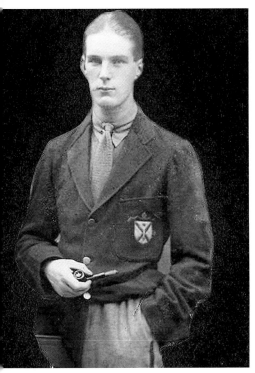

36. Lieutenant W. E. Watts as a prisoner of war at Schweidnitz in 1918.

37. Captain F. M. F. West as an observer with 3 Squadron, RFC in 1917. *(Photo via Chaz Bowyer)*

38. Sopwith Camel in flight.

39. Thomas Sopwith
in 1911.

40. Anna Malinovska with Sir Thomas Sopwith at his home, Compton Manor, in 1978.

happen, like the retreat from the Somme in March 1918 when the Germans had a dive for the Channel ports, we were going up perhaps six times a day. The German advance started on 21 March, and lasted for about nine days. The Germans couldn't go any further because they were running short of ammunition. They were low on water, too, so they rested for a while, and *we* were brought out for a rest on the Armentières sector. The Germans opened up their second offensive, and we were right in the thick of it.

We were machine-gunning advancing German troops. We'd been practising for this for some time, knowing that this push was coming. We used to go out with 4 pounds of Lewis ammunition and we had a new technique: troop-strafing. This involved rushing down at low altitudes and dive-bombing, either with one big bomb, or four 28-pounders. I don't know whether we killed many people like that, but a lot of the German transport used to be carried by mules, and I've seen the trouble a lot of raging mules cause when they're being shot at or bombed. They don't like it at all. It wasn't good for the Germans' morale, either. We used to dive down at terrific speeds. The Bristol Fighter had a top flying speed of about 110mph, but I've dived down at nearly 400mph. The pilot would be shooting all the way down, but you had to make sure you could pull back up again.

On the last flight I made, we'd still got the bomb on board when we crashed into the ground. The pilot dived too steeply, and couldn't pull out of it. The pilot had been shot, and the machine had been shot to pieces; we'd run into a nest of machine guns.

I was shot down when the Canadians took Passchendaele in October or November 1917. We were over Passchendaele reporting our own troop movements, and we were hit by anti-aircraft fire, of all things. We never used to take any notice of ack-ack. You'd see these little black puffs all around you, but you never used to worry about them. The Germans always said that they fired 2,000 rounds for every plane they hit, and our record was probably worse. I had a wonderful pilot at the time, called Lindup. Our machine stopped dead, 9,000 feet over Passchendaele. Lindup got ten miles with this dead stick plane, which takes some doing. The engine had been hit. He said, 'Look for a landing ground.' We were over all these trenches, and I couldn't see any landing ground at all. We managed to land, but the plane was all smashed up, and we were pulled out by some Canadian Light Railway chaps. I went to hospital with a broken nose, but I was only there three days before they sent me back to the squadron. I recovered from that.

On the other occasion, I was shot down by a German aircraft that dived on us when we were doing low-level photography. We were supposed to have Camels at 2,000 feet, and SEs at 4,000 feet to look after us while we were taking pictures, or low-level bombing, and this Jerry got through our defences and pumped it into us. We crashed on an advanced aerodrome. We counted twenty-seven bullet holes in our machine; he'd really given us a pasting. Luckily, I wasn't hurt. I didn't fire back at him, because we were concentrating on what we were doing, and this bloke came out of the blue. We weren't supposed to fight on that job.

The last time I was shot down, I was taken prisoner. It was night-time when the Germans got us out of the plane. I'd been knocked out, and had been there since dusk. We were pretty well smashed up. The Germans got us out, took us both on stretchers into a dugout, and brought a doctor who looked at our injuries; I had been badly wounded in the left ankle. They gave us some wine to drink. We were in that dugout all night, and our blokes started shelling. I thought, 'We're going to get killed by one of our own ruddy shells.' It worried me very much indeed that my mother wouldn't hear from me for a few days and then she would get a letter saying I was missing. From this dugout we were taken to Tournai, and I was a prisoner of war.

That was the end of my war service. I never did a day's soldiering after that, and it was a year before I finally returned home.

1st Air Mechanic Len Amioti

1st Air Mechanic Len Amioti, service number 9617, was born on 29 August 1897. He joined the RFC, and was sent to No. 1 Aircraft depot at St Omer, France. After a month he was posted to No. 15 Squadron at Léalvilliers on the Somme. Amioti encountered the un-cooperative attitude of the army towards what they considered the novel use of air reconnaissance. His experiences as a wireless operator reveal how far the value of the Flying Corps extended beyond the aerodrome.

Amioti was active in the Old Comrades Association in the 1960s. He was living in Mitcham, Surrey at the time of the interview on 27 March 1979. He died on 25 October 1981.

I turned eighteen the end of August 1915, and I had made up my mind to join the RFC when I was eighteen, so at the end of September that year, I went to Whitehall, where there was a regular recruiting office. At the first week of October I joined a party there, and marched to Waterloo. Then we went down to Farnborough, and there I was issued with my number and uniform. It was here that we did what was called 'square-bashing' and were made into soldiers by guards, NCOs largely, and then from there, somewhere about the end of November, I was posted up to the Regent Street Poly for training, mostly in sending and receiving Morse code. We were billeted at Earl's Terrace in South Kensington, and used to march through Hyde Park every morning, along Wigmore Street to the Poly, where we ate our meals, and we did our drill for about two hours every afternoon in Regent's Park.

The equipment we used for training consisted mostly of headphones, paper and pencil to take down the signals. We also used 'Morse-inkers'; these were machines with a strip of paper onto which a wheel would print a record of your transmission. They could tell whether your dots and dashes were the right length. By the time you passed out, you were expected to get up to about eighteen words per minute. We had hour-long lectures practically every afternoon.

An unfortunate incident occurred in February during my training period. I had a new pair of army boots and, putting them on one evening, I happened to slip down a flight of sharp-edged stone steps, badly injuring my knee. I had to go to hospital twice a week for about two or three months, and then I contracted mumps. I missed about two months' training, so I was a little behind the colleagues I'd joined up with. I went back to Farnborough and then did some field training. They took us out in a tender, and we had to put up a mast and a plane would come over and transmit Morse messages to us.

I was issued with a revolver and a pay book, and somewhere about 16 September 1916 I went to France, first to St Omer, where we had a little more practical training, and where I was detailed to look after a team of German prisoners who were led to the aerodrome. We got on quite well. After about three weeks I arrived at a railhead called Acheux, and when I got out of the train I had my first experience with Somme mud. You got out and your feet went down about six inches in mud, and there they remained.

The squadron was stationed at a very small village. They were just bringing out Nissen huts in those days, a kind of hut in wood and corrugated iron in which people slept. They had a lot of these huts delivered and they had to be erected. And again I was given a squad of German prisoners to instruct how to do it. Well, very fortunately for me, one of the Germans was a sergeant from the Black Forest, who spoke passable English, and I said to him, 'I don't know one end of these things from the other'.

120

And he said, 'That's all right, sir, you leave to me, I am carpenter.'

I said, 'All right, thank you!'

Around October, I was posted to D Battery, the 32nd Division, with 4.5 howitzers. I wasn't very popular there. Some of the officers, who had been in the Army some years, took the attitude that they didn't want wireless operators to tell them how to fire their guns. They had an OP up the front and they could jolly well do it themselves much better. They were most uncooperative. They put me in a cellar with two sheets of corrugated iron over it, and that was my accommodation. I was left high and dry practically. One morning, about a week after I'd been there, a plane called up to give me a shoot and, of course, I had no telephone, no wire and I shouted to one of the boys going by, 'Get an officer quick, I've got a plane calling!' And I put out a 'K' but it was no good. By the time he turned up, the plane had packed up, I'd put a 'T' out, and the thing was a fiasco. Then I had an angry call from the squadron asking why hadn't I cooperated. I explained what had happened, and that I couldn't get any cooperation. They came up and took me back to Divisional Headquarters.

It was really a waste of time as an operator there because by the time I got a call and they'd trotted out their guns, the target would have disappeared. At the end of February the Germans decided to go back to their Hindenburg Line, where they were really going to settle in. They'd built immense concrete trenches and dugouts. And they gave up about fifteen to eighteen miles in places to go back to this line. They sat there and of course we followed them up. The weather was terribly severe, we had very little shelter, and a really rough time. The Germans had burnt all the villages and destroyed everything.

Then I got trench fever, and was taken down to hospital at Rouen. I was there for about three weeks, after which I went to a convalescent camp. Trench fever was like a kind of glorified flu. You'd get it mostly from exposure. We'd been sleeping out in the snow, and the rations didn't come up very often; we were starving sometimes. I just collapsed.

At Christmas 1916, there were about twenty of us in a great big barn. We had a brazier. And we used to scrounge wood, and some-body got a can of petrol to help light the wood which was a little green. A new recruit had arrived the night before and of course he was immediately told, 'You get up in the morning and light the brazier and make tea for us.' So this poor lad attempted to light this wet wood and he said to me, 'I can't get it going.' And I said to him, 'Oh, there's a can of petrol there.' I said, 'Pour out about a couple of tablespoonfuls. Pour it on and put a match to it.' Well this boy must have misunderstood me. He grabbed the petrol tin, took the cap off, poured about two or three pints of petrol out on this brazier and put a match to it. I was up in flames, and lucky not to be burned to death. And my tuner got burned. The lid of it got all charred before I could move it. After that I was known throughout the RFC as 'the man who burned his tuner'.

After I came out of hospital, I went down to No. 2 Aircraft Depot at Candas. There was a very kindly regimental sergeant major in charge there, who called me in and said to me, 'You've had a rough time, haven't you lad?' I said that yes, things had been a bit rough, and I'd been ill. 'All right,' he said, 'You take it easy here. You can supervise the serving of the food in the Sergeants' Mess for a fort-night.' That was a nice, easy job. Of course, I got my food there, too.

In August I was posted up to the 59th Division, 295 Brigade. We had extended our front and taken over some more front right down to St Quentin. It was known as a 'rest' or quiet front, but that was one of the places where I had a dugout blown in. A lot of guns were brought up just before I got there and they had a little strafe on the Germans on this so-called quiet front, and that annoyed them very much. About a fortnight later, they had a strafe on this wood and put up what's called a 'box barrage', and they'd wipe everything out in it. I was in the centre of it with another operator, who'd only been out a day or two, poor chap.

They started this barrage in the morning, and about two o'clock it was getting a bit close and I said to this lad, 'Put your tin hat and gas mask on, and go out and see what they're doing. See if the battery's clearing or anything.' Well, he went out and apparently got lost. He lost himself. And he didn't come back. So for about another hour I thought, 'This is getting really hot; I think I'd better get out or do something.' So I packed up my tuner and phones, and while I was doing that a shell hit the corner of the dugout. Luckily it was in the opposite corner to where I was. Getting out I had a shell almost hit me.

I got out, left my tuner there and started walking down the road to see if I could contact anybody. An RFC tender came up, and I waved to them and they stopped. I explained what had happened and they took me back down to the central wireless station for the night. Next morning we came up again and went to my dugout. In the meantime, I'd become worried about what had happened to the other lad. We went round several stations, and we found him safe.

Right after that, we were posted up to Ypres, and got up there for the second Battle of Passchendaele. Then I was posted in a dugout in the ramparts at Ypres. Ypres was in a very ruined state at that time. The stump of the Cloth Hall Tower was still there, a skeleton, with the ramparts more or less intact. I did very little there. We had a room dug into the ramparts, with six wireless operators from different units, and we were all in it together. When I arrived, the sergeant who'd taken me up enquired, 'Who is the senior here?' We all gave our numbers and I was the senior, so he said, 'Well, you're in charge of this lot.'

We were there for about six weeks. Then there was the Big Day. I was told it was going to start that next morning or something, I said, 'Right. We'll have three tuners going, and three boys listening. Take down every signal you can hear, and if it should be any of your call-signs we must report it at once.' I had these boys doing this, and we had all sorts of signals and volumes of them all day. Next morning I was rung up by Central Wireless, which was down the road near Vlamertinghe. Directly this 'do' started, some aircraft came over and bombed and damaged their base. I had a telephone call very early next morning: 'Have you got any signals? We were bombed out first thing yesterday morning and we've hardly got any signals. We lost our tuner, it was bombed and destroyed, and we've had to get another one up.'

I said, 'Yes, I expect we got pretty near every signal on the front that was sent out, from the Germans, the French, the Belgians, anybody. I gave instructions that was to be done.' The officer came up the next day and thanked me. He said, 'That was a brainwave you had.'

I said, 'Well, it was just something I thought of; I knew it was an important business.'

He said, 'Yes, that was very good, I'll see you get some recognition for it.'

And I was promoted to 1st A.M. for that.

At Ypres we used to have what they called wagon lines, where the horses were, because we were horse-drawn in the Field Artillery. And they had horse lines and an ammo place for getting ammo and rations which used to be brought up to the batteries at night-time. We had an 18-inch Naval gun on wheels, which would come up about 7 o'clock in the evening and start strafing over in the German lines. This used to annoy them, and they used to send planes over to try and bomb this gun. They never succeeded in finding it, but they did find the wagon lines. In fact they found ours, and dropped a bomb right in the middle of the horses. That was a most terribly shocking sight. About forty or fifty horses were killed outright, and the remaining thirty had to be destroyed.

Shortly after that do I was sent up further, right up where the guns were at Wijtschate. It was a well known place; there was a big dugout there, which had been constructed by the Germans originally. I should think it must have been several hundred yards long. Of course it was almost impossible to construct dugouts in the Ypres region because it was running with water, and dangerous. I mean if you fell in it at night-time you might very well sink down in the mud and never be seen again, as some chaps were. We kept at that part of the line and we started to use it, but it had to be drained all the time. There was a gully that went all the length of the gallery, and I was at the top end of this just in a little niche at the top of the stairs. I had a lad attached to me then but he didn't stay long, because he got dysentery. After he'd been with me about three weeks, he said, 'I feel very ill,' and I said, 'All right, tonight about 5 o'clock pack up and I'll take you down to the Forward Dressing Station.' They used to have Red Cross dressing

124

stations for seriously wounded men and they used to bandage them up before they could transport them down the line. The doctor examined him and said, 'You're isolated'. So I had to leave him there and go back.

I stayed there about a month. I only did about one shoot while I was there. We didn't do many shoots, because our guns hadn't a very big range, only about 2,500 or 3,000 feet. The howitzers had a little more range than the 18-pounders, and of course a howitzer does more damage than the gunshot. The gun goes over in a complete arc, and it hits the ground and it's slower. But a howitzer goes up, and then drops; it makes a bigger hole and does more damage. Mostly, though, we were used for wire cutting and anti-trench mortar work, but not a lot of counter battery work; that was done by the heavier guns, and they worked all day.

The dogfights were very interesting to watch; very interesting. I saw one very big one. This was later when we were down on the Bullecourt section one morning. There were anything up to a hundred planes, both German and British, in a dogfight one morning. The sky was black with them. I saw one or two over Ypres, too, but that one was really something.

About the beginning of November we left the Ypres sector and we went into the Lens sector. I was at a place called Liévin. We overlooked the mines in Lens, and I was there for a little while. It was pretty quiet there. One evening they came along and whisked me away to go on home leave. This was my first leave from France, after about two years. They came up in a motorbike and sidecar and took me down to the squadron and gave me some money. We missed the leave train so they packed me in a goods wagon, which was freezing. I was very near frozen to death when I got out the other end at a place four miles outside Calais. It was just about getting light, about half past six in the morning, and I started walking down a road towards the docks. After I'd gone about a mile I saw a shop with a light in it, and I went in and it was a barber shop, there were some chaps being shaved there. I was perished with cold, and I said, 'Can I come in and get warm for a little while?' I spoke French, so the man welcomed me, and said, 'Sit down.' And presently he said, 'I'll give you a shave,' and he served me a cup of coffee and that got me going and thawed me out. When I got down to the port I found out the boat wasn't going so I'd got a couple of hours to spare so I went in what we used to call a 'caff' on the Front. And I had a nice breakfast – eggs, bacon and coffee. I returned to England for ten days, then rejoined D Battery, the 59th Division, 295 Brigade.

There was a question whether they might send us to Italy because the Germans had made a big strafe on the Italians and driven them back and they were sending British divisions down there to make the line good. The plan to send us was in the air for about a fortnight, but it fell through.

The Cambrai show happened about that time, and I think that was the first time tanks were used in great quantity. They went over and drove the Germans back quite a way. But the tanks in those days were very slow moving, and were big targets, so got hit quite quickly. The Germans made a terrific counter-attack about a fortnight after we'd made ours, and virtually drove us back to where we'd started. Some of our boys got very badly mauled, and the Germans used quite a lot of gas in that attack. We were suddenly hurried out from Arras down into the Cambrai sector, at Havrincourt, near Bourlon Wood. Bourlon Wood was reputed to be full of gas shells; we were told of it and wouldn't go in there. We got there just before Christmas, and were pulled out in January, when we were sent to Ivergny, a very pleasant place, for a month's rest.

The adjutant there called me in and said, 'Look, Sparks, we're going to open a canteen and get some stuff and sell it to the boys. Would you run it for us, and look after it?' So I agreed, and he gave me 1,000 Francs and I went out with a mess cart to a depot, and I bought a lot of chocolate, cigarettes and sweets. I opened the canteen for an hour each midday, and for a couple of hours in the evening. This went on for the best part of our month's rest. It provided a good trade, and I realized about 800 Francs profit on it, which was used to buy goodies for Christmas. We had lots of little luxuries that we didn't normally have, like beer and wine. These could be purchased down in the villages away from the line. Mostly there were what they called estaminets, like pubs where you could go for a drink. They weren't supposed to sell spirits to the troops, but used sometimes to risk it.

After that we went up to a spot near a place called Croiselles, which was facing Bullecourt. Bullecourt was taken and lost two or three times. You never knew who was in Bullecourt about that time. Around the middle of February I was up at the front with D Battery, 295. The commander of that battery was one of the finest gentlemen I've ever met, Major Bates. He was interested in wireless; sometimes he used to come in and sit in my dugout, and I'd give him another pair of phones, as we could put two phones in our tuners. He'd listen and I'd explain what was going on to him. Then came the offensive of 21 March. And that was my second dugout that was blown in. Again, I was lucky; I got out. But I could tell shells were falling close to it and that I'd better go and see what's happening.

When I got out, my mast was smashed and on the ground, and the Major saw me and he said, 'Oh, don't bother with listening any more, boy!' So I went in a gun pit and gave a hand with the guns.

I'd been in the gun pits occasionally; I used to go in and they'd let me load the gun and pull the trigger. They started this barrage at 5 a.m. on 21 March, and a terrific barrage it was, too. We had four guns where I was, and there were two guns up at the forward position, which was quite a common arrangement with the field artillery. Sometime about 10 o'clock the boys with forward guns came trekking back with the four guns because they'd been blown out and then we saw our infantry on a ridge a mile and a half away. The Germans came over and we started firing with what they call 'open sights'. When you're firing with open sights you can see the shell leave the gun and trace it to where it detonates. We fired on the Germans, but they came on, and on, and on. By about 1 o'clock we just had to give up. And they blew up the guns.

A rather dreadful thing happened then, because we had one very narrow passage to go through some barbed wire entanglements to get out away from the battery. Two German machine gunners came along and trained their guns on this gap. As our boys went through it many of them were shot down in the legs. Some got through, and then there were about a dozen boys shot through the leg and they couldn't move. There was a very big, dry shell hole there. And there was an officer with me, one of the battery. I said to him, 'Look, sir, do you think we ought to lift these boys up and put them in that shell hole, so they won't get shot anymore?' So we did that, we put in several men, about ten or eleven. Then we managed to get through ourselves. One of the battery boys was carrying a breech block, and he was shot down in front of me. I could see he was dead, so I grabbed up the breech block and the officer and I escaped unscathed. Next morning we packed up and went right back to somewhere near a place called Doullens, not far from Amiens. And I didn't go into action for a long while after that.

It must have been around that time that I had my pony. An aeroplane got shot down, and it landed just by our lines. The two officers were fortunately unhurt, save for a few bruises, and our officers took them in. They said to me, 'Get your pony'. They wanted to send a message down to squadron. So I got my pony and rode down to squadron with a message asking for help. It was some while before I went back, in fact it was on into April before I went back to the front.

In the main, we were in two or three positions; we were always moving. I used to spend my time mostly putting up my mast and taking it down again. In the early summer, the Germans strafed. Some divisions of Portuguese troops were serving on the Western Front, up in front of Armentières. The Germans turned on them and gave them a terrible time. Of course they were annoyed that they should be there, that the Portuguese would fight them, so they got spiteful. And these poor devils were just practically pounded out of the line. We had an urgent message, 'Up you go to step in.'

The Germans weren't very effective after that. Everyone knew the end of the war was coming. The Germans were slackening off their attacks and things got fairly quiet. From there on I moved up to various places, from Armentières we went up to Hazebrouck and Niep Forest. The Germans really started their retreat back, and we chased them up from about the end of August to 11 November. We were some of the first troops to relieve Lille, the big city in the north of France, which I was very pleased about, because I had an uncle and two aunts living in Lille. After the Armistice, I contacted them and went to see them twice.

When the Armistice came, I was at Tournai, in the south of Belgium. There's a hill there called Mont St Aubert, which is quite a high hill, about 600 feet high. In Flanders, it looks like the Alps. I got the message about quarter to nine on 11 November. A message came through to the effect that all hostilities would cease at 11 o'clock. I reported it to the officers. About ten minutes later it came through to them on their telephone. That was that. They emptied the guns.

Corporal William Elvin

Corporal William John Elvin was born on 21 December 1898 in Lawes Height, Suffolk. The son of an engine driver, 'Joe' worked as a joiner at Boulton and Paul's in Norwich before joining the RFC in 1917. He became a corporal on 19 October 1918, and continued with the RAF. On 6 December 1919 he married Grace Mary Lamb. They had one son.

Elvin was promoted to sergeant on 22 October 1923, and served in India from 1921–27. He was discharged on 19 May 1928. He remained in the RAF until 1952. Elvin died on 15 April 1994 and is buried in the Rosary Cemetery in Norwich. He was interviewed on 8 June 1980. His experience is important for its insight into contemporary practices of aircraft inspecting and testing.

I was working as an apprentice carpenter at Boulton and Paul's and I wanted to go into the Army as soon as I turned eighteen. A friend of mine, Al Chesson, came with me, and on 6 January we two lads went up to the Britannia Barracks at Norwich. We were duly booked in, given the King's Shilling and were in the forces. They asked my friend, 'What do you do?' and he said, 'I'm a clerk at the County Council,' and they said to me, 'What are you?' and I replied, 'I'm a carpenter at Boulton and Paul's.' They sent me to Woolwich.

This was the first time I'd ever been to London. I remember vividly, about 8 o'clock in the morning, walking across London Bridge to get to London Bridge Station, and down to Woolwich to take this trade test. I didn't go much on London; I thought it was pretty awful, too big and too dirty. I was obviously out of my element. I went into the YMCA to have a little wash up. I'd come that morning from Norwich, and there was no soap to wash my hands with. I went to the counter and said, 'Please, may I have some soap?' And they brought me a plateful of soup. They weren't used to my Suffolk speech at all. But, any rate, we got that settled. I went to Woolwich, did my trade test and passed it. I had to make a three-barred light, which was part of a window. Then I joined a queue and the chaps in front of me went to various regiments, like the Ordnance, the AFC and the Engineers. It came to my turn and they said, 'Only got the RFC left. So will you go in the RFC?' I said, 'Yes, certainly, I'd like to.'

I went to Farnborough and there I had to pass another trade test, be examined by a doctor and I was in the RFC. It was terribly crowded. I lived in tents on Queen's Square, and there were fourteen of us to a bell tent. There was a foot of snow on the ground outside. We started with square-bashing. The sergeant major was a man named Cook, an ex-Guardsman, and he was a bit of a Tartar. He used to chase us around a bit. He'd fall out the carpenters, and we'd fall out, and he'd say, 'Can you recognize timber?' You'd say, 'Yes, sir,' and he'd say, 'Well go and pick up the match stalks!' He used to catch us out on all that sort of thing.

One day they said, 'From here to the left, fall out, go and get your small kit, and fall in again.' We did this, got in lorries and went up to London. A lorry held about twenty chaps. We were detailed to move furniture from the Duquesa Hotel, which was on the Blackfriars Embankment up to the Cecil Hotel in the Strand. That was when the Air Ministry moved into the Cecil Hotel, because the Duquesa was too small. We were up there for a fortnight. We slept on the floor in the Duquesa Hotel which had a very nice plush carpet. We had our food there, too, which was very good. It was much better than being in a tent.

Then I went back to Farnborough, and while I was there I got put on a charge one day. Some leather-lunged sergeant would stand out in front and call out the last three figures of your number and your name. For me they'd say, '914 Elvin'. You'd then have to fall out for your posting to some school.

131

It was a bitterly cold day, and I felt something poke me in the back. It was an officer with his stick, and he said, 'Stand still. What's your name?'

So I told him and he said, 'You're on a charge, fall in at the office when you break away.'

So I went to the office and the sergeant major marched me in 'Left, right! Left, right! Left, right!' and they read out the charge, and I said, 'Please, sir. That isn't me.' It wasn't my name at all.

The captain said, 'Wheel him out.' So I got wheeled out, and never went back.

I did ultimately get posted, and I went to Reading where a school had been made into a comparatively new factory. There we were taught the components of an aeroplane, how an aeroplane flew, what all the various components did and the stress that they took, and how to inspect it. Ultimately we all sat this exam and I passed.

In due course I was posted to No. 5 Aircraft Acceptance Park at Filton, near Bristol, where the Bristol Aeroplane Company was building the Bristol Fighter. They had made other aeroplanes, the monoplane and the little Bristol Scout, but this was the FE2b. They were turning them out in big numbers, and sending them to us, about a mile away, to have their engines and guns tested before they were sent out to the squadrons.

When I joined up I was in the lowest rank, Air Mechanic 2nd Class, and I worked in a gang of four men erecting these Bristol Fighters. We reckoned to do one a day. The aircraft used to come from the factory on their undercarriages, and be wheeled down behind a lorry. And they would come with the parts as well, the wings, the centre section, the struts, the tail unit and all the various components. We would then assemble the components and true them all up. That is to say that we'd ensure that the main planes had the right dihedral, the right stagger and so on. This was done by adjusting the landing and flying wires. This was one of the arts of rigging an aeroplane, so that it would fly properly. In those light, wooden aircraft, you could twist the wings and do all sorts of things with them, and then they wouldn't fly right. A common thing to happen would be that you would send the machine up on test, it would be perfectly all right and the pilot would come down and say it's flying left wing low. In other words instead of it flying level and hands off, the left wing would go down, and you'd have to adjust for that. It's a simple adjustment but you had to know just how to do it, and how much to do it. That's where the art came in, to be able to see with your eye whether it was all right before you sent it up. Because although you measured it with instruments like inclinometers and levels, when you got practised, you could see if a plane was without any twists.

That's where my former training came in; that's why they put me, who was a carpenter, as a rigger. If a carpenter is making something, he sights it, not only to see if a piece of wood is straight but if, in the case of two pieces of wood, they line up together. You get used to looking for these sort of things. So when I started working with aeroplanes it came as second nature to me. There were four gangs in the shed where I was, and if we didn't have an aeroplane we just used to sit down, and in the winter time we used to go in the boiler house and keep warm.

I stayed at Filton until the beginning of December. I still belonged to No. 5 AAP, but was sent to a school of inspection at Watford. There were many different aircraft there: the Sopwith Pup, Sopwith Camel, FE8, half a dozen types. We were taught how to inspect them. In those days there were no such things as inspection schedules or repair schedules. You inspected your aircraft on your knowledge as a tradesman. Nobody laid down what you should look for, or how you should look for it. At Watford they still didn't bring out what I would call an inspection schedule, but they did teach a method of inspecting all the aircraft so you didn't miss anything. We'd check split pins, locking nuts, the tension of the tyres, the fabric and the elastics in the undercarriage; whether the plane was true, whether the controls were set accurately and working properly . . . everything. I did this School of Inspection Course at Watford for a month and, in January 1918, I passed out. I have a certificate which reads: 'Rigging Inspector's Certificate 1st Class. This is to certify that Elvin, W.J., 1st A. M. has qualified as a first class rigger and has passed the necessary tests; also shown ability expected as a First Class Rigging Inspector for the following aeroplanes: The De Havilland 4, RE8, and Sopwith Camel.'

I returned to Filton and carried on with erecting Bristol Fighters. That lasted about three months. Then, quite out of the blue, I was sent to Inland Area at Uxbridge to meet a certain Captain Stagg, and be told of a special duty. And when I got there, I met up with a Sergeant Greenaway, and a fellow called Griffiths. Our little gang of four was to inspect Handley Page aircraft. I hadn't come across these machines before, and can only assume that I was chosen because of my training as an inspector. We four formed a little party to go and 'accept' Handley Page 0400s for the Royal Air Force, the twin-engined Handley Page. It had a 380-horsepower Rolls Royce Eagle engine, and was a biggish aeroplane for those days.

First of all we went to Messrs. Handley Page at Cricklewood and spent a fortnight there learning everything we could about the 0400, how they were made and what they were like, and the snags in them and that sort of thing. Then we went to Birmingham, where we were housed with the Warwickshire Regiment. This lasted only about a week, as we couldn't get transport or anything from the Army, and their mealtimes were not suitable for us going to factories. So the four of us were moved into the YMCA in the middle of Birmingham. We lived there for some weeks. Again, though, it was always difficult to get transport because both the factories were a long way from the centre of Birmingham. We got moved again, to No. 14 Aircraft Acceptance Park at Castle Bromwich. This was a much bigger unit than No. 5. They were receiving aircraft of all types from factories in and around Birmingham. There was a medley of aircraft there: DH10s and DH10as, Bristol Fighters, SE5s and SE5as.

The Metropolitan Carriage Company erected their first Handley Page at Castle Bromwich and put it up to the four of us for inspection. We went over it with a fine-toothed comb. I found fault with the flying controls. The flying controls in those days were nearly all made of flexible steel cables, and for the fittings at the end you had to make a splice. You took a brass thimble, wrapped everything around it, held it tight around the thimble, and then spliced it. When I went round this one from the Metropolitan, I found all the thimbles were loose. I could push them out with my thumb.

134

Well, that wouldn't have done. Of course the cable goes a long way through a plane, and it was a big plane. If a thimble had caught up in the stringing of a plane for instance, it might have caused a serious accident. So I wouldn't pass the splicers. This meant a big setback, because the aeroplane was finished. Not only that, but the same fault would probably be found on many more aircraft coming out of the factories. So, of course, they would all have to be changed. This didn't please the firm, and they kicked up a fuss. Sergeant Greenaway backed me up, but the firm wouldn't accept that, so we sent for Captain Stagg, our boss in the area. That put the Metropolitan Carriage Company back weeks.

We still used to go out in a Crossley Tender to the Birmingham Carriage Company which was out at Smethwick, and do whatever work came along. But it became an awful bore, going backwards and forwards, so they said we'd split forces. MacPherson and Griffiths would stay with the Metropolitan Carriage Company at Castle Bromwich, while Greenaway and myself would go out to the Birmingham Carriage Company and live out there.

Well the sergeant had got his wife up and he already had accommodations so he was all right, but I had to be found accommodation out there. I took a chit of paper out to the local Bobby and a big policeman took me round to find a billet. I was only a little chap, very slight and very young and he took me into a baker's shop first of all, and said to the lady in the shop, 'I want you to give this young lad a billet,' and the woman said, 'I'm not billeting anybody; I've got enough to do with my work without seeing after anybody else.'

He said, 'You've got a room, haven't you?' The woman said yes, and he said, 'All right, he's yours.' And he left me with her.

The woman said, 'How much do you pay?'

I said, 'I think the rate is 19/6d.'

She said, 'I can't keep you for a week for 19/6d!'

I said, 'I don't earn much, but I'll give you two shillings more if that'll help.'

She said, 'All right, we'll settle for £1/1/6d.'

So I was in. I had a beautiful bedroom on top of the shop. I'll always remember the big brass bed; all the knobs had blue ribbons on. I'd never lived so well in all my life. There was plenty of good food, and they really looked after me. I got my bike up from Norwich, and could cycle to work at the Birmingham Carriage Company.

The Birmingham Carriage Company had a small field from which to test their aircraft. When the first one was finished, we pushed it across the main road, up a little bank for about a hundred yards, onto this flat field. Straight ahead was a raised roadway about six feet high, with a light railway running along the top. To the left of the field was all a very deep cutting, the main railway line to the north. To the right of this field was West Bromwich Albion football ground. The pilot arrived, we looked at this field, and I said, 'It isn't very big, sir, is it?'

He said, 'Don't worry; we'll be all right.'

In due course, we started up. There was a wobble pump in the Handley Pages, that you had to wobble to pump the petrol from the main tank to the centre section, and then the petrol was fed to the engines by gravity. Once you got in the air a mechanical pump would do that. But until you got airborne somebody had to work the pump. So I went to work the pump. The pilot got in, I got in and we took off. You had flow meters as they called them which were just optical glasses that looked black when the petrol was coming through. We flew round for about half an hour, I gave a little pump periodically, and we duly landed. The aeroplane was all right.

We got out, the pilot and I, and all the big bugs were there. And they patted us on the back; we were heroes. The managing director took us in his office, all posh leather, and he produced a bottle of whisky and some very big cigars. I had a couple of tots of whisky; I don't think I'd ever had any before. I'm afraid I got a bit tight. It was all very successful, and the pilot flew the machine away. And the next one came up, he went up again, and we did the same thing again. The third one came up. This time, a different pilot came. I said, 'Excuse me, sir, I'll show you this field; it's a little bit tricky.' And he went out and looked at it. 'Oh,' he said, 'We can land these things on a cabbage patch.' I said, 'All right.'

Once again I went up to work the pump. We hadn't been up

more than five minutes and the pilot asked, 'Where are we?' I thought, 'Well you're a bright one, you are.' But knowing West Bromwich Albion football ground by now, I said, 'That's where we've got to go.'

After about half an hour's flying he came in to land. He did what I call 'floated' it. I mean, he couldn't put it on the ground. He floated it across the aerodrome about six feet off the ground. He was coming in too fast, and couldn't get his tail down properly. At the last minute he opened up his engines, and he just missed the raised roadway. We went round again, came in again, and he did exactly the same thing. He opened up his engines, went round, came in a third time, and plonked it on the ground much too fast. We were howling towards this raised roadway, and we had no brakes. He opened the starboard engine and swung to port to avoid this roadway. I should think we finished up about ten yards off this cutting. It shook me a little. And then the damned man said it was flying right wing low. I could have kicked him. Anyway, we got it in the hangar and chocked it up. He said he'd test it again after lunch.

So he went off, and I adjusted this aircraft. One of the civilian inspectors asked if he could go and work the pump. I said, 'It's all right as far as I'm concerned, if your firm agrees.' So he asked permission, and went in my place. The pilot took off. He did exactly the same thing as he'd done before. This time, on his third attempt to bring the aircraft down, he hit the raised roadway, wiped his undercarriage clean off, shot over the road and landed in the field on the other side. The machine was smashed up. The only serious damage was that the bloke who was in my place broke his leg. After that they never landed again at that field. They took off from it, but never landed. So they used to fly to Castle Bromwich and land there.

I was out there nearly until Armistice Day. Then I was promoted corporal and went back to Castle Bromwich and continued there working on various types of aircraft, DH9, SE5s and SE5as. When I was there as a corporal, they asked me if I would go and help out in the technical office. It was a hut, of course. We used to keep a record of all the aircraft that came in as they went through all the various sections, and send off a daily report to the Air Ministry. That was one of the main parts of our job, to do all the paperwork relating to the fifty or so aircraft that were coming in each day. Directly the war finished, they were still coming in, and there was a question about what to do with the aircraft. On 11 November we had about thirty-five Handley Pages at Castle Bromwich, and they were all in separate canvas hangars, Bessoneau or Herveaux hangars which had been erected at the far end of the aerodrome. We just couldn't fit any more in, so we took over an aerodrome at Monmore near Shrewsbury. All the aeroplanes were tilted on their noses with their tails up, and all pushed up close together like sardines. Their wings were taken off and stored separately. There were hundreds of aircraft. Eventually, contracts were stopped and they could stop the planes coming, but for a while, it was quite a problem.

Later on, I was posted to Uxbridge, the depot for RAF personnel in those days. I hadn't been there long when I was posted, with three others, to Inland Area Convoy. Our job was to go round all the stations in the south of England disposing of surplus equipment after the war, everything from aeroplanes to beds. We had lists of what we had to keep and what we had to dispose of. In some cases we burned aeroplanes. All the technical equipment like tools which had to be disposed of had to be put in a big hangar at Manston, near Ramsgate. We had what we called the 'underground hangar' there. It wasn't actually underground but it was below the level of the ground. You could see the roof but it cast no shadow and it was very difficult to pick up from the air, being the same colour as the ground. This is where we used to dump all the stuff.

When I originally joined up and signed on in the RFC, I had to sign on for what they called 'ordinary enlistment' which was four years with the colours and four years with the reserves. They could have kept me until 1921, but in 1920 I signed on for another four years. I was quite happy. The war was over and there wasn't much in the way of work outside. I remained on this inland area convoy for about nine months. Even though the war had ended some time before, it wasn't slack for me; there was still plenty to do.

But the service laid off quite a few people when the war ended. In many cases it was the senior NCOs who wanted to stay on. They'd had fairly quick promotion during the war, got to flight sergeant, which was a relatively good job, and didn't want to leave. One of the consequences was that there was very little promotion because the senior posts were all full, so it was difficult for the rest to rise up.

Flight Sergeant Frederick Lang

Flight Sergeant Frederick Joseph Lang was born on 11 July 1893 in Lancashire. He enlisted on 12 October 1914 as a fitter. His account vividly describes the life and daily routine of a mechanic, and affords insights into the relationships between the crew and the pilots. Assigned as fitter to Albert Ball in 1916, theirs was probably one of the closest bonds of its kind despite the social barriers of rank.

He was interviewed in Garstang, Lancashire on 11 July 1978. Lang died on 10 September 1984.

I joined up as a regular, for four years in the service and eight years on the reserve. I wanted to do the work I was used to, having served a full-time apprenticeship as a fitter mechanic. I was posted off to Farnborough for three weeks' basic training, then sent on a rigging course at Upavon, before being transferred to Netheravon, where I first came in contact with aircraft. There were all sorts there including the Maurice Farman Longhorn, the Henri Farman Shorthorn and some of the old Blériot types. I had my first flight at Netheravon with a Lieutenant O'Malley in a Maurice Farman. It took about ten minutes to get up the air. We didn't get to a great height at all, and we made a bit of a bump coming down, but it was a good start and I really enjoyed it.

From Upavon, I was sent on two courses, one on rigging, at the Aircraft Manufacturing Company in Hendon, and one on engines at the Daimler works in Coventry. I got a good grounding in these, and was pretty well established as a recognized fitter. Then I was posted to No. 13 Squadron at Gosport in Hampshire, as a fitter on the BE2c. The BE2c had a 90-horsepower, V type, 8-cylinder, air-cooled, magneto ignition engine. The engine was very efficient, and the BE2c was a very fine machine. It was very stable; it could loop, sideslip, nose dive and was extremely manoeuvrable.

I was posted out to France with No. 13 Squadron, and we were stationed at Vert Galant. There were no runways as with a modern aerodrome, and you had to land according to what we called the 'sausage balloon', which showed the direction of the wind. Aircraft had to land against the wind; if they started to land the other way, they'd be tipped over. The same applied to taking off, of course.

When an aeroplane was due to take off, the pilot would sit in the seat, and the mechanic would stand by the propeller. In front of the wheels there were triangular chocks with ropes. At the tips of the wings, there'd be some riggers, and a man would hang on the tail to keep it down when the engine was started. I would say to the pilot, 'Ready, sir?' The pilot would reply, 'Yes' and I would say, 'Switch off. Suck in.' He would repeat these words. I would get hold of the propeller, and revolve it several times, sucking in the gas to facilitate ignition. Then I would say, 'Contact.' In other words, it was ready for starting. The pilot would speed up his engine to see if it was doing the necessary revolutions, before he'd accept that the machine was fit for flying. As soon as he'd done this, he would raise and lower his hands as a signal that the chocks should be withdrawn. The chaps on the wings would hop off, and we'd say, 'Good luck, sir.' We'd make our final reply to every pilot that took off, 'We wish you good luck, sir.' The pilot would respond with a small salute, and up in the air he would go.

The next thing was waiting for him to return, if he did return, that is. Then we'd go out and meet him and bring him in. 'Any complaints, sir?' Perhaps he'd say 'no' and we'd come back and find a lot of holes because the planes were all duck canvas. And the little bit of shrapnel that pierced used to leave a mark. Then it's the rigger's job to patch them up.

We didn't have much spare time at the aerodrome, though we did occasionally play bingo, cribbage and brag for small stakes in the hangar. We were only getting 2 bob a day and I was allocating a shilling a day for my parents, so I had only 7/- per week to spend on cards, dominoes, and the occasional pint or two. Sometimes we'd go down to estaminets, and consume half a dozen eggs with a *vin blanc*. That cost about 4 sous, and a sou was equivalent to our ha'penny in those days. We couldn't really do much, as we were on duty most of the time.

We left Vert Galant, and went to a place called Marieux, where I met Lieutenant Albert Ball. He'd had full training in England, and was a qualified pilot. I was designated mechanic for his machine, and we got on very well indeed. From time to time he would treat us to a display of looping and diving.

All mechanics were required to go up with the pilot to check that everything was all right with the plane. I once did a repair for him, and Ball didn't ask me to go up. When he returned, I asked him why he hadn't taken me up. He said, 'I went to have a look round.'

I said, 'Well you can see enough up in the air, sir.' 'Well,' he replied, 'I landed on enemy land to have a look round.'

The fellow had absolutely landed on German territory and he came and told me this secretly.

He says, 'Don't tell any of my superior officers; I'd rather just keep this to myself, and you're the only one I've told about this.'

That's just the type of fellow he was. He was a good lad, and we all recognized him as having a great future. I don't want to state what actions he'd taken because that was very secret among the pilots. Their news was not confided much to the staff. Sometimes he'd say, 'I had a bit of a do today,' or something like that, but I never queried him or asked him anything. He never mentioned anything at all, and I don't know to this day how many enemy machines he brought down.

A Bristol Scout arrived, and this was allotted to Lieutenant Ball. The machine had an 80-horsepower Le Rhône rotary engine with a two-bladed propeller, fitted with a Constantinesco gear to allow the Vickers gun on the left of the fuselage to be fired through the propeller whilst in flight. I was with him when we transferred to No. 11 Squadron. They were on the same aerodrome as we were, so it was simply a matter of transferring my Bristol Scout to B Flight of No. 11 Squadron. Ball didn't like this Bristol Scout, though, as the Nieuports were much faster and had a higher ceiling. They could fly from ninety to 100 miles per hour, whereas the old BE2c could only do about seventy. It was a different plane altogether, pure and simply a fighter. And that was Ball's job, and I could see he was destined for it. He was going to make a name for himself, and it was whispered among all the mechanics and everything.

One day we saw a German kite balloon about five miles in the distance, just over the enemy's side of the lines. Ball had a look at this, and said, 'I'd like to have a go at that fellow.' Normally, it would have been pure suicide, as the balloons were covered by fighter pilots and anti-aircraft fire. We converted one of the Nieuport Scouts to fire rockets, fitting three tubes on the struts of each wing, aligned at a slight upward angle. Our flight commander, Captain Cooper, took the plane up to try it out. Unfortunately, he got into a nose dive, came down and was killed. I went out there to the body, and saw him all mangled up. I know the doctor came out, and I could see, he just put a needle into him as much as to say he was done.

Ball said, 'We'll have another go.' We modified another Nieuport to fire Le Prieur rockets. These were fired electrically by the pilot, and pointing upwards for him to get high enough to get out of the machine-gun fire, or the anti-aircraft fire. Ball went up and got the hit first time. We could see the smoke and the flames ascending, the Jerries climbing out of the basket – I think they had parachutes in them days. Ball had been away for only ten minutes – another ten minutes he was back. When he returned, he jumped out of his machine, and danced about with joy; he was on top of the world. And we clapped and we cheered; everybody on the aerodrome turned out, even the 13 Squadron. Wonderful feat.

He was extremely friendly towards me, and even took me down to a local estaminet for a few glasses of *vin blanc*. There was a limit, though; officers and mechanics had to keep a sort of distance, because discipline had to be maintained as much as possible. He had a little hut on the aerodrome, and that hut was sacred. He didn't like anybody at all coming in. If I was wanted, he'd come for me; I wouldn't go for him. Sometimes he'd come at all hours. An alarm would come through, and he was immediately on the warpath, straight out of bed, still in his pyjamas, but with his leather jacket and sometimes goggles, sometimes not.

I found a notice posted on the board which read: 'F.J. Lang, No. 1812, Secondary Mechanic, will be posted to England.' A week or so later, I sailed across to England, and was posted to Kings Lynn in Norfolk. There was a BE2c there, ready to fly, and who should come out to fly it but Lieutenant Ball. I looked at him in astonishment, and he broke into fits of laughter. He said, 'We're here again,' and I said, 'Yes, sir, and I'm right pleased to see you.' He said, 'Come on; I'm going to take you up.'

So he took me up, and we had the final flight, finishing off with the flourish of a sideslip and I think about half a dozen consecutive loops. You didn't need to be strapped in for a loop; it was done so quickly, that you could just grip the seat. We used to put the belt round, but you could loop without worrying about the strap or anything.

He came down and then he confided to me, 'I've come over for promotion, and then I'm taking another machine back. I've always thought you deserved promotion, which is why I arranged for you to come here. You'll be posted away from here soon.' That was the last flight I had with Captain Ball. I never saw him again. The last I heard about him was that he'd gone off, disappeared in a cloud, and wasn't seen alive again. He was a wonderful man. Wonderful man!

I was sent to Hythe, to the first School of Aerial Gunnery, and got promotion in less than six months, jumped from corporal to sergeant, and became a chief mechanic. I was in charge of the flights of about twelve machines. I also had under my charge a platoon of sixty Americans. We had DH5s and DH6s there, and my duties included supervising these machines and taking up observers on training courses and firing practice. Every morning, I met with my flight commander, Captain Hopkins, and we used to plan together which machines were to go out. They had to be logged, and reported, and they had to be sheeted, and I had to write this all down. I had a marvellous time at Hythe, and was billeted at the Ship Hotel at Dymchurch, a beautiful little village nearby.

Eventually, demobilization happened. Some of us went on the rant. Four of us found a fellow working on the road with a steam-roller, commandeered it, and drove round for a few hours. We ended up at the canteen in Hythe, stuffing our bellies with beer and whisky, and were just as rowdy as they are after football matches today.

When I got home, though, I noticed a change of attitude among working people. There had been a lot of grumbling about conscientious objectors, and that people making munitions had been earning vast amounts of money, sometimes as much as five pounds a day, whereas starving second mechanics had to get by on two shillings. I went into business with my father. We had two filling stations at Garstang. I worked with my father until the strike in 1926. Then Army papers landed through my letter box; I was ordered to report to Shrewsbury. The RFC had become the RAF, and my title of chief mechanic had been scrapped. I was now flight sergeant, which was still the highest rank of NCO. I went down to Shrewsbury on my motorbike, and was involved in overhauling aircraft engines in a workshop there.

War service certainly changed my life. It made me realize that there was something more to life than just breathing or socializing. The war made a great transformation not only in me, but in people generally. I'm sure that there will be another war at some point; maybe not in my lifetime, but perhaps in fifty years or so. Anyhow, I can't consider the future; it doesn't bother me. I've got to this age, I've led a good life, and I've enjoyed it. I hope I've done what the Lord ordained me to do. I've tried my best. I've found friends and companions, gained knowledge and instruction, and most of all, I've discovered that there are far nicer people than me on this earth.

Remembering Ball

From private conversations with F.J. Lang

He was brave, right from the day he first flew.
He was always brave . . .
The good always die young.

145

In 1916 it was difficult for a pilot's mechanic to attain any higher posting. In Nos. 13 and 11 Squadrons, Albert encountered in his air mechanic someone with whom he could be at ease and forget the implicit class structures of the day, which were noticeable even in the markedly unstuffy RFC. Fred was an intelligent man of whose expertise and reliability Albert could be assured both on the ground and in the air. There existed between the two a reciprocal devotion and respect not afforded Albert amongst his squadron peers, despite his unassailable reputation for reckless courage.

He was angling to ensure me a promotional posting back to England – to the School of Aerial Gunnery at Hythe. This took longer than he anticipated, and betimes he would report to me his progress. On one occasion, frustrated by the lack of headway, he addressed me as 'Fred', lamenting the slow advancement of his efforts on my behalf. How the CO would have disapproved to hear an officer addressing another rank so intimately.

Albert's efforts on his behalf resulted in Fred's posting to Hythe School of Aerial Gunnery in July 1916. There he remained for the duration of the war, later being promoted to flight sergeant. In March 1917, he had his final and unexpected encounter with Albert, who greeted him without any formality, and invited him up for a flip in a BE2c. He gave Fred his uniform hat, which was later donated to the RAF Museum. Flight Sergeant Sharp, also stationed at Lympne, offered Fred a recent photograph of Albert which has hitherto remained unpublished.

The last time I flew was with him at Lympne, subsequent to the posting and promotion he had arranged for me. He insisted that I go up for a flight with him before he left for France. He shook hands with me, and I never saw him again. From that day to this, I have never flown, and have never wanted to fly.

Fred was not alone in benefiting from Albert Ball's humanity and attention to the needs of his comrades. Though an efficient killer, by late April 1917 Albert Ball had come to detest this role and was convinced that he would not survive. His frustrating period of enforced absence from his previous active service in France had seen not only significant developments in aircraft design, but also the rapid evolution of tactical deployment and strategy in aerial combat. Albert returned to France in 'Bloody April', when a radically enhanced pace in combat fighting against larger groups of enemy aircraft militated against any expectation of a pilot's surviving. Even the most skilful and admired asset of the RFC could not hope to pull through, given that he was taking on such odds daily, and courting danger with increasing disregard for his own safety.

Fred, who remained unmarried, was educated at a Quaker School, which may have furnished him with the breadth of imagination demonstrated in his various writings. Born in Garstang, near Cumbria, he lived for nature, delighting to roam the Pennines, and averaging fifty miles weekly in earlier days. An avid photographer, he wrote extensively on themes such as early transport, the Lancashire countryside, astronomy and his time as a choirboy. Of Edward, Prince of Wales, he remarked that there 'was nothing in that head at all'. He described the famous Vert Galant Aerodrome as 'a rotten field with a lousy slope on it'. When offered a post as warrant officer in the Second World War, he felt obliged to decline, as 'the family business would have suffered'. However, he did serve as a special constable for some years. Fred's collection of cigarette cards was renowned, as was his mynah bird, later banished for its less than hygienic habits. Having driven since 1910, Fred abandoned the practice aged eighty. After demobilization he was employed in the management of a garage and workshop.

Lord Harold Balfour

Harold Harrington Balfour was born in Camberley, Surrey on 1 November, 1897, the son of a colonel and great-grandson of Field-Marshal Lord Napier of Magdala. He was educated at Chilverton Elms, Dover, and the Royal Naval College at Osborne. He joined the King's Royal Rifle Company in 1914 and transferred three months later to the Royal Flying Corps. He served in several squadrons, most notably Nos. 40, 43, and 60. During the war he achieved eleven victories and was slightly wounded on 24 April 1917.

Balfour received the Military Cross on 26 May 1917, with a bar added on 22 April 1918 for ' a reconnaissance in which he bombed two guns and silenced them, bombed large bodies of troops in a market square, and fired into the hangars and huts in a hostile aero-drome'.

After the war, he achieved a distinguished career, serving as a Member of Parliament, before becoming Parliamentary Under-Secretary of State for Air in 1938. He was retained by Churchill in 1940 in a secondary role, and was active when France fell, and during the Battle of Britain. In 1941 he was sworn to the Privy Council. He was a member of the mission to Moscow headed by Lord Beaverbrook, and toasted Stalin. In 1944 Churchill appointed Balfour as Resident Minister in West Africa. Created Baron Balfour of Inchyre, he returned in 1945 to serve in the House of Lords.

After the war he maintained his interest in journalism and flying, as President of the British Society of World War 1 Aero Historians. He was interviewed at his home in London on 30 September 1978. Lord Balfour died on 22 September 1988.

148

I was interested in aviation from the age of seven. I can remember Blériot landing at my preparatory school near Dover. We were taken out to see his aircraft. Then came World War One, and I always wanted to fly, but I joined the 60th Rifles as a young subaltern on my seventeenth birthday. I used to sneak over to Farnborough. And I remember being taken up by a very famous man called B.C. Hucks who was a pre-World War One pilot. Then I got three weeks' leave from my regiment, and borrowed £75 from my father, who lent it to me very reluctantly. I said, 'I want to go and learn to fly to get my Royal Aero Club certificate.' I went to the civilian schools, to Hendon. In those days there were four or five such schools, all along a row of hangars. There was I, in plain clothes, a boy of seventeen, with £75 in my pocket.

All the schools wanted my seventy-five quid! I came to a thing called the Binky Wright's school; they had an old Wright biplane. It had a 50 Gnome engine and twin propellers run by two bicycle chains. There was an American instructor who wanted my £75 very much. He said, 'Young man, come to this school! Learn on a Binky Wright. It's a wonderful aircraft! All right at thirty-five miles an hour, dead man at thirty-four!' He didn't get my money. I went to the Ruffy-Baumann School which had fifty new Caudron biplanes. I had about two and a half hours' dual, then I was sent solo, and I took my ticket, Nº 1399, on 5 July 1915.

I returned to my regiment hoping to transfer to the Flying Corps. But the battalion was just going to France, and the colonel said he'd take me to France though I was really far too young – just seventeen and a half.

I had about two or three months in the trenches. It was very uncomfortable, very dangerous, and extremely dirty. I came to the conclusion that if I were going to be killed, which seemed at that time pretty inevitable, I'd prefer to be killed in comfort. One day, a circular letter came around inviting any officer who had a pilot's certificate to transfer to the Royal Flying Corps. I transferred as second lieutenant, seconded from my regiment.

I was sent to Shoreham at the beginning of 1916. There, we had old Maurice Farman biplanes, they were nicknamed 'Rumpties'.

From there I went on to Gosport where I flew more modern aircraft, the BE2c, the old 80 Gnome Avro biplanes. I even went up once in an FE2b which was a great big pusher, but I was destined to go out on what they called 'scouts' in those days. A man called Major Waldron who joined the Flying Corps in 1911, was the commanding officer, and my flight commander was Bob Smith-Barry, who became a very famous man later on in the war. We had Blériots, we had Morane Parasols, and a Martinsyde Scout. I'd not flown any of these.

I went into my flight commander's office, saluted, and he said, 'Go out and take up that Martinsyde.' I thought, 'He won't even come out of his office to see me kill myself.' However, I got into the Martinsyde, managed to get it up in the air and get it down.

On another occasion, he said to me, 'I want you to take up this Grahame-White.' It was a middle-wing aircraft with an 80 Gnome, exactly the same aircraft that was used at Hendon before the war at all the flying meetings. When I looked in the logbook of this particular Grahame-White Morane, I discovered that it was actually the aircraft that had flown to Windsor, and looped the loop over King George V. It had been piloted by Gustav Hamel who disappeared into the Channel just before the war.

The Morane was a strange aircraft. You sat in your seat and your passenger sat behind you on the same seat and clasped you round the waist. It had what's called 'middle wings', several pounds of lead laced to the wingtip so it wouldn't drop when you shut the engine off. I thought I was a fine little chap then because I'd just got my wings and we were all very pleased when the infantry officers used to come up and watch us brave chaps take to the air. One man said to me, 'What's the aircraft?'

I said, 'It's a Morane. I'm going up, would you like to take a trip?'

He said, 'Yes, sir, I would indeed.'

He'd never been up before, and I'd never taken a passenger in one of those things. We got in and I started up. As soon as I left the ground, I knew I'd bitten off something more than I could chew.

I climbed very slowly over the Solent until I reached 1,200 feet. Then I slithered the thing round gently, brought it over the aerodrome and shouted to my passenger, 'Hold on! We're going to land now!' I knew that when I shut it off, it was going to drop like a brick and there was just one moment where I could pull the stick back and level out. If I chose that moment too late, we were going to hit the ground, and both be killed. If I chose it too early, I'd probably stall a few feet from the ground. That's what happened. I pulled the stick back six or seven feet up, and she just dropped, one wing dropped and we turned upside down. Petrol ran all over us; it's a miracle we didn't catch fire. We both escaped unhurt. I had to go into Bob Smith-Barry and say, 'Sorry, sir, I've just crashed the Morane.'

He said, 'I saw it; you're a bloody conceited little fool aren't you?'

I replied, 'Oh, I am, sir, yes.'

Then we had Morane Bullets. We got the first one sent over from France, and we were formed into three flights. I was in a flight of Bullets commanded by Smith-Barry. We went out to France by boat and collected our aircraft at St Omer. The Battle of the Somme was just going to start, so I flew in that. Then I came back to England in due course, and became a test pilot at Upavon. There I met a lot of interesting characters. Another character I remember was a chap at Gosport called Smith. He'd learnt to fly, and his father came down to see him. He said, 'Daddy, would you like a trip?' So 'Daddy' got in the Maurice Farman and up they went. Unfortunately he crashed and killed 'Daddy'. He was known thereafter as 'Baghdad' Smith.

Gordon-Bell was my squadron commander, and I was made a flight commander, acting captain, on my eighteenth birthday, which was quite an event for me. Gordon-Bell had had two crashes before World War One, in which he'd killed a couple of passengers and had been very much criticized for it. Unfortunately, plastic surgery was in its infancy, and they'd stuck his nose on very badly. He stammered, too, as a result of the crash, but he was a wonderful pilot. He had a girlfriend not terribly far from Upavon, whom he used to go and visit in his Bristol Scout. He'd fixed up a sort of spring attachment on the tail so he could start the engine up and come round and get in the aircraft, pull the spring, release the spring and take off like that. He had two little white dogs, and I remember one day, he came down the tarmac, and all the pupils stood up, and said, 'Good morning, sir.'

And he looked up at me, put his eyeglass into his eye and said, 'I wasn't saying g-g-good morning to you, I was saying g-g-good morning to the dogs! But good m-m-morning all the same.' Pointing at a 1½-strutter, he continued, 'Now Tommy Sopwith says the wings come off at 140 miles an hour.' He turned to one of the wretched pupils: 'Get in and w-w-we'll see.' However, they didn't come off.

Gordon-Bell was a beautiful fighter pilot. He had remarkable character. I'd first met him at Gosport when I was learning to fly. He used to come out, and smell the air. I remember him coming out one day and sniffing with his stuck-on nose, and he said, 'I smell blood today.' We killed four people before lunch that morning. Unfortunately, poor Gordon-Bell was killed just at the end of the war, in 1918. He flew into Villers-Bocage aerodrome, his tail came off and he was killed.

Smith-Barry was a remarkable man, too. He was one of the pioneers of instruction. And until one had been through Bob Smith-Barry's course at Gosport where, incidentally, I was one of the flight commanders in the summer of 1917, one never really knew about flying. Smith-Barry started what I call the analysis of flying; what the controls did and why. Before he started the school, he got three or four of the old flight commanders of squadrons in France, No. 60 Squadron, and others and we taught each other to fly. We did every sort of manoeuvre, and wrote down an analysis of our efforts. Finally, we had a sort of patter which we could give in printed form to every pupil. All the pupils were instructors from other stations. There wasn't one of them who didn't go away saying, 'I learned more about flying in the last fortnight than I ever thought possible.'

At the beginning of 1917 I went to France on these 1½-strutters with No. 43 Squadron. We formed at Netheravon; I was one of the flight commanders. The commanding officer was Sholto Douglas, later the famous Lord Douglas of Kirtleside who played a distinguished part as Marshal of the Royal Air Force, and Air Marshal in World War Two. He was a fine CO. The trouble was our aircraft were so inferior to the Germans'. Every morning we used to go out on defensive patrols or reconnaissance in our 1½-strutters. And there was Richthofen's Flying Circus, circling above us in their gaily-painted Albatroses, playing about like puppies, waiting in the sun to come down and meet our wretched 1½-strutters. We had thirty-five casualties in a month. We were just shot down.

All we could do when the Germans dived on us was to form a circle, follow each others' tails round so the six rear gunners could concentrate the fire of six Lewis guns on the Germans as they descended. And we'd edge the flight slowly round toward the safety of our own lines. We used to say to the young, inadequately-trained men, 'Don't worry if you can't keep up. Don't worry if you can't get the best power out of your engine. Dive down underneath us and we'll look after you. But do not straggle because I'm not going to spoil my circle, and get myself and five other people killed for one straggler.' Of course the wretched little boys did straggle; that's how we had so many shot down. They were either killed or taken prisoner. That was in January and February 1917.

By October, when I rejoined the squadron, I was shot down over Vimy Ridge. I was in a 1½-strutter, patrolling up and down the front lines, with the Battle of Vimy Ridge going on below me. Our artillery aircraft were ranging their guns, and I was up and down the line protecting them in case they were attacked. There was a strong wind blowing, and I suddenly found myself three miles over the German lines. I turned for home. I was up only 1,700 feet, and every cannon opened up on me. Before I could get home safely, they shot my engine. The engine stopped, and I'd just enough height to glide over the front line. I remembered a heated debate in the mess the night before, on the question of whether, if you crashed on Vimy Ridge, you would have your seatbelt done up or not. I said I'd have my seatbelt done up, but the general consensus was that you'd be safer with your seat belt undone because you might avoid the engine coming back and squashing you. So as I was coming down, I remember flicking my belt open, saying, 'Well, I'll go with the majority.'

We hit a shell hole, my observer was thrown out, and knocked his head. The poor chap was never the same afterwards, and was invalided out. I was chucked out, too. Luckily, the propeller had been broken, otherwise it would have sliced me into pieces. I was fairly unconscious, and the Canadians came and picked me up and carried me into a dugout. That night I was sent down to a casualty clearing station. I remained in hospital a few weeks, then went back to Upavon as a flight commander and joined Smith-Barry at the Gosport school. I went out to France again at the end of 1917, flying Sopwith Camels.

One day, Lord Dowding, who was my wing commander in the Somme, flew over in a BE2c to see Bob Smith-Barry, who was commanding the squadron after the death of Major Waldron. After he'd finished his inspection tour, he was going to fly back to Fienvillers, his headquarters, which was twenty miles away. He started up the engine of his BE2c and it was popping and banging. Obviously something was not right with it. The station commander offered his Crossley car to take Dowding back to HQ. Dowding said, 'Get somebody to look at the engine, put it right and send it over for me tomorrow.' Next morning, Smith-Barry said to me, 'I want you to take the Wing Commander's aircraft over to Fienvillers.' I enquired, 'Is the engine all right?' and he said, 'Well, go and see.' I got the mechanics who'd been working on it, and they said that it was all right. We revved the engine, and it was fine. I got in the machine and thought, 'Great fun! I haven't flown a BE2c for some time.' I took off, and had reached about forty feet when the engine stopped. There was nothing to be done except go straight ahead, which I did, removing most of the telephone wires which were confirming the Battle of the Somme, and put the undercart through the bottom of the aeroplane. So I went to Bob Smith-Barry's tent, saluted, and said, 'Sir, I've just crashed the Wing Commander's BE2c.'

He said, 'Well, your punishment is to ring up the Wing Commander and tell him yourself what you've done.'

So I telephoned Wing Commander Dowding and said, 'Sorry, sir, I've crashed your aircraft.'

He asked, 'How'd you do it?' I told him exactly what had happened.

He said, 'Did you ask if the engine was all right?' I explained that I had, and confirmed that I had run the engine up myself.

He said, 'Very well.'

There was never a single word of rebuke. From that moment on, I was Dowding's slave.

I knew this chap called Robert Loraine, who commanded No. 40 Squadron at Aire on the same aerodrome as our 1½-strutters. When we got out there in the terribly cold, bitter winter of 1917, there was nothing except empty huts, no furniture, no cookhouse, nothing. A chap came along, saluted, and said, 'Major Loraine's compliments. There is hot lunch waiting in the mess.' This was indeed a wonderful invitation, and we lived in No. 40 Squadron's mess for a day or two. He was a great chap, very theatrical. He was an actor. I saw him after the war in *Cyrano de Bergerac*. But I remember his being especially dramatic when a hangar of No. 40 Squadron caught fire. We were comfortable in our own mess at the other end of the aerodrome, when suddenly there was a fire alarm. We all left our dinner and rushed out across the aerodrome. One of the hangars of No. 40 Squadron was ablaze, with aircraft burning inside, and we heard the popping of machine-gun bullets as the heat got to the ammunition. Nobody could do anything. Some little sergeant rushed forward and started to throw out bits of something, which was of no earthly use at all. Loraine rushed out into the fire-lit circle and said, 'Away, my man. Away. If this is anybody's place, it's mine.' He proceeded to perform a perfectly natural function in the firelight to the intense admiration of all the other men watching. He was a great chap.

I knew Lord Trenchard, too. He was known as 'Boom', and his morale-making was wonderful. When we were at our worst, with Sopwith 1½-Strutters at the beginning of 1917, Boom came round the squadron, with his faithful ADC Maurice Baring, and we thought we were going to have some words of sympathy, and some understanding of our problems. Not a bit of it! We all got a hell of a telling off. 'Squadron's got to be better. Too many casualties. Must be more aggressive.' This was probably very good for us. Maurice Baring, always following behind, comforted us, saying, 'Don't worry; the old boy's in a bad temper today!' He handed out Russian cigarettes as he spoke to us. Then he told us how he had Field Punishments Nos. 1, 2 and 3 for Trenchard. No. 1 was to hide Trenchard's pipe when he came down for breakfast, No. 2 was to say, 'The motorcar will be late today because of a little engine trouble,' and No. 3 was to say 'Maurice Baring put his elbow though a window'! Trenchard was a great man and a great leader. Leadership is contagious. Trenchard could come into a mess, and you'd know at once that a great personality had arrived.

Sholto Douglas was a fine leader, too. I knew him as squadron commander, and he's been a friend of mine always. He was a fine pilot, and did marvellously in World War One, wonderfully between the wars, and rose ever higher in the Royal Air Force. Then when I suddenly found myself Under Secretary of State and Vice President of the Air Council in 1938, Sholto Douglas was at the Air Ministry as the Air Commodore. Then he was made Air Vice Marshal. All the men under him loved him because they knew he would never let them down, and would always accept the blame and responsibility for any errors they made. After the war, he was made chairman of British European Airways and I happened to be made one of the non-executive government directors. We never dared to look at our chairman's expense account, because whenever we had a new inaugural flight, he used to fill the aeroplane with tarts and champagne. Anyone who knew the man loved him and trusted him. I had to give the address at his memorial service, from the pulpit of Westminster Abbey. It was not easy, because dear Sholto had had three wives, and was also an admitted atheist, but I got away with it.

Smith-Barry had the idea of trying to break the New York Stock Exchange. He put his mathematical brain into predicting which way stocks were going to go, and invested heavily. Unfortunately the stocks went the wrong way, so he lost an awful lot of money.

Then he fell ill, and died in South Africa. As for Trenchard, I went into the House of Lords in 1945, after the election, and he was there. He used to speak periodically, with great authority, on defence and air matters. He was never a 'good' speaker, but what he said was always sound, and listened to by the House with due respect.

At the beginning of 1918, for about three or four casualties in a month, we got twenty Germans down. That shows the tactical superiority of the Camel over the German fighter at that time. The great thing was to have an aircraft which was technically superior in performance to that of the enemy. Our morale was always good, even when we were being shot down like rabbits. But morale improved considerably when you had a better aircraft than the enemy and you could shoot them down. The Sopwith Camel was a lovely aircraft. I don't suppose it brought down as many enemy as the SE5, but on the other hand, the Camel didn't have the casualties the SE5 had because you could turn a Camel inside the turning circle of any German. During a severe fight, you had infinitely better chances of salvation in a Sopwith Camel than you did in an SE5. Once you knew a Camel, it would talk to you. I could do anything with a Camel. At the beginning, for the new chap, it was very tricky, and had a lot of torque. Taking off, if you tried your right hand turn, the nose would go down and the pilot would probably kill himself. A left hand climbing turn was beautiful, because she'd go up naturally against the torque. Well, these little boys who had had too little experience thought they could take liberties with it, but the Camel could turn around and bite you unless you were careful.

The Camel was my favourite plane to fight. But for pure joy of flying, give me an old Avro 504. I was teaching after the war, as instructor at the Cadet College in Cranwell. Portal was chief flying instructor. We had the mono Avro, the same as during the war. It would never turn and bite you like the Camel. It was the most honest flying machine I ever flew.

In May 1918, I was ill, and shipped back to England. I became Chief Fighting Instructor at Seaford in Norfolk, and I was made an acting major. I was only twenty, so I reckoned I could call

157

myself a minor major or a major minor. I stayed on as an instructor at Cranwell, and I left the service in 1924. We were still teaching on the Smith-Barry system until 1924. Indeed, in elementary flying, the Smith-Barry system still exists.

Dear Smith-Barry! We were both flying after the war. He commanded a station at Gravesend, where he had an aircraft called a Defiant. It was a four-gun fighter, and he went out in it to Dunkirk, where he shot down all sorts of Germans because the Germans never realized that he had four guns at the back. The next day, though, the Germans retaliated and all the Defiants were shot down.

Directly after the war, I personally tried to hide myself in work I enjoyed, teaching cadets at Cranwell to fly, and trying really to take shelter from the realities of what was going on; industrial unrest, rising unemployment, poverty and starvation. I tried to protect myself for a period of time, and I suddenly woke up to it, left the Air Force and went to work as a journalist on *The Daily Mail* at £3/10/- a week. Then in 1924 I fought a parliamentary seat in the East End of London, Stratford West. I got within 1,200 votes of the seat, and I went on working in the aircraft industry. I took a seat in Parliament in 1929, and then Chamberlain asked me to go to the Air Ministry in 1938.

I kept my flying up all the time. I was with a firm called Whitehall Securities, and we started a thing called British Airways. The British Airways of today pinched our name! We had British Airways running against Imperial Airways from Croydon to Paris, ran a service to Hanover and we acquired Saunders, a company which built flying boats on the Isle of Wight.

When Churchill became Prime Minister, I stayed on at the Air Ministry until 1944. I gave up flying as a pilot in 1946; I flew from 1915 until 1946. I didn't miss it, though. I realized flying was ceasing to be a hobby; it needed to be a full-time job, and I decided to call it a day. I had a lot of fun flying every sort of aircraft. I flew about seventy-five different types of plane. Of course, in the days of World War One, to fly a new type of aircraft was just fun. You got in it, asked somebody what speed to land at, what to bring her down at, what her vices and virtues were, and how the engine functioned. Then you fastened your belt, opened her up and flew. Even later on, as aircraft got more complex, it wasn't too difficult to learn to fly a new type. In my office in the Air Ministry, where I was Under Secretary of State, I wanted to fly a Typhoon. I sent for the Typhoon papers and read what a Typhoon's characteristics were, went up to Duxford a few days later, borrowed a Typhoon and flew it.

Today, a chap has to do a conversion course lasting months before he can learn to fly a new type. I've just been to my old squadron, where they have Phantoms, and when an experienced pilot comes to them he has to go through a Phantom Operational Training Unit to complete three or four months' hard training before he's allowed to go solo on one. Flying today is so complicated and difficult compared to what it was in my day. On the other hand, the boys there told me they still get the joy of flying, even flying one of these Phantoms. Today you can't crash an all metal aircraft without probably killing yourself. In those days, if you crashed an aircraft, it was wooden, and if you were lucky, you'd get away with it.

The war certainly changed society. When King Edward VII died, Edwardian society finished. When World War One ended, the differential in gaps between social classes and industrial conditions started to alter, and has been altering ever since. But I'm quite sure that the social revolution we are now seeing commenced in the 20s. The Second World War did the same, in a way, as the first war; it intensified social change. This was illustrated in the 1945 election, when Churchill, though revered and admired by the whole community, was nevertheless defeated in favour of social reform. It has nothing to do with flying, but when I went into the House of Commons in 1929, as the Conservative MP for the Isle of Thanet, I always blamed myself and my party, the Conservative Party, for not having a realization of the misery that existed in the depressed areas.

An experience like World War One taught one real values. One had the sort of friendships and loyalties in World War One which are an anachronism in peace time. One thought it likely that one would be killed. You were sad when somebody was killed, but you were selfish enough to say, 'Well, I'm glad it wasn't me' and 'It will probably be me next time'. You grieved for them when you saw empty places in the mess at night. But it didn't stop cheerfulness. I say, it was bound to have an effect on one's character for the rest of one's life. You were very much up against reality in World War One. When you think that the next day, you're probably going to be done in, you think of the essentials. Character at its best, I would say.

Captain Robert Halley

Captain Robert 'Jock' Halley was born in Perthshire in 1895. After eighteen months in the 2nd/1st Highland Cycle Battalion, he transferred to the Royal Flying Corps around the end of the Somme Campaign. He served on long distance bombing, a strategy highly promoted by Sir Hugh Trenchard, and was awarded the DFC on 3 August 1918. His citation read in part: 'a gallant and determined leader in long distance night bombing most successful in many of these raids.' Halley's last bombing raid lasted eight hours, a considerable amount of time for early bomber pilots flying in open cockpits with no oxygen.

Halley was interviewed on 7 January 1979. He died in the Royal Air Force Association home, Sussexdown, on 13 December 1979.

I joined up in 1915. I was a 'mud student' learning farming at a farm near Montrose in Angus. I was twenty years old, and joined the 2nd/1st Highland Cyclist Battalion as a dispatch rider. I had difficulty getting in because I only stand 5 feet 3 inches high. They wouldn't have me at first, but as I had a motorcycle and they were keen on taking on as many motorcycles as possible, I said, 'If you want my motorcycle you'll have to take me as well.' I got in. I went to the Quartermaster's stores and was issued with a couple of tunics, breeches, buttons, boots, socks and the usual stuff. I was also issued two chevrons. Next morning on parade, the sergeant major came round. He was a great chap; we called him 'Wee Hughie'. He'd been sergeant major of the 42 Black Watch for twenty-four years, had retired, and joined up again on the outbreak of war. He hadn't seen me on parade before. He had a cane in his hand and he tapped his leg and tapped my chevrons, saying, 'Do you know, my boy? It took me thirteen years to get that chevron.' I'd got mine overnight.

I did a year and a half as a dispatch rider, then four of us got commissions in the Navy. We did our ground training at the Crystal Palace. We had lectures on the theory of flight and the maintenance of engines. We were then posted to Vendôme in France, about forty miles south-west of Paris, where the Admiralty had a flying training school.

It was great fun going over. We were in Naval uniform. We were known as probationary flight officers. We had a little brass Albatross on our left sleeve, and looked like we were officers. Going over in the destroyer, the journey was very rough and we didn't behave as naval officers should, I'm afraid.

It was quite interesting at Vendôme. We had Caudrons, Maurice Farmans, and an American Curtiss JN-4 for training. We were given a medical examination and then had to go through a test for air sickness. This entailed getting in a Caudron and going up to a fair height. My pilot for this exercise was a warrant officer who had risen from the ranks. He said, 'Halley, get in the front seat.' I put on a flying helmet, and he said, 'We'll just go up and fly around. Take notice of what you see on the ground.' We took off. The height didn't affect me very much, and we got up to about 8,000 feet. Without any warning, I heard him shout, 'Jesus Christ! I'm on fire!' Well, that wasn't very comforting on a first flight. We landed in a small field about twenty miles from Vendôme. He leapt out, and I saw him dancing about, stripping off all his clothes, his leather coat, monkey jacket, pants . . . everything. He was swearing with a most extensive vocabulary. He happened to be a pipe smoker, and his pipe wasn't fully extinguished when he put it in his leather coat pocket, and it burned right through to his skin.

We did all our initial flying at Vendôme. After two and a half months, I was posted to Cranwell. There, I started on a BE2c, and then went on to an Avro and a Bristol Scout. These machines varied tremendously; they had odd tricks of their own. The Bristol Scout,

162

for instance, used to swing to the left when taking off , so you had to put on full right rudder. When I flew the Bristol Scout first, I started at 5:30 in the morning. I approached the plane, which was sitting up on its nose after the last pilot's particularly inept landing. I got into this machine. There was no adjustable rudder or seat, and given my lack of inches, they had to put a cushion in. This wasn't sufficient, though, and the flight commander said, 'Get another cushion'. Eventually I had four cushions. Just before I was ready to take off, the flight commander looked in and rather upset me by saying, 'Can you do with any more upholstery?' I took off, and went for about twenty miles in a straight line before I had the nerve to turn. I got round, came back and did quite a reasonable landing.

From Cranwell, we went to a place called Freiston on the Wash, which was a bombing and gunnery school. They used to put up hot air balloons and we had to go and shoot them down. An amusing incident happened there. There were targets anchored out on the Wash, on which we had to drop our bombs. I remember a Canadian lad called Causton going up to do his bombing practice. It was low tide, and out on the Wash was a fishing smack, almost the identical size and colour of the bombing target. Causton went and bombed this fishing smack. We observed all this through field glasses. The skipper and the crew were going mad on the deck, waving sheets and things, but he didn't seem to see them. Anyway, he got in another couple of bombs without any great accuracy. When there was enough water to get ashore, the boat's captain came to our commanding officer and made a complaint. It worked in our favour because Causton was given duty officer for the rest of his stay at Freiston.

At Freiston I got my stripes for flight sub-lieutenant, my rings, after which the Admiralty posted me down to Manston. I really wanted to be a fighter pilot, but it was just as well that I was posted to Manston, because I would never have made a fighter pilot.

I remember going down to Margate from Victoria. It was in the summer, and I felt like the 'cat's whiskers' in my Naval uniform with a bright gold ring and a white cap-cover. There was another PFO on the train, and we met at the exit to Margate station. His name was Walterton, and he was well over six feet tall. We must have looked a strange pair; I was the shortest officer in the Royal Naval Air Service. Walterton said, 'I'm going to Manston, have you heard of it?' I replied, 'Well, I've heard of it, I believe the new Handley Pages are there.' We got on a Wolseley tender together. It was rather late in the afternoon when we reached Manston, and the CO wasn't available. There was a delightful billet there which had been taken over by the Admiralty, called Rose Cottage. It had period furniture, and it's still there today.

We had a good night's sleep and reported to the CO in the morning. I knocked at his door first. He had his feet up on the desk, and he was behind the *Daily Telegraph*. He looked up, and exclaimed, 'Good God.' Then he looked at Walterton and cried, 'How extraordinary.' He must have been thinking about the type of machines we were going to have to fly, with their 101-foot span. He added, 'Anyway, you'll do your best; it's all right. There'll be nothing doing today; I'll take you up in the morning in the Handley Page. Now there are a couple of BE2cs at your disposal; you can fly all day and night as far as I'm concerned. Eventually there will be a Handley Page available for you.' We had great fun on these BE2cs. Our main delight was to go around the piers at Margate and Brighton, and pretend to shoot all the people up on the beach. Nowadays anyone would be court-martialled for that sort of behaviour.

There were about six or seven of us at Manston. The cottage was ideal and we had a steward there who'd had a catering position at the House of Commons. He gave us everything out of season, curried prawns, larks' tongues and all that sort of nonsense. I managed to wangle a job as intelligence officer; well, looking at me you could see what a farce that was. Basically the job involved holding the keys to the safe. What that safe contained, I never knew. I was eventually relieved of that job, but I had been keen on getting it, as the intelligence officer never had to act as duty officer.

Now and then I did a bit of ferrying from Manston, taking Handley Pages from Cricklewood to Coudekerque where the first squadron was – No. 7 Naval. I would go up to Cricklewood to collect the machine and bring it down to Manston to be fitted with Lewis guns. A crew would come aboard and we'd fly over to

Coudekerque. I took on this job from a man named Baedeker who took the first Handley Page over to France. He went along the coast with the intention of landing at Coudekerque. However, owing to bad weather, he landed at Berg aerodrome. He was immediately approached by some German officers, who said, 'This is a very nice machine.' After that, I was given the job.

I remember Sir Godfrey Paine, Director of Aviation at the Admiralty, coming down and talking in hushed tones to the CO. Clearly, something big was going to go off, but we didn't know what our target might be. Then the Huns started bombing the Thames towns, carrying out a very heavy raid on Chatham. There was an outcry from people at home, 'Oh, we must retaliate, you must bomb a Hun town.' The situation changed entirely. We were made up to squadron strength, one or two pilots came over from No. 7 Squadron, and we were sent up to a place called Auchy, in the Vosges, not far from the Franco-Swiss border.

We found ourselves on a French aerodrome with the usual 'French' comforts: empty wooden huts, 6-foot GS tables, no other furniture . . . and French rations. Owing to the bad weather, we sat there for three weeks. The bombing at home was intensified by the Huns and eventually the order came through: 'Bomb Saarbrücken'. Seven machines took off. I'd never flown at night before. My observer was a pilot who hadn't flown at night before and I think there were four or five others who hadn't, and we were just sent off. There were no meteorological assets in the way of weather reports and the bad weather generally came from the south-west. We went up, oh, in reasonable enough weather, but what a fright I had. It wasn't a clear night, nothing to judge your equilibrium by, or stars or anything. And there we were, flying a machine at night, loaded with bombs – a heavy machine. Anyway, we didn't get there, so we turned back and then we came into this bad weather. We flew with Flavelle, a Canadian pilot. I remember flying for over half an hour with the altimeter below zero, and in thick fog. The instrument lighting went. It was just sort of flying – groping – and getting the wind up and then taking up into height again. And eventually this went on until I knew there wasn't much petrol left, so I gradually came down, thinking, 'Well, I probably

165

have another two or three hundred feet to go' when it just crashed into the ground.

I was pinned in. The back of the seat caught me round the back of the leg. Flavelle was thrown out. But the revolver that I'd put in the locker at the back of my neck – the locker lid flew open and the revolver sort of came forward and just landed at my hands on the ground. There was a light in a cottage. It was a hut – it wasn't glass in the windows but fabric. This was an advance post for anti-aircraft; they'd been firing at us. So we crawled up, Flavelle and I. We had a sort of get-together and we worked out that he was to go up and rap at the window and if it was a Hun I would shoot him. Turned out to be a Frenchman. So that was my first experience on my active service.

It didn't worry me much. I think we were all the same; we were a good breed of chap, you know, and there was great *ésprit de corps*. Each raid had to be a longer raid than the previous one. And I remember when I was home on leave, I'd read in the press that a target like Mannheim or Karlsruhe or Saarbrücken had been bombed, and I'd think, 'Damn it all. I ought to have been on that raid.' The only time I was worried was going home on leave from King's Cross to Scotland. I always thought I'd be bombed on the train.

I was with No. 16 Naval Squadron, which later became No. 216. Although we were a Naval squadron, we had four RFC officers on transfer to us. They were very unpopular; we didn't like being mixed up with the Royal Flying Corps. In fact, when I first joined up I'd cross the street to avoid saluting anyone. Anyway, I got a wonderful observer, an American millionaire called Bobby Reece. As a young man, he was head of the Reece Buttonhole Manufacturing Company, and he'd come over at the beginning of the war, long before the Americans came in, and joined the LaFayette Squadron, but he was a rather ham-fisted chap. He was a bit of a burden on the rates and he crashed too many aircraft, so was transferred to No. 216, and he became my observer. He looked bleary-eyed all the time because he sat out in the open without goggles. He was a rather bloodthirsty chap; I used to want to do a couple of runs over the target, but he would do four. I was always scared stiff. He was a delightful companion, clumsy to a degree because when he hopped through the cockpit where he sat beside me – in the front cockpit to do his bombing – he'd turn off all the pressure taps. A bulky chap, you know. He sat on the top of the cockpit with his feet at my level, and there he would direct with his hand. I remember that we worked well together and were fairly successful. The observers didn't get the recognition the pilots got. When we were both awarded the DFC at the same time, I think he was probably the first American to get one. He had a tremendous appetite for beer, too. My father sent us out some tankards, and we used to have our raids inscribed on them. After the war was over, I used to hear from him: 'The tankard's in the air!'

It was about this time that I met Sir Hugh Trenchard. He came out in charge of the Independent Bombing Force. One morning my chief petty officer came to me, and said, 'I'm afraid your machine will be unserviceable tonight. The fuselage tank is leaking and the men are all undoing the rigging and the fuselage in the centre section, and it won't be ready.'

I said, 'Are the other three machines serviceable?'

He said that they were, so I said, 'Put all the men you've got on that machine and get it ready, and I'll come up and stand by.'

I didn't have a decent sleep, and I went up to the aerodrome. We were in camouflage in the woods, and the aerodrome was some way off. I fell asleep, face down, below the wing of the machine that they were working on. Something hit me on the back. I said, 'For God's sake, clear off.' It happened again, so I looked up. There was Boom Trenchard at the end of a shooting stick. I got up and I said, 'Good afternoon, sir.'

He said, 'They tell me this is your machine! Why are all the men working on it?'

I said, 'The other three are serviceable, sir, and they've got to get this one ready tonight; the fuselage tank is leaking and they've got to work on getting it prepared.'

He said, 'Oh, where did you go last night?'

I said, 'Mannheim, sir.'

'Oh, yes. The night before?'

I said, 'Mannheim, sir.'

'Night before that?'

I said, 'Mannheim, sir.'

He said, 'That's the stuff, keep it going!'

He was a great man.

We were the first lot in France, and then down came No. 55 Squadron with their DH4s. Then came No. 100 with their FEs. We had great fun with them. They weren't all that good at landing at night, but were excellent machines for night flying. At Auchy, the Huns tried to wash us out. They sent down a couple of Gotha squadrons that operated just on the other side of the lines, and they came over every night.

We had a lot of contact with the French. We got all our rations from them, and were in French Territory long before the Independent Force started. They used to call us the Bedouin squadron, on account of our nomadic movement between different aerodromes. If the weather was too bad for flying, we used to go into Nancy for the evening. We used to hop into a restaurant called the Liègeoise. The tacit understanding between us and the Germans of 'don't bomb Nancy and we won't bomb Metz' broke down, and they bombed Nancy the night that we were there. They blew the Liègeoise to smithereens. But the piano was left and also a couch, which eventually became the 'sacred couch' of the Bedouins. We 'won' that; that was the word used, but really we had pinched it.

The senior officer in the squadron was the 'Chief of the Bedouins'. We had all sorts of rituals. We had a 'sacred camel' made from esparto grass. The Chief of the Bedouins wore a 'sacred blanket' and he had a hunting horn. When he blew his horn, it was the signal for a sing-song or a get-together. We made honorary members, and they had to go through a ritual; they were laid flat on this couch and tossed up to the ceiling. Then they were given a chit saying that they were accepted as good and worthy members of the Bedouin squadron. General Newall, the commander of the brigade, was very annoyed that he hadn't been asked to be made a member. We made him a member eventually; he came up one night, booted and spurred, and we tossed him on the sacred couch. He was delighted! We also had a decoration known as the 'Order of the Waning Moon'. If you did any special work, you were given a corkscrew – we had to buy expensive bottles of 4711 lavender water to get the little corkscrew which in those days was attached to the bottle. Then an Italian squadron arrived, flying Capronis. They were a jolly good crowd; they couldn't fly for toffee, but they were very sociable and we awarded our decorations to them.

I remember I bought a couple of pigs and we were going to fatten them up, because the rations were so bad. The men took charge of them, and when we were mobile, they insisted on taking them with us. When we stopped, they let the pigs out, and they ran all over the countryside with the men chasing after them. Within about six weeks, the pigs were thinner than greyhounds. But they were great fun, and amused the men.

The 550 bomb came out, but my machine couldn't take the bombs. I kept an 0/100 machine until they were washed out and they introduced the 0/400. The CO ordered that I carry out a raid on Stuttgart. The target was the Bosch magneto works. Well, looking at the Bosch magneto works at Stuttgart was like looking at a pinprick on a billiard table. Anyway, we got there and Reece made an awful mess of the bombing; the bombs went anywhere but near the target. On the way home, we got lost, and I think we were up for about seven hours.

I was in the special Bomb Berlin flight at the end of the war. I remember coming back from a raid over Mannheim. The other flight commander and I each had a Primus stove, and made a breakfast which consisted of French rolls, rancid butter and lovely Gruyère cheese. We were digging into this, when an orderly arrived. He said that Brigade Headquarters wanted to speak to us on the telephone. I spoke to General Newall, who said, 'Look Halley, we've got a job for you. You'll go home tomorrow morning, and you'll come and see me on the way.' It suddenly struck me that this might have something to do with Berlin.

General Newall gave me a letter to deliver to Colonel Newlock at HQ. I was sent up by train. The RNAS had a Paris office at 14 Avenue de Clichy, one of the roads that goes up to the Arc de Triomphe, and I got instructions that they would give me a car. I drove up to Dunkirk, and there was a destroyer waiting there.

I crossed the Channel, and there was a car waiting in Dover. It took me up to the Air Ministry and I gave the letter to Newlock, who told me what was happening. They were getting ready for a raid. I was to say nothing, and I motored up to Bircham Newton, where I found a veritable hive of industry. There were three machines, with men swarming all around; fitters, riggers and electricians, all getting in each others' way with this great idea to bomb Berlin. These were the four-engine V/1500s. It was a wonderful sight.

Halley's career continued into 1919, when he had the distinction of ending the Third Afghan War. In May 1919 King Amanullah of Afghanistan declared war on British India. Afghan troops seized a large tract of land near the Khyber Pass. Skirmishes ensued and the British ordered five RAF squadrons into action against Afghan hill tribes in the difficult terrain. An airfield was laid out near Dakar from which BE2cs, FE2bs and DH9as flew bombing raids on the tribes. However rifle fire from the tribes was too dangerous and, more definitive action being called for, Brigadier General McEwan decided to bomb Kabul.

On 24 May, a lone bomber, the V/1500, piloted by Captain Halley, and known as the Old Carthusian dropped four bombs on Kabul, forcing King Amanullah to call a truce and withdraw troops from the Indian-Afghan border on the Northwest Frontier. This event proved the full potential of the aeroplane against colonial tribal warfare.

Robert Halley, always known as Jock, had decided to retire to the RAFA home at Storrington so that the nursing needs required by his fragile health could be more conveniently furnished. Although mostly confined to a wheelchair, he liked to escape from the home for reunions, lunches and outings into the surrounding countryside. On such excursions, he was driven at great speed by a friend who had been a fighter pilot in the Second World War, and who owned a rather sprightly sports car.

Jock's recall of his war service was both vivid and formidably accurate; it was curious to think that this diminutive officer had piloted a large Handley Page bomber sitting upon several cushions.

Jock, a confirmed bachelor, made this author an unexpected proposal of marriage – gently declined – shortly before his sudden death at Sussexdown on 13 December 1979.

170

1st Air Mechanic William Harris

William James Harris was born on 13 June 1898 in London, and joined the Royal Flying Corps months after he finished school. He was posted to No. 57 Squadron and served with the 5th Canadian Siege Battery. He married in 1921, and had four children. He and his wife, Ada, divorced and he remarried. Harris worked for London Transport in charge of the Bus Department. He was appointed MBE in the 1970s for his work at St Dustan's with those blinded in the war. Each year he participated in the London to Brighton walk for the blind. He was interviewed on 3 March 1979 at his home in Purley, Surrey. He died on 20 September 1986.

I was seventeen in October 1915 and I tried originally for the Royal Naval Air Service. I had a medical examination at Brook Green near Hammersmith. I passed the medical, and they said to me, 'Come up tomorrow morning with your birth certificate and two references, one personal and one from your firm.' That killed that idea, so I tried for the Royal Flying Corps. I went up to Whitehall to the big recruiting office. The same thing happened there; they wanted sight of my birth certificate, so I was snookered again. Then I heard that they were taking chaps at eighteen, but you had to sign for four years in the Colours and four in the Reserve; they called it ordinary enlistment. I returned to the recruiting office and told them I'd just turned eighteen. I took the plunge, and was accepted as a 'wireless learner'.

The main wireless school was at the Regent Street Polytechnic, and I thought, 'Oh, boy, that's all right. I could have weekend leave, and possibly get home every day.' But I was posted down to Farnborough. The wireless operators, amongst the ordinary rank and file of the Flying Corps were perhaps a different type of chap, insofar as most of us had a better education. A wireless school had started at Farnborough, so my dreams of training in London went for a burton. All our NCOs were pre-1914 Guardsmen. You can imagine the type of discipline. There was a flight sergeant called Stone. He was a fine specimen of a man, but he was a soldier rather than a gentleman. He'd been yelling his lungs out all morning, posting different people. One mild-mannered looking chap went up to him, and asked in a polite way, 'Please, Flight Sergeant, is the Kite Balloon Section being posted?'

Stone looked down at him, and said, 'Did you see that poster in London: *Your King and Country Need You*?'

He said, 'Yes, Flight Sergeant.'

Stone yelled, 'Well, I wish to Christ you hadn't!'

We were the first wireless bunch to go through this new school. All our instructors were ex-Post Office telegraphers. Their job was to teach us sending and receiving Morse. We had a technical officer, Lieutenant Perrin, who used to teach us the technical side, explaining the elementary principles of electricity and wireless, and then we used to have flashlight training. Of course, we used to do drills as well. To pass out, you had to have reached a speed of twenty words per minute, both sending and receiving. I passed out.

We were then sent over to France, ten or so chaps at a time. When we left for overseas we were told we would get shellproof and soundproof dugouts. We left from Southampton, went up the Seine to Rouen, and disembarked there. From Rouen I was posted to No. 1 Armoured Division at St Omer, then on to No. 2 Armoured Division at Doullens on the Somme front. I was attached to No. 9 Squadron. From Doullens, we were taken up the line in Crossley tenders. Three of us went out, and as we were getting near the firing line and approaching Guillemont and Ginchy, ahead of us was a place called Combles. We didn't know which were shells bursting and which were guns firing, all we knew was it was a terrific noise. We were on the extreme right of the British line and the French were intermingled with us. And we agreed to toss a coin, the odd man gets out first. I was the unlucky one – as I thought at the time. The Crossley tender stopped; the officer said, 'Come on, let's have one of you.' I got out of the car, and followed him, all spic and span, fresh from Blighty. I followed this officer, round the tops of shell holes and saw the wireless mast. Suddenly, I saw him disappear into a hole. And this hole was the so-called soundproof and shellproof dugout – it was about five foot deep with about three layers of sandbags round the top, and ordinary corrugated iron put over as a roof with a few sandbags to stop the wind blowing it off. Consequently, No. 1 gun was, oh, maybe twenty yards away. Every time the guns fired, the roof lifted and came down – crash. And of course with condensation in the wood, you sat down there with rust drops dropping all over you.

The two chaps with me were Merritt and Natterley. I went to No. 147 Siege Battery, 6-inch howitzers. Merritt went just to my left, no distance away – a matter of yards I suppose. The wheels on the guns were almost touching. And within two weeks, poor old Merritt had a direct hit on his dugout. Blown to smithereens. Natterley went a little bit to my right and within about the same period he had a direct hit on his dugout. I understood that he had both his legs pretty well blown off. This was my baptism of fire on the Somme. Of course, this made me a confirmed fatalist. I just thought, 'If a shell's got your name on it, so what? It'll find you.' I didn't really have any contact with any of the other RFC personnel apart from my wireless operator colleagues. The only Flying Corps people we saw were pilots and observers, with an occasional visit from the patrol corporal. Otherwise, we were with the gunners all the time. I only spent the occasional night at an aerodrome.

We had been trained in a certain amount of jamming, but wireless in those days didn't have the fine tuning you get now. It was a busy front, and when you picked up the headphones, it sounded just like a jazz band. There was an experienced wireless operator there, George Robey, who was writing down where he was picking the signals from. I couldn't pick them out at all. 'Oh,' he said, 'well as soon as the wireless officer comes round, I'm recommending you be posted away from it, because you're a washout as a wireless operator.' After about a week, though, it was second nature to me, and I was posted to take the place of poor old Merritt. We had a 30-foot mast, which was in six sections, and we were connected to the battery commander's post by a field line. We had what we called Mark III tuners. They were crystal tuners, of course. We also had ground strips which we used to put out to signal back to the aircraft. We had to do minor repairs on the equipment, too. I had my mast blown down more than once, and I would have to mend aerials and simple things like that, but if the guts of the tuner went wrong we'd have to requisition a new one.

I moved up towards Combles, which was a bit further ahead. When it was dark and the planes had gone in, you were free. In the evening we mainly played the card game, brag. I knew there was a brag school going on at the battery not far from me in this wireless operator's dugout, so I went over. On my way there, I heard a shell coming over and knew from its distinctive whine that it was a howitzer. I threw myself into a hole. The shell burst fairly close, too close to be comfortable. I'd have probably got hit if I hadn't dived in. When I got out of the hole, the stench was indescribable. Next morning when it was light, I thought, 'Let's have a look what I dived into.' And oh, God! There were the bodies of four Germans, rotting, and teeming with black maggots. For years after, if I concentrated sufficiently on this incident, the stench came back to me. At least I was young. How we came out so healthy, sleeping under the conditions that we did, I don't know. It was worse if you had any leave, because you dreaded going back. And of course the men's minds got into a state there. Nobody knew what shell shock really was, and some poor devils were shot for cowardice in the face of the enemy. It was a very hard war. I don't think there has ever been a war, or ever will be a war where men suffered such privations. Death was common. There were so many casualties on the Somme front, they couldn't be buried. There were rotting bodies lying all over the place, and rotting horses, too. The human bodies stank a lot worse to me than those of the horses. It

174

was the mud mainly with the poor horses. They'd sink up to their belly in mud. There was nothing to do, and no crane to lift them out, so they would have to be shot; poor devils would have to be shot.

There was a lot of aircraft activity at that time. We had the Sopwith Camels, and they had helped us regain supremacy in the air. Towards the end of 1916, though, it was terrible with that Richthofen Circus. He had the knack of synchronizing his machine guns through the revolution of the propeller. Our poor devils had the old pushers. The machine gunner was right out in the nose, and the pilot was unprotected from the back. Half a dozen shots and a tracer bullet from Richthofen's mob, and they went up in flames. Richthofen challenged Albert Ball to a duel over the Arras-Douai battlefront. I saw this happen. They fought until their ammunition ran out, and then they wheeled and swung round towards one another. Richthofen went back to the Jerry lines, and Ball came back our way.

We stayed on the Somme right through December 1916. It was bitterly cold. Everything was frozen solid, and we had the added discomfort of rats and lice. Everybody was alive with lice; all you could do was keep them down. In the evenings we'd light a candle, and pass it over our shirts. It was like miniature machine guns going off as these lice were popping. You'd lie on your ground sheet in the dugout, and you'd feel rats running over you. One bit of fun we used to have was to organize a rat hunt. There were holes in the ground, and we used to stuff these with strips of cordite. We'd man all the surrounding rat holes, armed with sticks and shovels, and ignite the cordite. There would be a small explosion, and green vapours would come from the holes. The rats would stream out of the holes. That was our bit of fun in the winter of 1916.

In February 1917 we were on the move. We were on our way to the Arras-Vimy Ridge battlefront. On the way, we rested for a couple of weeks at Béthune. We were drunk nearly all the time we were there. The first place I went from there was the village of St Catherine, on the Arras-Lens road. After a while, I was posted to Central Wireless Station at Mont St Eloi. It was a monastery,

175

actually, a ruin of the 1870 Franco-Prussian war. Then we moved up a bit further forward to a place called Roclincourt, which was just behind two little villages, Oppy and Gavrelle. I spent Christmas 1917 there. We weren't far from Arras, just walking distance anyway. In the evening, we used to go down there; there were still one or two estaminets open. We used to enjoy a few glasses of *vin blanc avec citron* and we got friendly with the old dear who ran an estaminet. We asked if she could make us a Christmas dinner, and she cooked us mutton with caper sauce, and potatoes. She wrapped this up, and we carried it back on a long pole. It was quite a reasonable Christmas dinner, and even after the half-hour walk back it was still hot.

I returned to the Arras front at the time when the Germans were making their big advance, about March 1918. We were in a place with dugouts in the Arras-Douai railway cutting. The Germans were advancing so much so then, that our howitzers were firing point blank at them.

I had an accident on the Arras front in June 1918. I found a tin of fifty rounds, and was getting some shooting practice done, firing at a jam tin in the trench. I went to go back into the dugout and I saw a crow on the barbed wire. I said to Jock, my assistant operator, 'Fleeting opportunity, Jock – a crow on the barbed wire.' I loaded a round into my revolver, to the left of the barrel. When I cocked the revolver, I thought I'd loaded it to the right of the barrel, so took the muzzle in my left and proceeded to pull the trigger five times. Of course, it went off first time, and shot me through the side of the hand. It wasn't too serious, though; if it had gone through the middle, it would have blown my hands to pieces. Jock, who was an ex-Naval man, and had lost two fingers as a youngster in the Battle of Jutland, looked at me and said, 'Christ, man, self-inflicted wound.' I knew what he meant, because all self-inflicted wounds were automatically considered the result of wilfully maiming yourself with the intent of making yourself unfit for service. And of course the penalty was very severe; in the early part of the war, you could be shot at dawn. I said, 'Oh, take no notice, Jock.' I got my old field dressing out, smashed the bit of iodine we had, and put it on. Of course my hand was all charred, and the cuffs of my tunic were all charred. Jock said, 'No, I'd better report it.' He rang the commanding officer of the battery, and put it in a very blunt way: 'Harris has shot himself, sir.' He received the reply: 'Take him back to the first field dressing station.' This was a place called Morel. When I got there, the first chap I saw was a Canadian doctor, who said, 'Ah, silly things to play about with, these guns. How did it happen?' So I told him the truth; I thought, 'If I tell the truth, they can't do much to me.' I didn't know whether the story sounded a bit too good to him, but he started to make a statement, writing down: 'I was cleaning my revolver, and I didn't know it was loaded.'

I said, 'I knew it was loaded, sir.'

He repeated it: 'I was cleaning my revolver, and I didn't know it was loaded.'

I said, 'Begging pardon, sir, I *knew* it was loaded!'

He repeated it for the third time, and the orderly, who was standing behind him gave me a bit of a wink. Finally, I understood the score, and we had to build up a story before the field general court martial.

I was posted to No. 12 Stationary Hospital at St Pol. I went to the RSM, and said, 'Look sir, it's only a slight flesh wound; can't I go back to my battery?'

He said, 'No. You're off to St Pol.'

Oh, God, it was heaven, getting out of the line, English girls helping you, VADs and nurses – pure heaven. There were two big wards there at St Pol. All the chaps there had self-inflicted wounds, and most of them were deliberate. With a self-inflicted wound, the charge would show up on your skin. One of the tricks was to tie a bully beef tin round your arm and fire through it; you'd get a clean wound then. It takes some pluck to shoot yourself, though, and gives you some idea of the mental state that the chaps were getting in.

The court martial was quite fair, open and above board. I was asked if I wanted to employ civilian counsel, but I declined this. I said that the battery commander would speak for me. The chairman was the brigadier general, and they had 'Exhibit A' there, my revolver. He asked, 'Are you left handed?'

I said, 'No, sir.'

He said, 'Then how do you account for wounding yourself in the right hand?'

I said, 'Well, sir, unless you're left-handed, to break open the revolver, the main action is with the right hand.' I got away with that question.

Sergeant Baddeley, who was defending me, said to the brigadier general, 'His assistant operator was wounded in the Battle of Jutland and lost some fingers on his right hand, yet that does not incapacitate him from carrying on his duties as wireless operator.'

The Chairman said, 'Oh, yes, it's quite obvious he didn't do it wilfully, but the charge is now amended to "negligence and conduct prejudicial to the good order of military discipline".'

I couldn't get out of this, and I had twenty-eight days' No. 1 Field Punishment. In the early days of the war, this entailed being tied to a gun wheel for a certain number of hours a day. I never actually did my twenty-eight days, because they had pretty well expired by the time I left hospital. You were under close arrest all the time you were in hospital. Even if you wanted to go to the toilet, somebody went with you. Then I came out and returned to the squadron. The next morning I had a special parade in front of the entire squadron. I had to march a number of paces forward, and the corporal grabbed my cap and took it off. Then the charge and punishment were read out, and I was released. So I had a field general court martial and a special parade.

We had some heavy casualties amongst the wireless operators in the trenches. At one point, we were losing about 400 wireless operators a year. When I say I was in the line, I was in the firing line with the guns, but the infantry was in and out, in and out. You'd see them coming back, coated in mud up to their thighs, but still singing some of the old songs . . .

I want to go home,
I want to go home,
I don't want to go in the trenches no more
Where the Jack Johnsons and Whizz Bangs they roar.
Take me over the sea, where the Alleyman can't get at me.

178

Oh my, I don't want to die,
I want to go home!

Far, far from Ypres I long to be,
Where German snipers can't get at me.
Dark is my dugout, cold are my feet,
Send o'er a Whizz Bang and put me to sleep.

Then there came our big advance. The barrage opened up not far from the Forêt de Mormal. It was a forest about ten miles deep. We'd had the hell knocked out of us the night before. The wireless operators were issued with a revolver and twelve rounds of ammunition. We were given no instruction except to get in some practice when we could. The battery commander came to me, and said, 'Sparks, you got any arms?'

I said, 'I've got a revolver, Sir.'

He said, 'Get it slung round you; tomorrow we're going to do the mopping up.'

I expected it to be a very quick retreat of the Germans, and this proved to be the case. I was with 251 Brigade then, Royal Field Artillery. I even had my own horse. Odd thing to see a Flying Corps bloke sitting on a horse. Had to put me puttees round the reverse way, the artillery fashion, otherwise they unrolled.

We went right through this Forêt de Mormal, and we expected quite a lot of resistance. It was certainly a quick retreat and finally we stopped, and the OC told me to rig my aerial up, no need to use the mast, I just slung it across the street, and that's where we heard the news that at 11 a.m. on 11 November, hostilities would cease. We were all so fed up. You imagine, we'd got so far in front, we were out of touch with everybody. We had no fags. Officers would come up and try to scrounge a fag from us. And then on iron rations, just bully beef and the old hardtack as we used to call it, dog biscuits, that's all they were, and tea without milk and so forth.

You can imagine the mental state that we were in, mainly we wanted the fags. And they were sitting out on the floor playing cards, I called out to them 'It's all over, boys!'

'Oh, is it?'

That was their reaction because we were so fed up to the teeth – not a cheer. I don't know, there was always the lighter side, usually in our dugouts.

The observers were called 'Piccadilly Johnnies,' but my God they had some guts. They probably only had a couple of weeks' instruction in Morse, and we had to guess at a lot of the letters that they were sending. They would transmit about eight to ten words a minute. And we had to pass out at twenty. It was awful for those chaps, though. Once, I saw a flight of five planes going out. I saw the chap starting up the prop, and the other chap who took the chocks away. And I saw this particular pilot shaking hands with the two chaps, just ordinary mechanics . . . shaking hands. They knew they were going to their deaths. God Almighty. And we used to look at them as Piccadilly Johnnies. If they went out in a flight of five and two came back, they were lucky. At one time in France, the life expectancy of a pilot was reckoned to be about eight days.

Harris, who enjoyed a stiff Scotch, reminisced most vividly while smoking ceaselessly. He was a tireless walker, of Olympic standard, practising daily both indoors and out. Notwithstanding his experience with the emergent Wireless Telegraphy Operation in the RFC sixty years or so before, his house in Purley boasted a potentially lethal example of wiring (a toothbrush serving as plug in a two-pin socket) which troubled him not a bit.

180

Lieutenant Hamilton Hervey

Lieutenant Hamilton Elliott 'Tim' Hervey was born on 6 November 1895 in Southsea and educated at Sedbergh School in Cumbria. In May 1914, he started a three-year course in engineering. On his nineteenth birthday, he joined the RFC, in which he served first as a rigger and gunner-observer, and subsequently as flying officer observer and flying officer pilot. He received his commission early in 1916, and was awarded the MC and bar as observer. Hervey was mentioned in dispatches for attempting to escape from Germany.

In December 1918, he joined a training squadron, and was demobilized in September 1919. He rejoined the RAF in 1940, serving until the end of the war. He wrote a book about his prison experiences, *Cage-Birds*, published in 1940 and was instrumental in the British programme to assist escaped prisoners of war.

Hervey married twice. His first wife, Beatrix Coldstream Tuckett, died of tuberculosis in 1934. They had one daughter, Felicity. He was remarried in 1937 to Constance Masters and had a second daughter, Rosamond. He was interviewed at Billington, Bedfordshire on 17 September 1978. He died on 30 May 1990.

My first interest in aviation came when the master of our school let us write a paper about the Wright Brothers' flight. I was about nine years old then, and there was nothing I wanted to do except fly. As it happened, I was able to do it earlier than I expected. I had my first flight in 1912 at the Grahame-White School in Hendon. When I left school, I joined the Bristol Company for a three-year course, but then war broke out and I joined up so I never completed the course. My ambition was to become an aircraft designer. The chief designer was a Romanian called Henri Coanda and his second in command was Barnwell, who designed the Bristol Scout and the Bristol Fighter later on. He was with the first squadron I was in; he was learning to fly there, and we had a Bristol Scout in the squadron.

I joined up from the ranks in November 1914. It was very hard to get into the Flying Corps, which was very small, and I had to do a trade test first. I joined up as a rigger. Our first training consisted of a fortnight at Farnborough at the recruits' depot. I got double pneumonia at the end of it as a result of drilling in the snow. When I'd recovered from that, I was posted to No. 1 Squadron Netheravon, pending the formation of No. 12 Squadron. At Netheravon we had a collection of different machines, some requisitioned from private sources before the war. We had a Blériot, a Morane, and one or two ancient Avros. Eventually we got BE2cs, and in late July 1915 I went out to France with BE2cs. This was with No. 12 Squadron.

My first station was at St Omer. The riggers and the engine men always slept with the machines in the hangars; the rest of the men were billeted in local villages. It was rather nice at St Omer, because we used to have our meals in cafés instead of going down to the mess. We were left alone and not bothered too much.

I stayed a rigger until about April or May 1916, and then became an observer. I'd done a bit of flying before as a passenger. You could cadge a flight. As soon as a pilot got his wings, he was allowed to take passengers up with him, so I'd done quite a bit of flying before.

As a gunner observer, your only duty was to fire the gun if you were attacked. But as an observer, later on when I got my commission, we used to have patrols along the line from dawn until dark. As one machine came home, another one was going out, and you just patrolled your own particular bit of the line. We often had to take photographs. We did bombing as well, up to about ten miles over the lines, and long reconnaissance missions, which just one or two machines went on. They used to send the gunner-

182

observers on those jobs really. If you were brought down, they hadn't wasted another trained observer.

The bombing was a rather hit and miss affair at the time. Of course, you didn't bomb from the terrific heights that you did in the last war, and we went over at about 6,000 or 7,000 feet. The planes couldn't get up with bombs aboard; in fact the pilots on the BE2cs never had an observer on board when they carried bombs, as he would have been too heavy.

After I got my commission in June 1916, I went back to England, and trained on BE2cs. At Netheravon, we did preliminary training on Maurice Farman pushers. After that, we went to Upavon to be trained on the machines that we would be flying, starting with Avros, then moving on to Sopwith Pups. The Pups were lovely machines to fly, and very light, particularly without their guns on. If you had the guns on it made quite a bit of difference because the windscreen was made smaller to accommodate the sight. I stayed in England quite a time. I was sent up to Turnberry to the machine gunnery school for aerial fighting, which was just started. I'd been there for only two days, when I was posted to France. They were having a lot of casualties out there at that time. I was posted to No. 60 Squadron, which had been having rather a bad time of it.

In the early days, you couldn't get a fight with a German; they'd always run away. I believe they were short of petrol at that time. But round about September 1916, they got much more aggressive. They had better aircraft and also they would join in the fight. We got quite a shock the first time we were attacked instead of attacking them. I suppose I was frightened sometimes, but it was very exhilarating and exciting, and as an observer I enjoyed it.

Once, we got into a fight with an Albatros, the first we'd seen. It attacked us on our side of the lines. We had quite a scrap with it, we were in a BE2 and it wasn't a very well-known aircraft from the point of view of fighting. There were so many wires on it, I often shot away my own wires in a fight 'cause they got in the way. But the Albatros went away again and just about a quarter mile off as we were patrolling up and down, it came over and attacked us again. Its engine was hit, and we saw the prop stop. It attempted to turn back towards the German side, we fired at it, and followed it down to the ground. It landed about three miles over our side of the lines. We landed alongside, and took the pilot prisoner. He was a youngish chap, and rather fed up at being shot down by a BE2. I remember we were a bit annoyed, because we asked if our German could come to tea and the authorities said, 'Yes, but you must try and get as much information out of him as possible.' We thought that rather unsporting; we really only wanted to give him a good time before he went away to prison camp, and thought it rather mean to try and find out information from him.

At that time, if you got down a machine you were allowed to claim some part of it; my pilot got the compass and I got the airspeed indicator. Actually, when I got back to England I was told to collect these things, as my pilot, Parker, had been killed in the meantime. He wasn't heard of again, and never confirmed as killed or taken prisoner.

I met Billy Bishop at Upavon. He'd been flying BE2cs against Zeppelins in England, and was doing a conversion course on Scouts. We were both in the same squadron, and in the same flight, so I saw quite a lot of him. He was mad keen on getting out to France, and when he got there, he did well from the start. I only joined the squadron about six weeks after he did, and he was already acting flight commander of 'B' Flight. When I arrived, he'd just shot down his first aircraft. He was an extremely good shot, and could hit things from a long way off.

Albert Ball was another famous character I met. He always got so close to the target, he couldn't miss. His favourite method was to get underneath them and then shoot up into the aeroplane. I knew him when I was in No. 8 Squadron. He had a row with General Higgins, and had been a bit perky, and given the General some 'lip', so he was 'rested' with our squadron for a while. I flew with him as an observer. He was just a kid, really. I remember we used to go out for walks in the evenings, and his idea of amusement was to throw stones at you. We'd walk on opposite sides of the road. Once or twice, he took a trip down to the trenches, and was found throwing grenades into the German trenches on the other side. Naturally, our troops didn't like that very much. It 'started' things. I remember doing one fairly hectic flight with him, balloon-strafing in a BE2c. I think the Germans did more damage to us than we did to the balloon. We didn't get it anyway.

Just before the 1917 Arras Offensive, Richthofen's squadron was opposite us at Douai. With all the casualties they'd been having, our new boys had to go in there almost straightaway, before they even got used to flying the Nieuports. Quite a few were killed, but also there were quite a number of RFC chaps taken prisoner, because nearly all the fighting was done on the German side of the lines. You were lucky to get a fight on your own side. We were flying Nieuports with No. 60, and they were very different from the Pup. The main thing that worried you was that the right and left hand turns were entirely different. When you climbed to the right, you were inclined to stall if you weren't careful; when you went to the left, you could get into a spin. We had never been taught how to spin; all we were told was, 'If you get into a spin, shut off your engine, centralize your controls, and hope for the best.'

We had one or two pilots who did very well after the Big Push, but they couldn't hit a thing. Grid Caldwell was a New Zealander who made good in this respect. He was a terrific chap. Eventually, he picked up about twenty-five aeroplanes, but in the early stages he'd always get into scraps but he never had the luck to shoot anything down.

On one occasion, I was in a fight and had my rudder controls on one side shot away. I spun from 10,000 feet down to 6,000. The Hun followed me down all the way and started firing again as soon as I'd tried to do a turn. I went into a spin again, coming down to 1,000 feet. I went through cloud and then suddenly saw this Hun turning away. If he'd come down after me again, I would have had to loop the loop. I was so sure I was going to be dead, that I wasn't terribly frightened. As soon as I'd come out of it, I staggered home with my engine hit and my heart beating like a pump. I think if I'd flown into the ground I don't think I'd have been very frightened. When I got back, my CO, said, 'You've had rather a rough time, so you needn't go on tomorrow's patrol.' But in the morning about 6 or 7 o'clock, Bishop called out, 'The Major's leading our patrol and he wants you to come along' so I had to hurry and get dressed.

There were five of us. I and a chap called Milo had the two rear machines in the flight, and were instructed that if the other machines were going after a German, we were to stay up top to guard their tails. Actually that's just what happened. Major Scott fired on a two-seater. Milo and I stayed up top and we were attacked by a flight of Germans who came out of the sun and Milo was killed almost instantly. I didn't know he had been killed but he was shot down and subsequently posted as killed. I managed to get away from these people, and I was hanging around over Arras where we used to rendezvous if we lost the rest of the patrol. I was thinking of turning for home, when I saw a flight of FEs being attacked by a lot of Germans. The FEs were fairly obsolete in those days. They used to fly round in a circle, like goldfish in a bowl, so that the observers could aim at the enemy in almost any position. Germans were attacking them from all directions, so I went back to join in. On the way, I had a burst of anti-aircraft fire, and my engine stopped. I was too far over the lines to get back again, and I landed at an artillery dugout. Some Germans came out of the hole and grabbed me. I had lunch down in a dugout with these German officers, then I was taken to Douai where most of the RFC in that area were collected before they were sent to Germany. It was there that I met Leefe Robinson, the Zeppelin man. He was shot down just the day after I was, and we both went to the same camp in Germany. I got along very well with Leefe Robinson. He was very modest. I think when he got his VC, people often got fed up with him. He had so much adulation, you'd think he had a bit of a big head, but actually he didn't at all; it was forced on him more or less by publicity. He was a hero everywhere he went, and he couldn't get out of it.

We stayed at Douai for about a week, and we were in solitary confinement there. I think the idea was to make you thoroughly miserable and then send in an interrogating officer, thinking that after so long you'd be longing to talk to somebody. They hoped you'd give away state secrets. Then we were put in a cell together, where we discovered a microphone. The Germans had hoped the various people they put in there from the same squadron would talk, not realizing that they were being bugged. When you were interrogated, they would ask which squadron you belonged to, who your CO was, and so on. One question they kept asking, was whether I'd been up to Scotland. I'd been to the gunnery school at Turnberry and I was pretty sure that's what they wanted to know. They asked that same question in the next camp I was sent to, in Karlsruhe. It was a transit camp. We were so hungry there, we spent most of the time just lying in bed; there was no food there at all. The Germans were very short of food themselves.

From Karlsruhe I was sent to Freiburg in the Black Forest, because our aeroplanes had been bombing there. There was an aerodrome at Freiburg so they thought if they put the whole lot of RFC prisoners in the middle of the town it might stop the bombing. It didn't, really; it didn't have any effect at all. I met a chap there called McIntosh, whom I had flown with at Upavon. He had torn a map out of a railway carriage, and had also managed to conceal a compass. We planned to escape from Freiburg together. Our prison camp was the old University, a building which was joined to a church. We made a rope out of parcel strings, which took us ages, and eventually we managed to get up into the attic of the University. We broke through that into the church, got out of the window, and onto the main road.

Six of us got out that night, two with Robinson. Three of us had intended to try and swim the Rhine, as we were all reasonably good swimmers. The other three were going to try and cross the border into Switzerland where it jutted in on this side, but we found it too heavily guarded. We thought we had more chance if we swam the Rhine. So once we got out, we parted. However, all six of us were recaptured. We'd been out for a week, and were getting quite close to the frontier. But it was very wooded, and in the dark we couldn't really see where we were going. Suddenly, about fifty yards away, we saw a German sentry with a police dog. There was nothing we could do about it, and he took us prisoner.

We were taken to the local jail and kept there for about three days, until the authorities at Freiburg sent guards down for us and took us back to the camp. We weren't badly treated for our escape attempt. The camp commandant was very hurt about it, and shouted at us a bit. He said he had treated us very well and couldn't understand why we had done the dirty on him by trying to escape. We tried to explain that it had nothing to do with him, and that we simply wanted to get back to England. We should have been given a month's solitary confinement, but they had no cells. Robinson and his party were in the room upstairs, and we were in the adjoining room, and did our month's solitary in there. While we were in there, we made a hole through the wall into the next cell, and from there we made a hole which led up to the attic again. We hoped to have another shot at escaping, but our time came to an end before we got to use the hole. But the next occupants in the cell used our hole the night after we were sent off, and they managed to get away.

From Freiburg we were sent to Fort Zorndorf, which was an underground fort near Berlin, especially for escapees. The German idea was that if they put you in a very unpleasant camp, you'd get fed up with the idea of escaping, and settle down like good boys in a more normal camp. What happened, though, was when the expert escapers were together, they were so enthusiastic about escaping, that it didn't really work at all. We were allowed to write one letter and four postcards a month. I had a code with my girlfriend, which we'd arranged before I went to France. The first things I asked her for were a map and a compass. I told her to put the compass in a tin of jam. In due course, it arrived. At all these camps, when you got food parcels you had to open them in front of the Germans. They had a locker room where all your food was kept, and they opened the tins and emptied them onto plates in front of you. Once, I had some stuff sent out, and it wasn't sent in the way I'd asked it to be sent. I was horrified when I saw an enormous 'cucumber' being emptied out onto the plate, right in front of a German. A chap called Horrocks, whom at that time I hoped to escape with, was beside me. He saw this thing, grabbed hold of the plate and dashed off with it. It was a whole roll of maps of the area, disguised as a cucumber.

Another time, I got a pair of wire cutters which were sent in a ham, in place of the bone. I didn't know it was in there, and the Germans cut right down into the ham, thought it was a bone, and handed it over. When I got back to the mess, I found this great pair of folding wire cutters. Eventually I had a complete civilian suit sent out. It was dark blue, with a removable red stripe down the trousers. It had gold wings all over it, making it very martial. I used to wear it in the camp, and eventually used it to try to escape. I was never successful, though, and didn't get back to England until the end of the war.

I got back to England in 1918, just in time for Christmas. After I'd had six weeks' leave, I went to Croydon on a refresher course for Flying Corps prisoners. I stayed on in the Air Force for about a year after I got back, ending up where I'd started, at Netheravon. I wanted to go on flying, but it was terribly hard to get any job in England, particularly for a scout pilot. The only people they wanted at all, and there weren't very many of them, were people who'd been flying Handley Pages.

Eventually I went out to Australia and met up with a pilot I'd been flying with during the war. He'd taken a half dozen machines out that he'd bought from the Disposal Board at Croydon. They'd got quite a lot of machines that might be useful for commercial purposes of one sort or another, and you could buy them up very cheaply, with endless supplies of spares. He'd taken half a dozen Avros out and he'd also bought a De Havilland aircraft from the Australian Air Force at Point Cook. He started an aerodrome in Melbourne with a partner called Ross, who'd joined No. 60 Squadron with me. I got my commercial licence, and flew in Australia for about ten years before I came back to England again.

When I got back to England I was Chief Instructor at the gliding club at Dunstable. In the Second World War, I joined up with the Air Force again. I had a squadron down at Haddenham, training the Army to fly gliders. I was also involved in helping prisoners in France to escape and join the Resistance. When the Second World War broke out, I wrote to Gossage, my old CO at No. 8 Squadron, suggesting that a department be started to try to help people escape, as so little was done in the First World War. After some time, two Army chaps who'd escaped from Germany, did start a small section at the War Office in England. In fact, they were the people my girlfriend had got in touch with at the War Office. They knew exactly how to send parcels and how to label them. I'd got all my stuff through them.

Being a prisoner of war changed me a great deal. I often had the feeling that I wanted to be alone, and got fed up with people talking to me. It developed my solitary side, and this state of mind took some getting out of.

For Tim

Clouds hold him
cirrus and stratus
fold him
cumulus wrap around
hill mists and sea wrack
shroud the ground.
Sun take him
winds lift him
light fill him
– memory
stay with us.

© ANNE LEWIS-SMITH

This exquisitely appropriate valedictory was written by a close friend for 'Tim' Hervey on the occasion of his funeral. Hervey's commitment to various forms of aviation was precocious; at six he was already producing designs for potential aircraft. This dual interest in aviation and art would persist throughout his long and fruitful life. After his service with the RFC, and his memorable sequence of attempted escapes from various POW camps deep within Germany, his initiative in prompting MI9 to establish the Escaping School provided an invaluable contribution to POWs in the later war. He was to be a pioneer of both civil and sporting aviation following his emigration to Australia, where he became a founder-member of the Gliding Club of Victoria. Returning to England, he was appointed Chief Flying Instructor of the London Flying Club from 1936, and later joined the Balloon Club, reluctantly parting with his licence aged ninety. He had continued to design model aircraft, his first design having been published in *Flight Magazine* in October 1914.

'Tim' Hervey created his prized miniatures of varied fauna from natural objects until a short time before his death. He was a member of the Royal Miniature Society.

Major John Andrews

Major John Oliver Andrews was born in Waterloo, Lancashire on 20 July 1896. His father was a brewer in Manchester. Andrews attended Owens School from 1908–1911, then Manchester High School in 1912. He first enlisted in the Royal Scots Regiment at the age of eighteen, before transferring to the Royal Flying Corps. He received Royal Aeroclub Certificate No. 1924 on 15 October 1915, and served in Nos. 1, 5, 24, 66 RFC and 209 RNAS. Most notably Andrews was in the combat of 23 November 1916 with Major Lanoe Hawker in which Hawker was shot down and killed by the rising German ace, Manfred von Richthofen.

Andrews gained twelve confirmed victories in his career on fighter aircraft, and was awarded the MC in October 1916, with a bar added in December the following year. He received the DSO in July 1917 for 'conspicuous gallantry and devotion to duty in leading offensive patrols with great dash and success on over thirty occasions and taking part in over twenty-two combats'. He was gazetted major on 7 May 1918.

Andrews stayed on in the RAF until 1922, then served on the Aeronautical Committee of Guarantee in Germany as a squadron leader. He remained active in aviation, and served as Senior Air Officer in the Far East in 1938. During the Second World War, he was Air Commodore and Director of Armament Development at the Air Ministry. He was promoted to Air Vice Marshal in November 1940, and then appointed AOC of No. 13 Group in February 1941. He was interviewed on 3 November 1979 at Cookham, Berkshire. Andrews died on 29 May 1989.

Soon after war was declared in August 1914, I joined the Royal Scots (Lothian Regiment) as a 2nd Lieutenant. At this time, they were asking for chaps interested in secondment as potential observers to the very embryonic RFC. I thought that I might like to do this, as I had been interested in the emergent art of flight since I could remember so I volunteered and was sent to No. 1 Squadron RFC for training on 4 November 1914, and in January 1915 was posted to No. 5 Squadron to fly over the Ypres salient on the Western Front to observe on reconnaissance patrols for the Army.

At that time there was a problem with the armament in the aircraft and the other main worry in those early days was being hit by ground fire. The first plane I was observer in that had any machine-gun mounting was the Vickers Gunbus, a pusher. It was the first aircraft to be equipped with a gun with a proper mounting. Before that, we just used to tie them on with bits of rope. We did that before, with a DH2, in the front seat. You had a rope round the gun, pull-hoisted the gun up and made it fast, and then you could swing the Lewis gun round, but it wasn't particularly effective. Also, the weight of the gun impeded your rate of climb. Any weight of gun and ammunition in those days was quite a serious issue, when you only had 50hp Gnome engines. Some were 80hp. This wasn't such a problem when we had the Vickers. It had the mono engine, 100hp, which was much more powerful than the earlier engines.

It was towards the end of the summer, beginning of the autumn of 1915 when I decided to take my ticket and become a pilot. The war was obviously not going to be over by Christmas; Christmas had come and gone, and it was clearly not going to be over by the next one, either, so I thought that if I was going to fly seriously, I ought to become a pilot. I went to train at a place called Le Crotoy, which is a little aerodrome on the coast near the mouth of the Somme, and did my elementary flying course there on a Farman, and then went back to Farnborough where I did my so-called 'advanced' flying training. Most of my training was done on Avros. I got my wings at the end of 1915 after completing twenty hours' solo flying. Subsequently I was posted to No. 24 Squadron which had just been formed at Hounslow. There I did a bit of training on a pusher, a DH2. I flew a Vickers there, too, and then I went off solo in a DH2.

The DH2 was quite a tricky little aeroplane, very different from the tractors in which I'd done most of my flying. I had flown pusher types, such as the Farman and the Vickers, but she had a much smaller wingspan, was more heavily loaded, and the torque of the comparatively large engine in a small frame was somewhat unusual in an aircraft of that period. One had to get accustomed to that very marked engine torque, which rocked the aeroplane, and tended to turn the aeroplane instead of the airscrew. In those days, the rotary engines had no throttle; you controlled the engine by switching it on and switching it off. There was a switch on the joystick, a 'blip' switch, and if you wanted to cut the engine out, you couldn't throttle it back; you switched it right off, and when you wanted engine, you took your thumb off the switch and the engine came on again. It was either all or nothing, and whenever you changed from one to the other, you affected the lateral trim of the aircraft by the engine power suddenly coming on or cutting out, which was different, of course, from the stationary engine like the BE2 or the Maurice Farman; they had throttles. One got accustomed to it, though. You had to be very careful to take no risks near the ground until you got a proper feel for the machine. There was a particular problem with spinning. Any aircraft which stalled easily and which was laterally unstable on account of the engine torque, tended to get into a spin. With a DH2, things happened very suddenly because of this torque, and unless you spotted it and corrected it at once, you could get into a spin or stall the engine. It was a very handy little aeroplane when the engine was functioning properly, and it had quite a lot of horses for the size of the aircraft, so it gave quite good performance.

I don't remember many accidents with it in training. There were accidents soon after we got to France, though. We killed a chap at St Omer. We went from St Omer to Bertangles, which is down near Amiens on the Somme, and we killed another chap landing there, so two out of twelve aircraft, and pilots, were lost in a very short space of time. But people were getting accustomed to handling the DH2.

By this time, the Fokker Eindekker had made quite a nuisance of itself, shooting up our reconnaissance planes. We were the first squadron formed to tackle the Fokker; in other words, to clear it out of the way so that the Army Cooperation people could do their job. We certainly enjoyed meeting the Fokker, because we thought we had it cold. The DH2 was definitely a much better fighting plane than the Eindekker, the original monoplane Fokker. The Fokker had quite good performance, and a fixed gun which could shoot reasonably well through the airscrew disc. But we could out-manoeuvre it, and the great thing was that we could out-dive it. If the Hun tried to dive away, you sat on his tail and waited until he packed up. You could go just as fast as he could downhill.

When we went out on offensive patrols, we were sometimes accompanied by Major Lanoe Hawker. He had far too much on his plate with the organization of the squadron to come out very often, but he did come out with us from time to time. His morale was always very high, and he kept that of the squadron very high. He set a great example, and was never down or despondent. Technically he was very good. He was a Sapper officer, and had been technically trained more than the average Army officer. He was very useful in clearing up troubles we had with the engines, and devising gadgets to train people in aerial gunnery. He devised a model aircraft with an extensible rod in its tummy, which showed you where the aircraft would be at certain ranges and certain speeds, so that you knew the amount of deviation you had to allow for the speed of the target aircraft. The other thing he evolved was a wooden cell on the ground which rocked back and forth with the movements of the joystick, so you got used to aiming the gun, which was fixed ahead, by the movements of the control pillar. You aimed the aircraft, not the gun. Another innovation of his was that we used to have on the airfield what we called a 'Little Boche' with a couple of old wings, to represent the enemy and its direction of flight, and we used to dive on that and fire on it from the air.

As 1916 went on, the Germans got more effective aircraft. They dropped the Fokker and re-equipped with the Albatros and various Halberstadts; types of biplane. They had better performance and better gun-power. In No. 24 Squadron we were expecting to be re-equipped at some point, hoping all the time that we'd get something better, but when I left the squadron in December 1916, it still had DH2s.

Hawker was a very good pilot and a very experienced fighter. He had done quite a bit of fighting before his No. 24 Squadron days, in No. 6 Squadron. That's where he got his VC, flying a Bristol. All our patrols were offensive at the time. We did the odd escort occasionally, but usually when we went out on patrol, we were looking for trouble, and we got it.

It was my last patrol with Lanoe Hawker. My plane got shot up. The engine was hit initially because the engine was behind me, and the bullets came from the stern. The Hun came down on my tail. Usually the first thing to go was the engine or the tanks. It would have the same effect, because the tanks were pressurized, so if a bullet went through the tank, you lost pressure and you lost your engine because there was no petrol.

I had become separated from Hawker almost right at the beginning. What happened is that there was a palpable German trap near Bapaume, with a number of fat Army Cooperation Huns tooling about. There were also about six or seven single-seater Hun fighters about 4,000 feet up. The idea was that you'd go for the fat Huns, and the fighters would descend on you. Well, I could see what this was about. I turned toward the fat Huns and gave them a squirt at a distance of about half a mile, just to say: 'Well, you hop off home!' Then I turned to come back to reasonable safety, before the top Huns could descend on me. I thought I might have engine trouble; that's why I turned back, but Hawker went on after the Huns. I saw this and turned back to go with him, but by that time the top Huns were on us. I was shot to pieces from behind straightaway; tanks, engine and the rest, and all I could do was turn in the direction of the lines in the hope that I could run a straight glide. I'd got no engine to manoeuvre, and no height to spare, and I hoped that I could just scrape over the trenches, which is what I did. Hawker went on. I saw him go past me, and what happened to him after that, I don't know. I last saw him at about 3,000 feet near Bapaume, fighting with a Hun apparently quite under control but going down. He was shot down, of course; but how he was shot down, whether they got his engine early on, or wounded him, I don't know. I should imagine that his engine was shot away fairly early on, as that was the only reasonable method of shooting an aircraft in those days with your limited gun-power. You'd sit as close as you could to the target's tail, and pump lead into his backside. That's where your engine and tanks were. You were sitting in front of that, and the probability is that he was too low to have much chance to get over the lines. Whether he tried to and was hit from behind, or whether he was hit from the ground, which was rather unlikely, I don't know; having a Hun on his tail, they would not have attempted to fire at him from the ground.

The whole machine was riddled like a colander when I got it on the ground. I managed to land, though, and the right way up. I came down somewhere behind the French lines, and landed at Divisional Headquarters, somewhere among the French defensive system. They had a little emergency landing ground which they'd flattened out among the shell-holes, and I landed on that. I hadn't expected to be shot down, but you kept in mind where you could pop down, especially when flying a DH2. That's perhaps why Major Hawker was killed; he was in a machine that was outclassed. Lanoe Hawker's death came as a great blow, as everyone liked him, and had absolute confidence in him as a commanding officer.

I didn't get back to No. 24 Squadron that day. I was down, and a party was sent out to retrieve the machine if they could. Luckily, it hadn't been shelled in the meantime. We collected the machine and I went back the following day. I spent the night with the Frenchmen at Guillemont. This happened on 23 November, and I got back to the squadron the following day with the wreck of the aircraft. I remained with No. 24 Squadron for about a fortnight after Major Hawker was killed.

Soon, I was posted away from the squadron. I was pretty well due to come home anyway, because I was the last of the original No. 24 Squadron left. Some had been posted to promotion, and some had done their tour of duty and come back to be put on training jobs in England. Others had been wounded, but I was the last survivor of the original squadron. That's not to say that I was the last survivor alive!

When I came back to England, I had some leave. There were no more DH2s coming into service, so I had to learn to fly a tractor fighter again. There was, technically speaking, a 'conversion' course, after which I went to No. 66 Squadron which was just bringing in the Sopwith Pup, a fighter with a tractor engine. The Pup was a beautiful plane to fly, provided you flew it and didn't break it; it was very flimsy. It was a perfect aircraft; it had no vices, whereas with the DH2, if you didn't watch it, it could get the better of you. The Pup would pull you out of the most impossible situations. It had a better ceiling, too; it was very lightly loaded, and you could get it up to over 20,000 feet, whereas the DH2 would stagger, with the greatest difficulty and groaning, to about 15,000.

I got back to France in February 1917, and was with No. 66 Squadron until August. The pace of the war had accelerated a great deal by then, and there were quite a lot of machines flying around. I was there in April 1917, which was the really bad month for the RFC. There were a lot more casualties then. That was the Battle of Arras. There was a great deal of aerial activity. The Army was keen to get constant reconnaissance going, and we were keen to stop the Hun doing reconnaissance of our chaps. So there would be a lot of activity around any land offensives. The fighters always collected where ground activity was greatest, because that's where the Huns would be. We did quite a lot of escorts to long distance reconnaissances. We used to escort strategic reconnaissance aircraft to protect them from German attack, and also there would be a lot of activity against the Huns, who were trying to pick off our Army Cooperation aircraft. The fighters were organized in wings of three or four squadrons, and moved about to where the ground activity was greatest, either to the Hun offensive, as in March 1918, or to our offensive in 1917.

I had come back in September 1917 and was OC of a training squadron in Lincolnshire until January 1918. There were three or four flights. We used a mixed bag of aircraft. We had the chaps starting their advanced training on things like Avros, and BEs, and then we might have had some single-seaters, Bristol Bullets, to train some of them on to become scout pilots.

During the offensive of 1918, I was in No. 70 Squadron, with Camels. That was quite a thing. I was doing ground-strafing practically the whole time, because our opposition was very slight on the ground. The Hun came through in masses, in a rush, and there weren't the troops to put in front of him. We had to try to do what we could to help the wretched blokes on the ground, in clumps in shell-holes and the remains of buildings. There was no strongly held front line to oppose him; he'd got right through that. We had to shoot him up where we could find him, in small columns, worthwhile targets and so on, in the back areas immediately behind his front-line chaps.

After the Hun offensive packed up in 1918, and the Royal Air Force was formed on 1 April, I went to command a Camel squadron, No. 209, which had been RNAS, at Bertangles. We hadn't enough aerodromes, so they put extra squadrons on existing aerodromes. We were so jammed in, and were on the opposite side of the aerodrome from where I'd been with No. 24. I don't know what had happened to No. 24 by then. Where we had been, was I was now with a scout squadron again, doing offensive patrols. I was commanding them when the big attack of 8 August took place in front of Amiens, which was the beginning of the end of the German Army. But commanding No. 209 involved a great deal more paperwork than when one is commanding a flight. Of course, the most interesting job was commanding a flight, when you knew your five or six chaps, and you worked as a fighting unit. That was the exciting thing, but it did take a great deal out of one, and one couldn't go on indefinitely being a top-line flight commander. I think whenever one commanded a squadron, one got sufficient rest to recover the energy one had expended before. I was very interested in the development of fighter tactics while commanding the squadron, and saw a great deal of change in those since I'd been in. One saw far more aircraft activity, in a more or less coordinated way, on each side in the battle instead of one machine versus another machine, or a pair against a pair. It developed into a couple of squadrons on each side. The Huns would have up to twenty or twenty-four aircraft. The days of 1916 and 1917, when the lone fighter was effective, were definitely over by then. Of course, after you'd joined combat, then you'd split up. Then it became single combat. But initially, at the beginning of the fight, you had some more or less coordinated action by anything up to six or twelve aircraft. After the battle was joined, though, it was every man for himself until it was over, and then you collected up again and went on with your patrol.

I left No. 209 in about September and went out to the Near East, to the Aegean. I was posted out to command another ex-RNAS squadron, No. 220. There, we had DH9s, and there was a flight of Camels. So I collected a Camel for my own personal use. Actually, by the time I'd got out there and settled in, the war was over, because the Turk threw his hand in virtually. I think he threw it in officially in October and said he didn't want to fight any more. By the middle of September we had nothing to fight. It made a great change from being on the Western Front, where we were active all the time. We were left out on a limb, so a composite unit was formed out of various squadrons. There were three squadrons in the Aegean; two in Mudros, and mine, which was on Imbros, an island not very far away. We went up in December, through Constantinople to the Black Sea and the Caucasus, to join up with a fellow called Deniken, who was fighting the Bolsheviks in south Russia. I was on the western bank of the Caspian Sea, north of the Caucasus. I wasn't there very long, though, because I got typhus in June or July 1919, and was lucky to survive to get back through the Mediterranean and home.

There were very few units of any sort. There were a few training units, and very few squadrons. Most of the active squadrons were overseas in India or Mespot (*Mesopotamia*). I was commanding a squadron in India. I formed a fighter squadron out there. We had two fighter squadrons out there in 1919; one was formed in India, and the other in Basra, and the latter left Basra and joined up with the one in India. I was flying a Snipe. They were a little bit ham-fisted, but gave quite a good performance. But I was so used to flying light machines, like Pups and Camels, that the Snipe felt heavy to me. The other chaps didn't mind; they'd known nothing better. You had to be a bit careful out there in the hot weather at any altitude, because you started off at the equivalent of about 10,000 feet up, and consequently had to have a much higher speed to get your lift.

I soldiered on with the RAF. I went out to India for a short time, and then came back in the 20s to various training jobs in England. Most of the old fighters had been phased out by then. Gradually new types came in. Of course, the number of squadrons was cut enormously. The Sopwith Snipe kept going for some little time, and Hawker produced a fighter called the Fury. They were changing and gradually evolving the whole time. Bristol, who produced a Bulldog, were building all-metal aircraft by then. They were pioneers in all-metal work. The big step was the Spitfire and Hurricane, which developed from the civil aircraft that were entered in the Schneider Cup Trophy.

I'd spent most of my time in fighters, so I became very much involved in the layout and organization of Home Defence previous to the Second World War. It was very well organized; had it not been, I shouldn't be here today.

On 23 November 1916, Captain Andrews, commanding 'A' Flight of No. 24 Squadron, flew with Major Hawker VC on patrol, during which the latter was dispatched by Manfred von Richthofen whose gun jam cleared after a combat lasting thirty-five minutes. Both English pilots were flying the hopelessly outclassed DH2 pusher biplane. The fatal shot struck when Hawker had almost gained the safety of the British lines. Definite news of his death was not received until July 1917. Andrews did not fly a DH2 again, though he served with distinction in other squadrons.

Meanwhile, No. 24 Squadron, which had been ordered by Hawker to attack everything, and had destroyed only thirteen HA since his demise, was not re-equipped with an efficient scout plane, the SE5a, until the end of 1917. This improved their success against hostile aircraft immeasurably.

During the Somme battle, Andrews was approaching his home aerodrome, which consisted of a large field adjacent to an awkward, narrow sloping space next to the mess. In order to arrive at the mess more quickly, as an experienced pilot, Andrews decided to land on the difficult field. His engine cut out and he descended on a large canvas hangar used for aircraft maintenance. Fortunately, no-one was injured, though there was much shredding of rope and canvas. As chaps came running to see if anyone was hurt, Andrews calmly climbed down from his machine, removed his flying gloves, and remarked, 'I am pleased that you have arrived, Staff Sergeant. Get this mess cleared up!'

As Andrews was flying back from a patrol over the Somme, he noticed a flight of enemy aircraft above him, to his right towards the sun. Resolving to take no action until they passed over him, he zoomed and shot up the last machine in the flight from beneath, bringing it down. It transpired that the man he killed was a senior officer who had been escorting novice fliers on a tour to familiarize them with the battle area.

Lieutenant Wilfred Watts

Lieutenant Wilfred Edward Watts was born on 24 December 1898. He enlisted in The Artists' Rifles in 1915, transferring to the Royal Flying Corps in September 1916. He became a prisoner of war in 1917, and survived moves to several camps. After the war he devoted himself entirely to the Church and from 1937 was Rector in the parish of Hambleden for nearly forty-two years. Canon Watts was interviewed at the Rectory at Hambleden, Oxfordshire on 8 November 1978. He died on 20 April 1980.

To be quite candid, I enjoyed the idea of a uniform. I joined the Artists' Rifles in December 1915 while I was under seventeen. They found out my age, and then I joined the Royal Flying Corps in September 1916.

I first went to Denham where we did very little work indeed, just a bit of marching about the place. Then we got sent to Lincoln College, Oxford, in order to acquire some knowledge of engines. I was never very good at it, and know very little about engines now. Volunteers were wanted to become observers rather than pilots, and a few of us stepped forward; we thought we'd get to France quicker that way. So I became an observer first of all. I was sent just after my commission to the School of Aerial Gunnery at Hythe. There I met Malcolm Campbell, who said: 'I wonder if you'd be my observer.' I'd never met him before in my life but I'd heard about him; he was already making a name for himself as a racing driver. We did only three weeks at Hythe, and then we got sent to

203

Gosport. It was on our very first day there that Campbell and I went up to the aerodrome and saw something falling out of an aeroplane. To our horror we found that it was the observer who had fallen out. Naturally he was killed. It was a pusher machine, an FE2b, and the observer was in front, with nothing to hang on to except the gun mounting. The pilot, who was doing what we used to call 'split-arsing' in the air, turned his machine upside down and just crashed into the ground. Malcolm Campbell actually was a very safe pilot. I never thought that he would do anything which would make me fall out of the plane.

After a while we heard that a certain squadron in France had got badly knocked about, and that only certain people were going out, and Campbell was one of them who was left behind. That meant that I, too, would be left behind and so I took this as an opportunity to become a pilot myself.

I first learned to fly on Maurice Farmans. I did two and a half hours' dual, then flew solo and did about five or six hours on Maurice Farmans. That's all one did. The first time I went solo in the Farman, I pretended to myself there was someone else there. I thought, 'Well, I'm not alone'. I was alone, though, and went round and got down all right, without crashing. I don't think I ever crashed. I had many forced landings, but I always landed safely. I was a rotten pilot in many ways, but in some ways I might have been a good pilot. I didn't try to flatten out like some pilots did when they were six feet off the ground. Some know perfectly well how to do it, and others don't. It's a question of reaction, judgment and eyesight. You saw crashed machines all over the place.

Then I flew at Gosport on BE2cs, Avros, and a certain American machine called a Curtiss which was famous for having the joystick on a wheel. Very few people had ever flown a Curtiss and therefore I was asked to take the plane to a place called Southport. After about fifty miles I had a forced landing in a field. And I thought 'Can I get out of this field?' It was a very small field, but I just managed to get out of it. I went on to Castle Bromwich, stayed the night there and decided to go on to Southport the next day. But I was warned there was only two hours' petrol in my machine, and that I had to fly as high as possible over Liverpool because the engine might cut out. It did cut out, actually, and I looked at the Mersey, and I thought, 'Shall I come down there? Where shall I come down?' It looked very nice, but I thought, 'No, I don't think I will come down, I'm a very bad swimmer', so I thought I'd try to get somewhere near the sand. I just managed to get to somewhere near Southport. When I landed I asked someone, 'Where is your aerodrome?'

And I was told, 'There's no aerodrome'.

I said, 'There must be an aerodrome here; I've been told by my squadron leader to take this plane to Southport.'

They said, 'There's no aerodrome there.'

I said, 'Well, I'm not going to take it away again, what shall I do with it, then?' and someone said,

'Well, move it to my garage.'

And as far as I know it's still there today. When I was in France with Sholto Douglas, he said to me, 'You know that plane I told you to take to Southport? Well actually it shouldn't have been Southport at all; it's not your fault, but it should have been Southwold.' I'd love to know what happened to that plane. Where the garage was I haven't the slightest idea. I stayed, I always remember, at the Adelphi Hotel, which was the best hotel in Liverpool. I'll always remember the porridge and cream. Then I reported back.

At Gosport I learned of the first 'cure' for spinning. When you got in a spin and gave up all hope of surviving, you'd find your-self diving to the earth very quickly, but having gained flying speed you'd pull the joystick back and finally come out of it. We were all told to practise spinning. I had my first spin in a Sopwith Pup. I don't think it worried me very much indeed. I think I prefer spinning to looping; I didn't like being upside down very much. I loved flying. I must admit that, but when I was flying we always got into forced landings. Time and again your engine would cut out, but I was just lucky, and usually managed to find somewhere to land. Nowadays I don't like flying at all in these vast things.

I was flying Pups and Camels, which both had rotary engines. I preferred the Pup every time, because you could manoeuvre it easily. They weren't always that safe, though; I remember someone did a loop in a Pup and the wings fell off. You were always warned if your engine cut out when taking off, never to try to turn back to the aerodrome, but so often people did, lost flying speed, crashed to the ground and were killed. In 1917 as many people were killed learning to fly as were killed in France.

Soon I got my wings and was posted to No. 84 Squadron. There were eighteen planes in the squadron, six planes in a flight. I went from Lilbourne to Hornchurch, but there was a terrific fog and I arrived at Hythe, which was the next landing place. There I met Leefe Robinson, who got the VC for shooting down a Zeppelin. He was on his way to France, and was there only a very short time before being taken prisoner. He died as a prisoner of war.

We went out to France on SE5s. The SE5 had one great drawback; you had to put on a great deal of left rudder in order to keep the machine straight when you were getting off the ground. There was one fellow called Beauchamp Proctor who was always going round and round in circles, and we thought he was going to crash, and he said, 'I can't do this,' but actually he went on to get the VC. He was in No. 84. That was also Sholto Douglas' squadron. No. 84 Squadron was at a place called Estrée-Blanche near St Omer, the aircraft depot. I used to think how lucky we were in one sense. As short as life was, the average time being about twelve days, we usually had two breakfasts, one before going on early morning patrol, and another when we came back in. We were hungry in those days. But I remember seeing troops going up past our camp, often with horses, and going up the lines, and I used to pity them. I thought they were far worse off than we were. My brothers were in the infantry and got badly wounded.

You had your own rigger and your own mechanic, and I remember they always wished me good luck, as no doubt they did to everyone. I remember one saying, 'Oh, do come back. We'll miss you tremendously.' You relied entirely upon them. I mean, I knew nothing about engines in spite of the course I'd been on at Oxford.

We were billeted on the airfield at Estrée-Blanche, but I can't remember very much about that except the mess, and that someone called Rushton often used to play the piano. I remember quite a number of names, like Crowe, Rushton, Park and a few others. I know two of those were taken prisoner before me. I remember one fellow coming in one night, very smartly dressed in Indian Cavalry uniform with chains on his lapels. I never saw him again.

It's very difficult to say whether our planes were as good and as well developed as the German aircraft at that time, but I'd have thought probably as good. I don't think you can ever say that all along the German planes were better than ours, or ours were better than theirs. It happened that you might produce an SE5, which we thought were good planes, but I understand now that the Camels were better. I didn't particularly like a Camel; you were sitting up too high. The easiest plane by far to handle was the Sopwith Pup. You could come into your aerodrome and see fog, and you could side-slip down to almost a few feet from the ground and see where you were, and you'd land safely. The Pup never let you down.

I loved flying but I didn't like the thought of being shot down; I don't think anyone with any sense would. There was a certain amount of fear, but I think the only time you really thought about it was when you saw your friends who'd been wounded, and realized how lucky you were. Jolly lucky, really, because it was a very short life out there. Naturally some people survived, but nearly all the great aces got killed eventually. Ball got killed. McCudden got killed. In fact, I think they all were killed. I knew McCudden, who was on the same aerodrome as we were with No. 56 Squadron. He seemed a nice fellow. He was already a hero, when I was no one. He died in a very stupid accident, though. You were warned time and time again, not to turn back, not to do that. But even the very best pilots went and did silly things. The only time I ever even broke an undercarriage was when I landed in France at St Omer. And I remember it so well, because the mechanic said to me, 'Oh, God, you don't mean to say. We're so busy, you would go and crash yours!' I'll always remember that. I said, 'Well, it's the first time I've ever done it in my life.'

I hated the thought of coming down in flames; we had no parachutes. To be quite candid, I envied a friend of mine who'd lost his arm, because he was invalided out. If I had flown again I would have flown in a two-seater. There were no such thing as three- or four-seaters, not in my time. But you're very lonely. You're in the air completely by yourself, with no way of communicating with anyone. You're usually flying over the clouds at about 8,000 to 10,000 feet. It was a very lonely life there, particularly over enemy lines. At that time all the fighting was done over enemy lines. I never saw a German plane once over our lines; one was always over their lines.

The machine was as much your enemy as the Germans in a way, when you were flying in the First War. I got my joystick caught up in the fuselage of my SE5, and I was crashing down to earth. Sholto Douglas was watching, and I just managed to get out in time. And he said, 'Whatever happened?'

And I said, 'My joystick got stuck.'

He said, 'That's quite impossible!'

I said, 'No, it did. Try it.'

And for half an hour they tried it and it got stuck. I was sent on patrol, supposedly joining some bombers, but something was awry, because my machine, which ought to have taken two and a quarter hours' amount of petrol, only took two hours' worth. I told Sholto Douglas about this, so he tried it for two hours and said he thought it all right. But I still felt it wasn't. And that's how I got left behind. I couldn't get back, was shot at from the ground, and crash-landed onto the railway embankment. I don't remember very much about it, except I do remember coming to, and saying, 'Where am I?' and someone speaking bad English replied,

'In France.'

And I said, 'Thank God for that!'

And he added, 'But in German hands!'

I was taken prisoner on 20 October. I'd only had about a month's operational flying, and only a few combats in the air. I was very bad. Albatroses were the main scout the Germans had in 1917, but I never came across Richthofen. He was very much respected by our people. Most extraordinary, why there should have been this sort of feeling but there was at that time between the German Air Force and us. It was the idea of knights of the air, chivalry. But it rather wore off by the end of the war. I saw Sholto Douglas after the war, and he said things changed a lot. But during 1916 and 1917 there was a feeling of comradeship between the opposing sides.

I got taken prisoner and went to a German officers' camp for a while. They were very kind to me. Later, I was sent to a place called Douai, where I was had up, twice, before a board of German officers who accused me of using dum-dum bullets. As far as I know, I had no dum-dum bullets; I would never have loaded them in the drum myself. The Germans said, 'If you did, you'll be shot.' I think they said that to frighten me more than anything else.

First I went to Lille, and then to Douai where I was in solitary confinement for about two weeks or so. I was sent to a prisoner of war camp for Russians. That was at Berg, I don't think I could even find it on the map; it's somewhere near Berlin. There were about twelve British, about 1,500 Russians, and about thirty French. It was rather a difficult time altogether. We were very hungry; our last meal was about five o'clock in the evening, when we got a few carrots and a little bit of bread. It was a toss up whether we ate the bread that night, or saved it until the next morning. I was so hungry, I couldn't sleep. I was so cold; 1917's was a bitter winter. I nearly always ate my little piece of bread, and I had nothing to eat therefore until one o'clock the next day, when we had usually cabbage soup. Twice a week we'd have a little meat with it. I suppose the Germans were also very hard up for food. If we had been sent to an English camp it would have been OK, because in all the English camps they put aside our parcels and new prisoners shared with the others. But going to this camp for Russian prisoners, parcels were not coming through except that their friends had sent some parcels. But ours, for some reason were just listed 'missing' for a long time, and the first batch of mail I received was forty letters from my mother. I was absolutely delighted to think that I'd got all these. She wrote to me every single day, and believed somehow I might be alive.

One thing I remember very well, was I used to teach French prisoners English, and for that they used to ask me to lunch every Sunday. I used to look forward to that lunch, not only for the comradeship of the French but also for myself, as I felt rather hungry. One Sunday, they came round and said to me, 'We've got jugged hare.' And I thought to myself, 'This is marvellous,' and I didn't think where this hare might have come from. I was enjoying the lunch, there were about six of us, and there's not much on a hare, naturally, but just a little meat meant something to us. And I said, 'Where is pussy?' and they all laughed like anything. And I realized I was eating a cat. I've always been sorry for cats ever since, because I absolutely love cats. But the Russians used to eat anything they could possibly get hold of, even a mouse or a rat.

I found the Russians lovable creatures. They used to invite us to their concerts. I can't remember any instruments, they just all sang together, sang their local songs, you know, the Russian songs. They used to go, about 1,500 of them, and just sing in this vast place. I used to love their concerts. And I compose, actually. My father used to compose at Salisbury Cathedral, so it's in the family. I have composed settings for the Russian *Kontakion*, because it reminded me of those Russians. We hadn't got the slightest idea what they were singing, but they had lovely voices, and we appreciated it.

Their quarters were a little way away from ours, and were extremely dirty. But we always said they would give us their last shirt, and so they would have done. They were just ordinary Russians; not aviators, not even officers. It would have been at the time of the Revolution. What happened to them, I don't know. All I know is that there was a lot of disease in camp, of course, and vast numbers of them died from the influenza epidemic.

There was a lot of illness about. I have photographs of people being buried by different chaplains out there, and of one Anglican chaplain in particular, Father Eustace Hewell, who lost his arm on the Somme. He was taken prisoner in the German push in 1918.

I'd never been overweight. Now, I weight about 10st 6lb, but in the camp I weighed about 9st. I was pretty thin. About May or June 1918, we went to Schweidnitz in Silesia. That was the Richthofens' home. That was a British camp, where we lived in a barrack-like room. One of my great friends was a fellow called Con Smythe. Everyone knows him well in Canada; he was a great athlete, and captained Canada at ice hockey. There was another fellow called Broughall, who also was a great international ice hockey player.

We didn't know how the war was going, who was winning and

what was happening. But I do remember during the German offensive, the chaplain Father Eustace Hewell, who used to say a daily Mass, saying to me, 'This is the end of the war. We are going to win it.'

I said, 'Why, what do you mean?'

He said, 'This is the Germans' last great effort, and we are stopping them. There's nothing to hold us back now.'

I do remember that. I don't think the squadron knew I was prisoner for about six weeks. I was just posted 'Missing'. You were very deep into Germany, and if you had escaped it would be quite difficult to get through, almost impossible, and particularly from Schweidnitz, which was in a part of Germany that became part of Poland.

Regarding escape attempts, I can't remember one, except the only person who did manage to get away. That was Con Smythe. I think he was the bravest man I ever met. While we made an awful row our side of the camp, he and Broughall climbed the other side, but they only just got over. They were brought back immediately. We all thought that we must try to get away, and started planning something, but they'd always discover our plan. The only man who did get away was a person who could speak perfect German. I'll always believe that he was a German who was planted on us. He suddenly left the camp. There were two who left like that and weren't brought back. We always had our suspicion about one of them, and very much about the other, and they both left us. Perhaps they'd been informing on us the whole time. You had to be so careful. When I was in solitary confinement two people joined me, and I think in fact they were both planted on me. I never saw them again.

After the war was over, I spent nearly two months in Germany. We were told we mustn't try and get back on our own. And my name beginning with 'W', naturally I was one of the last to leave camp. The Army and the Air Force had the same system; they always started with the 'A' and went on. I saw a lot of the conditions in Germany after the First World War; people dying of starvation, children running up to you and asking for food, and we had very, very little we could give them. But even we prisoners in

211

the English camp had more, probably, than they had. I remember also that the German people were very friendly to us after the war. I don't think it was merely that they thought they ought to be friendly to us, because they'd lost the war, but they were naturally friendly. And I suppose at least 1,000 or 2,000 people used to come to the station and wave us goodbye, saying, 'No more war! No more war!' And when I came home, I was very much the idealist. One of my great friends was Malcolm Muggeridge. He was a bit of a Red and so was I. We thought we were going to put the world right. Very high ideals. And personally, I couldn't bear to see any food wasted at all; even at home if someone left a piece of gristle on the plate, I just couldn't understand it. Gristle. We would have eaten anything at all.

My uncle was headmaster of a prep. school, so just after I got back, and before I went up to Cambridge I put in a few months there, and took my degree in history and theology, and went back to teaching for three years, and I decided I really did want to be ordained, and I was ordained in St Paul's Cathedral by Ingraham who was, at that time, Bishop of London. I was at All Saints, Fulham. I considered joining the Cambridge University Flying Club, but I didn't do very much work at Cambridge, I must admit; I took a Second. But I think that at university the great thing is not just a matter of passing exams, but of getting to know people.

Somehow one lost touch with other people. But I still hear from Con Smythe, who was four years older than I. Every Christmas, even after all these years, he sends me £150 for my church. We call it the Con Smythe Fund, and we keep it separate and use it for anything of importance. It's a great help.

As far as I was concerned, the war changed me tremendously. I went into the war, as everyone did, with the feeling that we must win. After the war, one was thinking very much more in terms of internationalism. As far as I'm concerned we should all be Brothers in Christ. Some of my great friends were people like Studdert Kennedy, a great First World War poet, who stayed with me three days before he died. He was known as 'Woodbine Willy', and I have two books he signed on that visit. I used also to stay a great deal with Dick Sheppard of the Peace Pledge Union. He was vicar of St Martin's in the Fields. It was the Reverend F. A. Iremonger who said, 'You must be ordained.' He was editor of a church paper called *The Guardian*, which was a very progressive sort of paper. It had changed my life without a doubt. During the First World War, many people were killed. From this village alone, I think there were sixty killed in the First World War, and only eighteen in the Second.

I still feel that war is a tremendous waste of life, of everything. I felt no hatred; I never wanted to kill anyone at all. But you're just caught up in the whole affair. I think my brother would say the same thing. He was badly wounded in France, as a regular soldier. I think it made me realize that the world didn't consist merely of England, but of a much bigger thing altogether, than simply taking care of our own skins.

This interview took place on a day of late Indian summer, golden, hazy and dreamlike. Gentle, slightly remote and scholarly, Canon Watts was delightful to encounter. Soon afterwards he retired, using his brief remaining days to write a history of his incumbency in the parish of Hambleden and its valley, assisted by the organist of his former church, Ms Christine Wells. Music and composition were abiding interests for him, and a great solace. His proximity to Russian prisoners and exposure to their singing had engendered an interest in the musical form of the *Kontakion*.

His war service had altered his attitudes to the extent that, having been ordained into the Anglican church, Canon Watts had become a pacifist. Dick Sheppard, who is mentioned in his interview, was a leader of the Peace Pledge Union, with which Vera Brittain of *Testament of Youth* fame was also involved. Both appeared on the Nazi list of those to be removed, should a German invasion have occurred.

After the interview, when tea was served, Canon Watts clung on to his food in a most deliberate manner as though it was the last he might see for some time; clearly an effect of the time he had spent in POW camps.

Captain Ferdinand West

Captain Ferdinand Maurice Felix West was born in Princes Square, London on 29 January 1896. His mother was the Italian Comtesse Clémence de la Garde de Saignes, and his father was Lieutenant Francis West of the East Lancashire Regiment. When West was six, his father was killed while serving in the Boer War. His mother returned to Milan, with her young son. Educated at a private school there run by Swiss instructors, the boy became fluent in English, French, and Italian. He entered Genoa University in 1913.

After war was declared, West returned to England. He enlisted in the Royal Army Medical Corps, where his older comrades dubbed the eighteen-year-old, 'Baby'. Determined to be involved in the fighting, in May 1915 he transferred to the Royal Munster Fusiliers in the Loos sector. In 1917 he visited Amiens, where he was able to observe No. 3 Squadron, RFC.

He was posted to No. 8 Squadron on 8 January 1918, flying FK8 two-seaters, with Alec Haslam as his gunner-observer. West witnessed the death of von Richthofen, the Red Baron, and noted, 'He looked quite calm in death – he might have died in bed.' By summer he was promoted to captain and given a Flight. West received the Military Cross on 24 July 1918. On 10 August, while reconnoitring for a group of tanks, Haslam and West were attacked in their FK8 by seven German aircraft. West was hit in both legs, one being nearly severed, but managed to land. Canadian soldiers eventually pulled the two men out. For this action, West received the Victoria Cross. The citation read, 'Captain West . . . surpassing bravery and devotion to duty, manoeuvred his machine so skilfully that his observer was enabled to get several good bursts into the enemy machines, which

214

drove them away. Captain West then, with rare courage and determination, brought his machine over our lines and landed safely. Exhausted by his exertions, he fainted, but on regaining consciousness insisted on writing his report.'

Perhaps even more amazing was his determination to return to service flying, after losing a leg, and to serve in the Second World War, commanding a wing in the air component of the British Expeditionary Force. He was appointed Air Attaché in Rome in 1940, then ordered to Switzerland, effectively head of British Air Intelligence. His most successful covert mission was the retrieval of an extensive card index of Luftwaffe dispositions.

In 1946 he resigned his post and became managing director of Eagle-Lion Distributors with the J. Arthur Rank Organisation. He married Winifred Leslie, and they had one son. Interviewed at Sunningdale, Berkshire on 27 May 1979, Air Commodore West died, aged ninety-two, on 8 July 1988. He was the last surviving British VC recipient of the First World War in the air.

In December 1914, I was eighteen years of age, and joined the Army. At the beginning of 1916, I went to France to join the 2nd Battalion, Royal Munster Fusiliers, which was situated in the Somme area. I very much disliked this trench warfare, because we had to walk in mud all the time, and we had to share our meals with very unpleasant rats. We were fired on by the Germans day and night, and they were about 250 yards from where we were. Above all I disliked the lack of space. From the trenches, I could see airmen flying, and said to myself: 'If I ever get the chance to join the Royal Flying Corps, I shall certainly do it.' Luckily enough for me, sometime in 1916 a circular from the War Office was sent to the battalion asking for volunteers to join the Royal Flying Corps. I immediately applied and was accepted.

I was sent to Brooklands, where I had to learn how to cooperate with the artillery, how to use wireless, and how to read maps, which of course I already knew as a soldier. After about twenty-two hours' training, I was posted to France, to No. 3 Squadron, which was equipped with Morane Parasols. The name indicates that the aircraft was very fragile; it was very much like a parasol. It had a 90-horsepower engine, and it was rather tricky to land.

After about five months, I applied to become a pilot. Again, my application was accepted and I was posted to Grantham in 1917. I was given a DH6, which was a very easy machine to learn on and to fly.

I was enthusiastic and happy to be up in the air, and I know that this was the experience of all the young fellows of my age; we were delighted with our first experience of flying, and we loved it. Your fellow creatures are creeping on the ground while you're alone up there in the air, and you can feel a superior being somehow. After five hours' solo on the DH6, I was put on an Armstrong Whitworth with a 90-horsepower engine, and after about sixty hours' solo flying on that machine, I was posted to No. 8 Squadron in France.

No. 8 Squadron was an Army reconnaissance squadron, and naturally they liked to have pilots with Army training who had been in France, as we already had considerable knowledge of what we could expect from the air. Our squadron was earmarked to cooperate with the tanks. In those days, the means of communication between the air and the tanks was very primitive; it was by means of red, green and yellow flags. But these flags, when placed in a tank, would soon become greasy and dirty, and my colleagues and I could not tell what colour the flags were from the height at which we were flying, so I suggested to them that we could co-operate by means of wireless telegraphy.

However, the big battle of August 1918 took place before we were able to carry out these experiments. I was too young an officer to form too many opinions at the time, but I would have thought that the Air Force must have helped the Army enormously, in assisting the tanks and the artillery. Certainly this must have opened the eyes of senior officers to how great a future aviation had. I think the Army officers of my rank were very impressed with what flying could achieve, and were quite convinced that the Air Force would be developed and that the Army would need to rely on it more and more. I wasn't particularly interested in the Airship programme, though; most of us considered that the airship was too big, too cumbersome and too much of a target for enemy aircraft, and so could not be of any use in war. Also, the disadvantages of the fuel capacity and of strong winds, made them pretty much unserviceable in tropical conditions. I think that most of us thought that civilian flying from country to country would become a normal way of life, and somehow we felt that we were pioneering something that was bound to develop. That I think was the opinion of all my young colleagues.

Of course, we were subject to machine-gun fire, and rifle fire, but one expects to be shot at in war. We had to fly very low, and we were shot at from the ground fairly heavily, and my machine and those of my colleagues had hundreds of bullet holes. During the war, we were concerned with our own squadron, and we knew all that happened in our squadron and the particular front on which we operated, but all sorts of things were happening in France of which we had no knowledge. We were, to a certain extent, cut off from other squadrons. However, I remember Captain Ball and James McCudden, both VC chaps who were killed later, coming down to our squadron to give lectures on how they operated as fighters, and how we might best manoeuvre our aircraft to get away from the enemy. I remember talking to McCudden, and he said that it would be easier for the Hun if I flew low, rather than at 10,000 feet, as they could dive on me with much greater facility. As a fighter pilot, McCudden was very good indeed.

I spoke to Ball, too. He was a different type of fighter pilot; he was more interested in working on his own, whereas McCudden was more interested in formation flying as well. When they came to us, they didn't quite emphasize particularly how they attacked the enemy, though; they were interested in telling us what tactics to employ to make it difficult for fighters to attack us. Their talks were on that basis, not about how many aircraft they had shot down. I think the French, the Belgians and the Germans were much more inclined to use the names of their more famous pilots like Manfred von Richthofen for the purposes of propaganda. I don't think we boosted the names so much. We'd heard of Ball and McCudden of course, but I don't think the authorities boosted them as much as the Germans did. It was partly due to the character of the pilots; I don't think they wanted it themselves, either. The sort of worship that the Germans had for Richthofen certainly didn't trickle down to our squadron. I happen to be one of the few pilots who saw the crash of Richthofen and, in fact, the Australian gunners who claimed to have shot him down gave me a piece of his machine in the shape of Australia. On this shape of Australia they wrote: 'The Red Falcon, Baron von Richthofen, shot down 21st April 1918.' But of course, as you know, the Royal Air Force said that he was shot down by Captain Arthur Brown. I had no idea who shot Richthofen down, except that I knew that he had been brought down alive in our lines. Quite rightly, he had a funeral with full military honours.

The casualties in squadrons in 1917 and 1918 were very high, and I think that any pilot who managed to last three or four months was doing pretty well. We were very interested in our work, and when you're young you don't think much about death or accidents; you're interested in the adventure and the thrill of flying, and doing the job. When you come back and you're all together, you're happy. In my experience, none of the boys worried about death, and if they did, they kept it to themselves. Somehow, I think a chap in the infantry is more conscious of death, because he's stationary in trench warfare. But a pilot has to do so much; he has to fly his machine, to navigate and use his wireless, so I think that the danger side doesn't worry him very much.

The observer's main job was the protection of the pilot. If the observer starts looking down on the ground, he won't spot a fighter coming quickly out of the cloud. So all the experienced pilots made sure that the observer's eyes were trained to the sky. The average observer, being a human being, is interested in what's happening on the battlefield and what the enemy is doing. He wants to look around. But the pilot is interested in being safe-guarded; he wants to know that he is going to have sufficient notice from the observer that the fighter is about. If we saw him taking an interest in the ground, we shook the wings violently from right to left, to remind him that observing the ground was the pilot's job.

When I was an observer, my pilot, Captain Goldie, who un-fortunately was killed, had pretty much the same idea. I learned from him. I tried to explain to my observer, a Gunner officer, that his role was to look after the aeroplane and then himself, but I occasionally had the feeling that he had a jolly good look at what

218

was happening on the battlefield. We used to direct the artillery. We gave the order to open fire. The gun was fired and we flew over the target, and would tell them by radio whether the shell had landed on target or 100 yards or fifty yards or at 3 o'clock, and so on. They would use ground signals to tell us that everything was OK.

The photographic aspect of our work was not so difficult, because the main thing for photography in those days was to maintain a straight line over the area in which you were going to take the photograph. The anti-aircraft guns knew perfectly well where you were, and when they opened fire, and you saw those black puffs near your machine, you had to keep steady and carry on. If you deviated, you'd have to start all over again. The observer would check that the camera was in good order, and would put the plates in. The positioning of the camera, the placing of the plates in the camera, the removal of the film from the camera and the development of the plates had nothing to do with the pilot. All we had to do was keep in a straight line and bring these photographs back; everything after that was somebody else's job. The photographs were very good, with excellent detail.

We didn't do much night flying. We had a few trials, but we weren't equipped for night flying; you've got to have proper long exhausts and instruments, and the type of plane I was flying was not equipped like that, though we did carry out a few experiments at night. Nowadays, you're greatly helped with instruments and lights and so on, but in those days, we didn't have very much. We had to use impregnated cloths which would be set alight; we could see where to land by the flames and the smoke, and we'd flatten out.

During the course of the August 1918 battle, which lasted several days, I was shot down a couple of times. I was shot down twice behind the English lines. On the first occasion I was not hit in any vital spot on my body, or on the machine. But the controls became a bit difficult, so I had to go back before something dreadful happened.

The Army Commander-in-Chief had asked Sir John Salmond, who was commanding the Royal Air Force, for information as to where the German reserves were, so that he could forecast where the counter-attack would come from. Sir John came down and visited our squadron and other squadrons and told us: 'Your task is to locate the German reserves. That's what the Commander-in-Chief needs.' On 10 August 1918, my observer and I were able to locate a considerable group of German troops and transport, but the Germans were also aware of the fact that we had spotted them, and were determined that we should not take this information back. On our way back to our lines, we were attacked several times, and somehow, through the skill of my observer, I managed to land my aircraft just inside our lines. I know that the question of chivalry varies. My own experience is that I never came across it. When I was in a crashed aircraft, with the loss of a leg, the Germans dived down on us three or four times and fired a few hundred bullets into our machine. That's not exactly an act of chivalry, but it was war, and that's what you'd expect in war. Maybe others had other experiences. Unfortunately, I got in the way of several explosive bullets, which practically severed my leg, and as a result I had my left leg amputated.

I was in hospital in France for about a month, and apparently had lost large amounts of blood. I was extremely weak. It was only because I was very young and healthy, that I was able to survive, and when I had recovered sufficiently, I was sent to the London General Hospital, where there were hundreds of wounded officers, some blind, some who were missing limbs, and so on. I shall always remember the reception of my colleagues, the ones without arms and legs, on the day that I received my Victoria Cross.

I was placed on indefinite leave, pending the fitting of an artificial limb. And when this limb was fitted to me, I came across a man called De Souter, a Swiss chap, who was a great man on precision instruments. He produced his own leg, on which he was able to climb mountains. He told me that if I went to him, he would fix me up with an aluminium leg, much lighter than the one provided by the government, and that I would be able to fly again. This famous leg of De Souter then became the standard leg, and remains so today. My hidden hopes to be able to fly rose a great deal, and through the connivance of Sir John Salmond and Lord Trenchard, I was posted to RAF HQ, Uxbridge, with Air Commodore Hugh Dowding, who was known to us all as 'Stuffy'. I used to go to the aerodrome at Northolt, and started flying again. Much to my amazement, when the Air Ministry issued a list of officers granted permanent commissions, I was delighted to see my name amongst them. And I had their encouragement and blessing to make a career in the Royal Air Force.

When I returned from the war, I found that a lot of people had had their careers affected. Some chaps who had been students at Oxford and Cambridge Universities had left to go to war and were not inclined to return to study. The thing was to get a job. You had to decide what sort of career you were going to have. My recollection is that universities and the big companies like ICI were all very helpful to service people. But the question of finding jobs was a very serious one and, of course, a few years later came the big strike in England which paralysed the whole country.

My job was to fly newspapers which were printed by the government. I remember landing at Hawkinge, and being faced by a rather hostile crowd, so we suggested that we should have a football match and they all cheered up.

One of the sad things after the war is that the ministry concerned had to concentrate on discharging people. The big force of, perhaps, 30,000 had to be reduced to about 1,000. All politicians after the war were keen on economies on the services, and a great number of officers who would like to have remained had to leave. On the whole, those chaps who were working in the RAF were keener to remain and go flying, than those of the other services, who could not offer the excitement that young people like to have. The fact that it was a new service, and in the air, built up an allegiance through its excitement.

Young men were attracted by the sense of adventure that flying offered. Immediately after the war, we had to use up the equipment which was available until a few years afterwards. The development of civil aviation could only happen later in the 1920s. Anyone who had the good fortune to remain in the Royal Air Force was very interested in the new types of plane. We all wanted new types of aircraft, bigger aeroplanes, faster machines, and we could see that that was coming.

This was just the beginning of the revolution that happened between 1932 and 1940 in aircraft development. We knew that the technicians were producing bigger and faster aircraft; it was just a question of waiting for them to come into service. Naturally, the war demonstrated what use various types of aircraft could be put to, and most pilots understood that you've got to have a period of retrenchment, and that they would be marking time pending the arrival of new machines. This we had to accept. After four years of conflict, though, we weren't thinking about another war; all we were thinking was: 'What are we going to do now? What sort of jobs are we going to have? What professions are we going to follow?' I was one of the lucky ones, extremely lucky, in fact, because I never expected, with one leg, to remain in the Royal Air Force.

On an intensely hot, humid day while waiting for the video equipment to agree to register any image at all, the former Captain West rolled up his trouser leg to display the artificial limb acquired from De Souter after the incident of exemplary bravery for which he was awarded the ultimate decoration.

Though the delay caused him to miss the afternoon's racing, which he would infinitely have preferred to watch, he described in his mellifluous and charmingly-accented voice something of his subsequent career in the film industry.

He displayed an interesting souvenir of the last flight of Manfred von Richthofen, a piece of maroon fabric in the shape of Australia, cut from the Baron's Fokker triplane and given to him by one of the Australian gunners who claimed Manfred as their victory.

Captain West was a remarkable and most sophisticated man, the only surviving recipient of the VC from the war in the air. He was able to dismiss the difficulties consequent upon his near-fatal injury during the war, being of the conviction that, having been reprieved, the remainder of his life should be as diverse and significant as possible.

Sir Thomas Sopwith

No work of this kind would be complete without including one of the best known pioneers of design, Sir Thomas Sopwith.

Thomas Octave Murdoch Sopwith was born on 10 January 1888, the only son and eighth child of a civil engineer. He was forced to become independent when his father was killed in a hunting accident aged twenty-eight. His sisters offered financial support, and the seventeen-year-old Thomas went into business for himself. The next few years of his life included perfecting his skills as a racing car driver, yachtsman, balloonist and, finally, an aviator.

He founded The Sopwith Aviation Company in 1912, and started a flying school at Brooklands in Surrey. The 1965 film *Those Magnificent Men in Their Flying Machines* is based on a 1911 air race held there.

In 1914 The Sopwith Aviation Company went to war, providing an early scout called the Tabloid. For the next four years, various state of the art fighters emerged from the Sopwith factory – the Baby, the Pup, the first Triplane, the Snipe and the Dolphin. It produced the most famous British fighter of the First World War, the Sopwith Camel.

Sir Thomas was appointed CBE in 1918 and knighted in 1953. He married Beatrix Hore-Ruthven in 1914. After her death, in 1932 he married Phyllis Brodie Gordon, who died in 1978. They had a son, also named Tommy.

Together with Frederick Sigrist, Harry Hawker, and Sydney Camm, Sopwith continued to build fighters well into the 1930s, and stamped his name on the famous Hawker Hurricane of the Second World War as chairman of Hawker Aircraft Ltd. He was interviewed at his home, Compton Manor in Hampshire on 8 November 1978. Sir Thomas died in Winchester on 27 January 1989.

I had always been interested in aviation. In 1906 I had a balloon, the Padsop, and gradually worked up from there. I got my first plane in October 1910, a Howard-Wright monoplane with a 60-ENV engine, and this was the machine on which I took my ticket, No. 31. I learned to fly very quickly, effectively teaching myself. It was quite a nerve-racking business, as the machines in those days were built entirely by eye, and hadn't been stressed. We were flying with no instruments at all; few of the aircraft I flew had a rev-counter, and the airspeed indicator didn't come in for another two years. You had to judge your speed by feel alone.

It was this same Howard-Wright monoplane that I flew in the Michelin Cup in 1910. Cody won that, though. I won the DeForest Competition which was going on at the same time. Both these titles were awarded to the person who'd flown the highest; the Michelin Cup in England, and the DeForest out of England. Whoever was ahead by 31 December, won the prize in each case. I had two or three attempts at the Michelin, but each time I beat Cody, he beat me. In the DeForest, I was flying for about three and a quarter hours, and I had enough fuel to fly as far again. Nobody got off to much of a start in that race, which was dogged by misfortune. I got frightened because the sun went in, and I couldn't be certain of finding my way. I was getting into the hilly country, near the Ardennes, and it got very rough indeed. When you're sitting on the edge of a biplane, without even a belt, that's not very pleasant. I decided to call it a day and make a landing. I won, though.

After this, I visited the Blériot school at Pau in France, where I bought a 70-horsepower Blériot. In 1911, I took it to America. One of the things I did there was fly this machine round the City Hall in Philadelphia, which was a bloody foolish thing to do. At least I survived, though. On another occasion, I seriously crashed a Blériot, spinning it into the ground; I was very fortunate to escape with my life.

Late in October 1911, I returned to England, and started a school at Brooklands. I had the Howard-Wright biplane, the Blériot monoplane and the first tractor biplane that we built in the shed there. That was a three-seater, and had an interesting career. I eventually sold it to the Admiralty, and it spent years flying from

Eastchurch to Whitstable in order to collect oysters for the mess. My most famous pupil at Brooklands was Lord Trenchard. He had to learn in a hurry, because to join the Royal Flying Corps, you had to be under forty. He had only ten days before his fatal fortieth birthday, so we had to get him flying as much as we could in the time. We got him his ticket all right. He wasn't a very good pilot, but was a marvellous leader of men, and a tremendous character.

I founded the Sopwith Aviation Company in 1912. We built our first couple of planes in the sheds at Brooklands, and then took over a roller-skating rink in Kingston, turning it into an aircraft factory. My engineer in those days was Frederick Sigrist. He came from the West Country, and at the time we took him on, he was working on the bench at the Parsons Motor Company in Southampton. I remember that he had the magnificent salary of £2/14/- a week, and kept himself on it.

The Bat Boat was one of the first machines that we designed and built at Kingston. I had always been greatly interested in the sea, as well as the air, and the Bat Boat seemed an ideal way to unite these two things. It won the £500 Mortimer-Singer Prize, for the first aircraft to make a certain number of landings both on land and water. Originally, it had a 100-horsepower, water-cooled, Green engine. We had several different ones just at the beginning of the war, and actually sold them to Germany. We built a big Bat Boat with a 200-horsepower, water-cooled Canton-Unné engine. Subsequently, we built another with a 225-horsepower Sunbeam engine, and yet another with an Austro-Daimler engine. It was the Bat Boat that we entered for the Olympia Air Show in 1913.

By the summer of 1914, things were beginning to look pretty ominous, and the Tabloid, which we'd produced the previous year, was the first of our planes to see active service. This was followed by the Pup and the Camel. Our two-seater 1½-Strutter came in between, and was the first of our machines to have the synchronizer gear. In those days, it only took about six weeks to build and fly a new type of plane; nowadays, it can take more than six years. Things were developing at an astounding rate then. They were much more empirical aircraft too, and weren't nearly as complicated as modern fighters. On our early aircraft, I won't give full marks to anybody as being the designer. It was a conspiracy of three or four of us, and Harry Hawker and Sigrist both had a great deal to do with it. We gradually built up a drawing office, which had to commit to paper the ideas of the practical people. It's really a question of merging; we gradually merged into a fully fledged drawing and design office. Up to the beginning of the war, I was still flying, but soon gave this up in order to concentrate on the construction side of things. I reckoned that I wouldn't have the time to do both. Hawker took over from me as our chief test pilot. We'd stopped the competition flying at this point, and threw ourselves into the business of producing military aircraft.

One of our most successful and popular planes was the Triplane. Fokker's triplane followed soon after, inspired by ours, but not really a direct copy. The Germans were afraid of our Triplane when it first came out, because it had such a tight and quick turn. We tried to make that a feature of all our machines. We were very careful to keep our weights as close together as possible, and went very much for manoeuvrability in our designs. There was quite a strong movement for making aircraft automatically stable, but they found when they went to war with those machines, they weren't manoeuvrable enough. The BE2 was a case in point. That was the first biplane that went into comparatively mass production for the Flying Corps, but it was so stable that it was a perfect target. It was a fairly slow plane, too, and couldn't dodge. These were two reasons why it was mainly used for reconnaissance work.

Most of our aircraft seem to have supplied the Royal Naval Air Service, and there is a very good reason for that. I reckon the aircraft industry in this country owes a tremendous debt of gratitude to the Air Department of the Admiralty as it was then called, which was formed by three Naval officers: Captain Meyer, Commander Oliver Swann, his No. 1, and Lieutenant Cecil Malone. These chaps really kept the nucleus of our aircraft industry alive for a year or two before the war. So when the war broke out, most of our contracts were with the Admiralty. We started the war only building for the Navy, and then the RFC came along and bought quite a lot too.

I went out to France quite a bit during the war. I used to visit some of the front-line squadrons to see how they were getting on with our machines. I'll never forget going around the area, just after the Battle of the Somme, and seeing the complete devastation. Even the wood had disappeared. You didn't even see the trunks of trees; they were all stirred up in the mud. It was terrible.

By 1918, we had built two other works, and were employing about 6,000 hands. However, when the war came to an end, the bottom dropped out of the market overnight. It was frightful. It became clear to me that we were on the point of bankruptcy, and forestalled this by putting the company into liquidation. We started up again almost immediately. Four of us got together, Bill Ayer, Harry Hawker, Frederick Sigrist and myself, and we hired a quarter of the workshop from the liquidator, and started to play with aircraft in a small way. We called that outfit the Hawker Company.

The Harrier was marvellous. Millions had been spent by America, France and Russia to try to achieve a successful vertical take off, but the Harrier is the only one that has been a success. Not only that, it's quite easy to fly; anybody can fly a Harrier. The time I saw one flying in reverse, I thought I'd seen it all. Credit for the Harrier belongs principally to Sydney Camm, who designed the aircraft. He came to work for me in 1923, and was responsible for many of the inter-war designs, such as the Hind, the Hart and the Fury. Tragically, Hawker was killed, but not flying one of our machines. He was due to fly a Nieuport in the Aerial Derby of 1921, but it caught fire in the air, and he was killed. His was a great loss.

The Hurricane was another of our planes. It came out just before the Second World War, a year earlier than the Spitfire. That's why the Hurricanes had such high scores in the Battle of Britain. We had five times as many Hurricanes as Spitfires.

After the war, there were a lot of Sopwith planes which had been ordered, but never used. I think most of them were burned. For a long time I had the tail of my original Howard-Wright biplane, which lived up in the roof at the factory. I don't know what happened to it eventually.

Sir Thomas Sopwith, by 1978 the sole accessible pioneer aviator/designer alive, was an elusive quarry. He twice declined to be interviewed, and acceded only after special and protracted entreaties. On the morning of the visit, as we sat together in the spacious grounds of his estate, Compton Manor, he remarked rather sadly that he had become lost in his own garden earlier that day owing to his impaired sight.

A modest and self-deprecating man, Sir Thomas did not relish the attentions of the camera, either; in consequence he tended to extremely laconic replies. After lunch, preceded by industrial-strength rum cocktails, and followed by splendid Havana cigars donated by Fidel Castro, Sir Thomas became more expansive, and recalled his encounter over a drink with Anthony Fokker, a former rival in aircraft design, on the yacht *Endeavour* in 1937.

The mantelpiece of his dining room was adorned with a series of magnificent trophies for the Michelin and DeForest races pre-First World War, one of which was surmounted by a golden Caudron monoplane.

Fleeting though this reminiscence may have been, it was a great privilege to have met this most seminal figure of the aviation world.